SHOPPING ALL THE WAY TO THE WOODS

Shopping All the Way to the Woods

How the Outdoor Industry
Sold Nature to America

RACHEL S. GROSS

Yale
UNIVERSITY PRESS
NEW HAVEN AND LONDON

Published with assistance from the Louis Stern Memorial Fund.

Yale University Press books may be purchased in quantity for educational, business,
or promotional use. For information, please e-mail sales.press@yale.edu (U.S. office)
or sales@yaleup.co.uk (U.K. office).

Set in Electra LH Standard type by IDS Infotech, Ltd.
Printed in the United States of America.

ISBN 978-0-300-27008-2 (hardcover : alk. paper)
Library of Congress Control Number: 2023941910
A catalogue record for this book is available from the British Library.

This paper meets the requirements of ANSI/NISO Z39.48-1992
(Permanence of Paper).

10 9 8 7 6 5 4 3 2 1

For my parents: Sharon Rowe and Ken Gross

CONTENTS

CONTENTS

I had only been backpacking for one night in my life before I began to prepare for a yearlong backpacking adventure. With excitement and trepidation, I had accepted a fellowship that allowed me to spend my first year after college hiking alone on four continents to explore the idea of wilderness. Since I had been car camping over the years with my family, I knew that the first stop to prepare for the trip, after the library, was my local outdoor store.

The inspiration for this trip was partly intellectual: the history of wilderness is a central topic in environmental history, which I planned to study in graduate school. Before I started my studies I wanted a better understanding of the wilds beyond the United States. The trip was also deeply personal. Family road trips when I was a child shaped my romantic association with the wild and with mountains in particular. When I was ten or eleven I longingly read my brother's *Boy Scout Handbook* and ticked off the merit badges I imagined I would have earned if only I had been eligible to join that club. Ms. Guth's eleventh-grade history class introduced me to the Rocky Mountain School painter Albert Bierstadt and his oversized canvases of sublime mountain beauty in Yosemite. Camping trips with my parents and siblings in western national parks taught me how to set up a tent, poke at a fire, and wear a hat to keep warm at night.

For an urban upbringing, my young adult life was full of messages that the mountains were where to go to feel *real*. I listened to books on tape like *Hatchet* and *My Side of the Mountain*, where courageous boys (always boys) lived in trees and learned the ways of the woods. Our family calendar of black-and-white Ansel Adams nature photography taught me how to see natural landscapes as the opposite of my everyday life in Los Angeles. I had applied for the post-college fellowship because I saw it as my chance to become the outdoorsy person I wanted to be, which to me meant that I wanted to be self-reliant, brave, non-materialistic, physically strong, and competent at managing details and surviving.

Gripped with the desire to exude expertise that I didn't entirely possess, I went to Adventure 16, a Southern California outdoor retailer. Before I went I read guidebooks and imagined what I'd look like walking along Scotland's West Highland Way or climbing up Mount Kilimanjaro in Tanzania. But now, with the departure day only weeks away, I stood nervously at the wall of wool socks, comparing tan and brown. I reassured myself confidently that picking the right gear in that metropolitan store would be the key to my success in the great outdoors.

Ultimately, I chose an orange nylon rain jacket, some Capilene long underwear, and a women's down sleeping bag that was supposed to keep me warm down to fifteen degrees. Friends gave me old fleece gloves and an MSR Dragonfly stove, among many other items. I arranged this ensemble of new and old in my green, seventy-liter Gregory internal-frame pack, confident that checking the boxes on my packing list meant I was prepared *and* that the gear would bestow the power of belonging.

Of course, I chose wrong. The gear made my beginner status glaringly obvious. My spork snapped in half. My cornflower-blue shirt was too bright and clean to be worn by anyone other than a newbie. I also had more pressing concerns: I could light my stove, but didn't know how to fix it when it broke. Tucked into my lime green down sleeping bag, I was cold every night because I didn't realize the cold was seeping up from the ground through my thin sleeping pad.

Worse yet, backpackers I met along the way commented on my (poor) choices. From the Appenzell in Switzerland to Patagonia in Chile, I got the same questions: Why did you pack so much? Why did you pack *that?* Our conversations about equipment and clothing sometimes gave me insights into local hiking culture. At other times, however, they were condescending lectures intended to highlight the speaker's supposedly superior knowledge. People questioned my expertise because I was young and a woman, I knew. But I also learned something less obvious in those discussions about gear: what people brought on the trail was inextricably linked to the meaning they assigned to their outdoor experiences.

It turns out that my packing list was so very American. Not just the brands I sported—REI, Patagonia, Smartwool—but the ideas behind the gear: how to layer, how to deal with the rain, how to eat on the trail, the bromide that "cotton kills." Reading adventure fiction and scouting handbooks in my childhood had shaped my experience as a young adult traveler more than I realized. I believed that there was a Right Way to dress and equip myself, just as much as the folks I encountered around the world believed in a different "right way."

Over many months, I grew stronger shouldering my too-heavy pack, learned how to fix the stove so I didn't have to eat granola for dinner, and became more confident on the trail. Over many miles, I reflected on why I thought acquiring the right gear would turn me into the person I wanted to be. Where did my packing list come from? As it turned out, these questions would shape my academic research for the next decade.

The year after my great adventure, I began graduate school in Madison, Wisconsin, happy to begin writing about mountains rather than climbing them. Though I still hiked and dabbled in other outdoor sports, I didn't become the wilderness guide or park ranger that I'd imagined becoming as a teenager. Instead, I became a specialist in the meanings Americans attach to their experiences in nature. I am now a historian of outdoor gear—and the first person to claim such a job description. I'm an expert in unpacking the packing list, studying what Americans bring to nature and why that list of seemingly mundane goods matters.

When I combined what I learned in school—the cultural evolution of ideas of manhood, the search for authentic experience as a response to modernity—with my time on the trail, I finally began to answer the questions that followed me earlier. There are no "right things" to buy for the trail, since notions of what is right or even what is comfortable are specific to place and time. And stuff does not inherently define character—only my education in adventure fiction and scouting magazines, and comparisons of my tent with my neighbor's, had taught me that misperception.

Although my specific path to the woods might have been unusual, my quest to prove myself as an expert hiker—via shopping—turns out to have been a quintessential American experience. For more than 150 years, outdoor equipment and clothing has been a treasured and necessary component of the American outdoor experience. Indeed, many would-be outdoor enthusiasts in the 1920s spent more time shopping for a fringed buckskin jacket or an imitation Buck Skein™ jacket than they did wearing it on the trail. Why Americans go shopping on the way to the woods, and what the things they buy say about who they are, became the central focus of my research, as it had already been in my personal life.

For this history of the outdoor industry, I looked at a wide variety of archives and publications. I consulted historical documents such as Duxbak hunting apparel catalogs from the 1920s, guidebooks like *Mountaineering: The Freedom of the Hills* from 1960, and DuPont advertisements from 1980. I visited the archives of outdoor companies, viewing material historians had never looked at, such as old catalogs and advertisements at Adventure 16's headquarters in San Diego and the formal archive at the W. L. Gore & Associates headquarters in Newark, Delaware. I complemented this research with an examination of actual material objects such as a first-generation Gore-Tex rain jacket and a nearly disintegrating Trapper Nelson packboard, a wooden frame with straps used as a kind of backpack. I also interviewed outdoor enthusiasts who showed me their closets full of gear dating back a half century and shared what the shredded t-shirts and surplus pants meant to them. These oral history interviews with outdoorspeople active from the 1950s to the present allowed me to get at the most elusive aspect of any history of consumption: how actual consumers used and thought about the products they purchased. To trace the role of the military in the industry (and of the industry in the military), I used not just the widely known records of the ski troopers of the 10th Mountain Division but also the much bigger collection of the Quartermaster Corps, the home of research and development on uniforms and equipment for the U.S. Army.

This book introduces new characters alongside famous figures from the outdoor past. There are business owners whose now hundred-year-old businesses are still popular, such as Eddie Bauer and L. L. Bean. There are gear-makers Alice Holubar and Mary Anderson, who were as important to shaping the industry as better-known gear company owners Yvon Choui-nard of Patagonia and Johnny Morris of Bass Pro Shops. There are people famous for climbing mountains: Everest climber and REI manager Jim Whittaker, as well as famous people who climbed mountains. A young Robert Redford, for example, chose the college he attended based on his love for the Holubar Mountaineering shop. But most of the outdoorspeople are ordinary consumers: Pennsylvania hunter Harold Bomberger, who bought a red plaid Stag Cruiser in the 1920s and wanted to show it off to his hunting buddies, and Montana hiker Kristi DuBois, who sewed a jacket from a Frost-line do-it-yourself kit. The experiences of industry professionals and customers are at the heart of this story, for they are the ones, in the end, who created outdoor culture.

I didn't realize until years later that many of the items I bought for my backpacking adventure actually have origins in the U.S. military. I didn't understand that the synthetic fibers I took for granted in my long underwear had been part of a long trend of technical innovations in chemical companies. I hadn't considered how the prohibitive costs of the new goods I acquired—made possible in my case by the generous support of the fellowship—as well as the mystique of my borrowed goods necessarily excluded whole swaths of people from accessing these particular goods and looking like they belong. I shared this ignorance about my pack's backstory with most outdoor enthusiasts, who number in the tens of millions each year in the United States.

In the twenty-first century, as in the previous 150 years, Americans have learned to feel most themselves on the trail or river, in the RV, by the camp-fire. And for every family camping trip, for every backpacking excursion, for every fly-fishing afternoon, Americans go shopping first. This is, of course, because there is necessary equipment that makes the activities possible. But Americans are also hoping that the products that fill their backpacks, dry bags, or panniers will open the way to authentic experience. This book is written for gear-lovers by a gear-lover, explaining where all these goods come from and just why they end up on Americans' packing lists.

ACKNOWLEDGMENTS

Years of emotional, intellectual, and financial support from individuals and organizations made this book possible. Librarians and archivists, funding institutions, faculty advisers and colleagues, friends, and family have all enriched this project. They have been generous in sharing time and expertise.

A wide range of institutions supported me in completing this book. The Thomas J. Watson Fellowship stimulated my curiosity and introduced me to landscapes I never could have imagined. The NCAA provided important assistance in my transition to graduate school, and the Department of History at the University of Wisconsin–Madison and the Nelson Institute's Center for Culture, History, and Environment (CHE) supported me once I arrived. The Smithsonian Institution at the National Museum of American History (NMAH), the Lemelson Center, the Hagley Museum and Library, the Winterthur Museum and Library, the U.S. Army Military History Institute, and the Science History Institute (formerly Chemical Heritage Foundation) also provided assistance. Finally, the Rachel Carson Center provided the time, space, and community support to make crucial revisions on my manuscript.

Librarians and archivists around the country enriched the project from the beginning. At NMAH, thank you to Joyce Bedi, Pam Henson, Eric Hintz, Craig Orr, Alison Oswald, Katherine Ott, Jane Rogers, Jeffrey Stine, Roger White, Tim Winkle, and especially Margaret Vining for introducing me to material I never would have found otherwise. At the Autry National Center, Marva Felchlin was an early supporter of this project. Angela Snye at the Adirondack Library, Alex Depta at the American Alpine Club, Lisa Crane at the Honnold/Mudd Library, Emily Guthrie and Tom Guiler at Winterthur, Lucas Clawson at Hagley, Leslie Bellais at the Wisconsin Historical Society, Lynette Miller at the Washington State History Research Center, Alison Moore at the California Historical Society, and Susan Snyder at the Bancroft Library all shared their expertise with me. The staff of the University of Washington Special Collections, the Denver Public Library, the Boulder Public Library, the Oregon Historical Society, and the Chemical Heritage Foundation all made research trips as fruitful as possible. Jim Mead and Terry Embrey at Adventure 16, Will Shanahan at American Recreation, Colin Berg at Eddie Bauer, and Gene Castellano, Kevin Brown, and Steve Shuster of Gore welcomed me to explore company archives. I am glad to be partnering with Chase Anderson and Clint Pumphrey of the Outdoor Recreation Archive at Utah State University, where they are assembling a valuable resource for future generations of scholars.

Ingrid Guth taught me both to approach the study of history with the utmost seriousness and to tell great jokes (with a straight face) along the way. Model teachers Nancy Bristow and Doug Sackman guided me through my first research project. Lisa Steenport and Mark Massey helped me find my voice on the court, with immeasurable benefits for the teacher I hoped to become. I hope they will recognize their influence in these pages.

At the University of Wisconsin–Madison, I benefited from the feedback and guidance of many faculty members, including Bill Reese, Jennifer Ratner-Rosenhagen, Cindy I-Fen Cheng, Judy Houck, Suzanne Desan, John Hall, and Eric Schatzberg. Leslie Abadie ably guided me through the program. Susan Johnson's careful reading and commenting on my writing gave me a standard to aim for and pushed me to broaden my questions. Nan Enstad has enthusiastically supported this project since its earliest incarnation and motivated me to articulate the broader contributions of the project.

As an adviser, Bill Cronon has been an intrepid guide. He taught me to read and write more critically. In addition to his intellectual guidance throughout, he has shared countless primary documents from his own collection, from 1970s pamphlets on "How to Stay Warm" on the trail to his old army surplus hiking outfits. The ultimate lesson I've learned from him echoes across both his work as a scholar and as a citizen. It is not an assemblage of dates and names but a deeply held manifesto: you can only love and care for what you know, what you are connected to. Thank you, Bill.

I've been lucky to be a part of several writing groups over the years. They've helped me keep on track and inspired me with their research and writing. Thanks to Meggan Bilotte, Brendon George, Ariana Horn, Jillian Jacklin, Chong Moua, Megan Stanton, and Britt Tevis; Alex Rudnick and Kate Wersan; and Grace Allen, David Harrisville, Terry Peterson, Ben Shannon, and Nick Strohl. As deadlines loomed, Katherine Charek-Briggs, Jillian Jacklin, Teresa Uyen Nguyen, Lisa Ruth Rand, Rebecca Summer, Irene Toro Martínez, and Melissa Charenko gave their time to my writing. Other friends and colleagues have patiently listened to me describe my ideas and consistently improved them with phenomenal insight. Thank you to Cam Anderson, Nathan Barker, Rachel Boothby, Andrew Case, Andy Davey, Jesse Gant, Daniel Grant, Spring Greeney, Brian Hamilton, David Harrisville, Dan Liu, Adam Mandelman, Garrett Nelson, Tony Pietsch, Sarah Robey, Andrew Stuhl, Naomi Williams, and Anna Zeide.

In more recent years, remote work sessions with Lisa Ruth Rand and the impressive insights of the Wisconsin Brain Trust—Britt Tevis, Christine Lamberson, and Debbie Sharnak—helped the project mature. Colleagues near and far have made my time in the profession a stimulating place and given generously with their feedback, support, and camaraderie, especially Peter Alagona, Chloe Chapin, Mike Childers, Leisl Carr Childers, Annie Gilbert Coleman, Steven Corey, Bart Elmore, David Farber, Eric Hintz, Roger Horowitz, Matt Klingle, Reinhild Kreis, Joy Parr, Sarah Pickman, Michael Reidy, Jesse Ritner, Carolin Roeder, Adam Rome, Sherri Sheu, Amy Slaton, Susan Strasser, Jay Taylor, Phoebe Young, and Terry Young. Keira Richards and Meghann Brown ably assisted in the research. Kyle Volk and Anya Jabour helped me integrate smoothly into academic life at the University of Montana. Christof Mauch and the community of scholars at the Rachel Carson Center, especially Kelly Bushnell, Angelo Caglioti, Matt Klingle, Neil Maher, Anna Pilz, Mark Stoll, Xiaoping Sun, Louis Warren, and Kate Wright welcomed me to Munich, commented on my work, and motivated me to finish this project. At the University of Colorado Denver, I am lucky to have such generous colleagues as Chris Agee, Nicky Beer, Cameron Blevins, Edelina Burciaga, Michelle Comstock, Ryan Crewe, Fei Gao, Sarah Hagelin, Bryn Harris, Lisa Kelley, Peter Kopp, Pam Laird, Marjorie Levine-Clark, Carrie Makarewicz, Dale Stahl, Gillian Silverman, Esther Sullivan, and John Tinnell. When final deadlines approached, Stas Budnitsky, Ariana Horn, Peter Kopp, Christine Lamberson, Lisa Ruth Rand, Debbie Sharnak, and Britt Tevis stepped up again to provide crucial feedback.

Don Fehr helped me navigate the world of publishing, Pamela Haag sharpened the manuscript with fantastic insights, and Jean Thomson Black and the team at Yale University Press guided me through each stage of the review and editing process. Anonymous reviewers for the press as well as anonymous reviewers at the comprehensive review stage at CU Denver improved this book immeasurably with their generous insights. Thanks to the Johns Hopkins University Press and Editions Eska for permission to use material previously published in *Technology and Culture* and *Entreprises et Histoire*, respectively.

I am grateful to the friends who have been supporters and welcome distractions over the years. Thanks to the Milken crew, Elissa Gysi, Marc Marrero, Andrew Nahmias, Aaron Ordower, and Lauren Wolman; my favorite teammates, Ann O'Connor and Kristina Randall; and my favorite fan, Katie Cordingley. Britt Tevis and Stas Budnitsky reminded me to celebrate every step on this journey and to think about life beyond the book. Irene Toro Martínez has been an editor, consultant, critic, audience member, and cheerleader.

While my family members have not been directly involved in this project, their interest and support sustained me and helped me reach the finish line. My grandparents, Audrey Rowe, Peggy Gross, z"l, and Barney Gross, z"l, supported my progress. The Colorado family as well as the soon-to-be Colorado family, Rebecca, Oren, Emet, and Ilon Friedman, and Benjamin Gross, made time away from the project enjoyable. My parents, Ken Gross and Sharon Rowe, helped kick-start a life of learning by letting me get away with reading under the covers as a kid. When I was fifteen, I had only recently graduated from the whining, dirt-kicking stage of family hikes, but my mom agreed to take me on a trip to the Yosemite backcountry. That trip unlocked many of the interests that led to this project. My dad has been invested throughout in learning the intricacies of an academic's work and job application process. My parents have attended my presentations, read my writing, and listened to countless practice talks and lectures via videochat. The environment of reading and learning lishma they both created—"nu, did you ask a good question today"—set me on this path. It is to them this book is dedicated.

Introduction

Amid the postwar enthusiasm for outdoor recreation and camping, a guidebook poked gentle fun at the outdoorspeople who took their afternoon hikes "a little too seriously." The authors wanted to make sure their readers would remember to have a pleasant walk, rather than approaching recreation with solemnity. They described capital-H Hikers who knew that there was "only one right way" to be an outdoorsman. These Hikers calculated trail mileage and tore through their itineraries with no time to dwell on a picturesque view or a chirping bird. They followed the capital-R Rules of camping—don't set the woods on fire, for instance—not because it was common sense but rather so they would never be "branded an ignoramus." Above all, Hikers carried the right gear. Their peers, mere hikers, might find any old tent design acceptable, but for Hikers, the right gem of a tent, ideally from an obscure store, was the only way to be a "properly equipped member of the band."[1]

What is telling about this description three-quarters of a century on is how aptly it continues to capture outdoor culture in the United States. There are indeed certain customs that govern the way of the woods and ensure that participants avoid looking like neophytes. The guidebook authors, though they did not endorse the attitudes of the cliquish Hikers, recognized the powerful draw of fitting in and looking like something other than a tenderfoot. Embracing free time outdoors meant and still means learning about the right clothing and equipment. Tracing the development and growth of the outdoor business in the United States reveals how the industry and its consumers created and normalized an outdoor identity—the intangible promise of camaraderie, belonging, and skillful outdoor knowledge described by the authors.

The outdoor industry is predicated on creating functional equipment and on selling authenticity to consumers. Shopping for the woods was about being—or becoming—the right kind of person by buying the right things. From the late nineteenth century onward, the industry perpetuated the idea that buying gear conveyed expertise. Buckskin shirts sewn by Native women, Abercrombie & Fitch canoe camping gear, White Stag hunting coats, and army surplus tents imbued their owners with historically specific mantles of authority and proficiency. Outdoor enthusiasts did acquire new technical skills, of course, but those skills were largely of secondary importance according to the lessons passed in catalogs and outdoor stores. This book shows that most consumers, whether they helped to shape or conformed to evolving outdoor archetypes, enjoyed dressing the part.[2]

The first of three important elements of this outdoor identity was a masculine ideal. Being outdoorsy was not equated with being a man, but rather the aesthetics, values, and even the approach to shopping became linked with performance of a certain type of manhood. In the nineteenth century, outdoor recreation promised the benefit of sober, masculine values to temper the risks of newfound leisure time. These outdoor tourists turned to working-class rural activities such as hunting, fishing, and camping to express their feelings of disconnection with modern American life. Outdoor adventure in the West was meant to quell anxieties about American men getting too effete in their urban East Coast lives. Nostalgia for an authentic American past, the days of the robust pioneer on the frontier, accompanied skepticism about the trappings of modernity. Yet this attitude toward modern life and wilderness revealed a series of ironies: The regeneration and renewal drawn from wild lands was only available to a leisure class of men who had the means to make such a temporary escape. What is more, excursions to Adirondack great camps as well as guided hunting trips required a modern tourist infrastructure to support them. Even in geographically removed places, tourists were consumers, seeking to collect experiences and landscapes and turning very often to modern clothing and equipment as an emblem of the primitive.

Nineteenth-century outdoor attire evinced a rugged masculinity that reinforced the wearer's authenticity and mastery over nature. Guidebook authors such as Nessmuk and Horace Kephart, outdoor icons such as Theodore Roosevelt, and the men who read their writings all made outdoor goods popular. In doing so, both industry leaders and consumers forged and then upheld links connecting a masculine ideal, authenticity, and consumption of outdoor goods. In the first half of the twentieth century, the masculine ideal at the heart of the outdoor identity drew sustenance from its association with the U.S. military. Later, adherents to the countercultures of the 1950s that shunned the conformity of suburban life adopted surplus military attire as the emblem of their grubby, salt-of-the-earth aesthetic of making it outdoors. The legacy of the masculine outdoor identity endured even as both men and women were drawn to this aesthetic. Throughout these periods, men considered their choices in clothing and equipment rational, steady, and unemotional, for they were buying necessary hardware for survival, in contrast to the flighty impulse purchases of female shoppers. This notion that historical actors conceived of male consumption as outside traditional market relations is useful for understanding the evolving idea of the masculine outdoor identity that so often viewed male consumption as essential, in contrast to the feminine excesses of luxury consumption. Ultimately, understanding the gendered ideals of the outdoors reveals how colliding interests and objectives among manufacturers, consumers, retailers, and self-identified outdoor experts produced an American cultural identity.[3]

The second element of the American outdoor identity is that it is deeply tied to material things: specifically, how consumers acquired their identities through the purchase of particular goods. Although the 150-year period under study here included phenomenal growth in the number of participants in outdoor activities, the outdoor identity was focused less on outdoor experience than it was on the gear users possessed even while not recreating. In the twentieth century, a sleeping bag sewn by the renowned gearmaker Alice Holubar, a used pack acquired at an Adventure 16 swap meet, or a Frostline vest sewn at home was a signal of community connection, savvy discount hunting, and craft skill in an age of mass production. Clothing and equipment operated as emblems of belonging, or at least as bids for belonging. In the second half of the twentieth century, many outdoor companies that had once served a niche market of mountaineers and climbers, including Recreational Equipment, Incorporated (REI), evolved to serve much broader audiences. These new recreationists displayed their investment in the outdoor identity by purchasing high-cost, high-performance products to wear at home and at work as well as on the trail. The cultural trend linking belonging to owning the right gear was deeply felt in the recreational community, even though a subset of recreationists have never subscribed to it. Not all outdoorspeople expressed a gearhead's enthusiasm for the latest and greatest. Documents harder to uncover in the historical record might reveal others who purchased equipment and expressed resistance to the overwhelming culture of consumption in outdoor recreation. Nonetheless, the tremendous growth of the outdoor industry in economic size, political impact, and geographic spread suggests that millions of Americans did buy into the notion that gear mattered deeply.

Finally, the outdoor identity, firmly linked to the masculine ideal and a culture of consuming, is also deeply entwined with American national identity. There are outdoor leisure seekers and outdoor clothing companies and recreational habits across the world, to be sure. This book focuses on what is uniquely American about the rise of its national industry. The notion of western landscapes as a proving ground for white manhood and the imagined emptiness of newly founded national parks that protected wild lands were both predicated on a disappearing or disappeared Native American population. The liberal appropriation of supposedly Indigenous aesthetics and technologies reveals how national historical narratives of white conquest continued to appear well into the twentieth century. Nineteenth-century narratives of outdoor recreation abounded with stories of racial passing and mistaken identity. The punch line of many of these accounts was that the buckskin-clad horseman viewed from afar was, in fact, a white gentleman, showing how chroniclers of outdoor culture embraced class and whiteness as markers of belonging in American narratives of recreation. The link between conquest and outdoor recreation is not buried in the long-ago past. Into the twentieth century, American military ties to outdoor sports and outdoor industry have remained, with overlapping participants and sensibilities. National boundaries cannot contain the ambitions of brands or athletes, and indeed this book shows how American entrepreneurs in the middle of the twentieth century had great success importing European goods. Nonetheless, the mythologies of the American frontier and fetishization of Native American knowledge and aesthetics show how the outdoor identity sold by industry and embraced and refined by consumers came to engage with stories of who belonged in the nation. This book unearths the origins and evolution of this identity.[4]

To trace the evolving elements of the outdoor industry, the book uses catalogs, national magazines, corporate and military records, and interviews with business owners to show how outdoor merchandise was produced, stocked, distributed, and marketed. The outdoor identity was not merely a manufactured tale of artifice emanating from industry interests. Both manufacturers and consumers were arbiters of authentic experience and belonging. Other types of sources include consumer letters, diary entries, and beloved attire from individuals' closets. In considering these personal accounts and physical objects alongside corporate materials, the book shows that the ideologies of consumption are not so neat as to allow for a story of market control or consumer-constructed meanings alone. Manufacturers made outdoor goods and experiences accessible to expanding communities of consumers at the same time that they and their consumers defined those communities in racialized, classed, and gendered ways. Products derived meaning and value from how they were produced and marketed, enabling consumers to claim special status from the relationship to the outdoors the products represented or made possible. A diverse source base that includes both corporate and consumer points of view makes clear that messages about products' meaning emerged from the pages of *Backpacker* magazine and other national publications, discussions with gearmakers and guidebook authors, and interactions with other outdoorspeople. Overall, this book demonstrates that the ever elusive search for authenticity was not something passed down from on high from outdoor companies or something that solely bubbled up from the masses.[5]

Shopping All the Way to the Woods examines the American outdoor identity by tracing the development of a nascent industry in the late nineteenth and early twentieth centuries, the influence of World War II on its growth, and the postwar boom years of outdoor businesses. The book begins by examining the origins of outdoor recreation in the United States and the creation of an accompanying industry. Chapter 1 starts in the late nineteenth century, when elite travelers debated what new and old clothes, buckskin hunting suits, and bloomers might say about their gender and class identity. In that era, the American wilderness served as an exclusive getaway for the wealthy, particularly white men. Many nineteenth-century guidebooks advised these aspiring hikers and hunters to avoid buying too many gadgets. Such purchases, these books suggested, would preclude loftier pursuits at the heart of the back-to-nature experience. Then, around the turn of the century, a handful of outdoor clothing and equipment retailers and manufacturers in the United States upended that idea. As Chapter 2 argues, outdoor companies began to respond to the growth in outdoor recreation and presented their stores on the boulevard as a necessary first stop on the road to the blazed trail. Abercrombie & Fitch and other regional mail-order outfitters sought to convince Americans that, by going shopping, they could embody a celebratory history of the frontier past. They made jackets, tents, and boots that functioned for leisure and work alike, and marketed those products using appealing stories about the wild as a proving ground for manhood. Alongside iconic outdoorsmen such as Theodore Roosevelt, shopkeepers became arbiters of how to master the outdoors. Chapter 3 offers a new archetype of the outdoorsman for the 1920s and 1930s: the outdoor worker, whose need for functional equipment proved to be a useful advertising message for companies selling recreational attire. As new technologies such as the Trapper Nelson packboard and Buck Skein jackets debuted in the marketplace, outdoor companies played with consumer nostalgia as they stretched the boundaries of what counted as real and authentic equipment.

The middle section of the book examines the changes in technology and outdoor culture wrought by World War II. The war introduced new methods for testing clothing in laboratories rather than in the field and contributed to the wealth of new outdoor technologies Americans bought in the postwar period. Chapter 4 traces the U.S. military's development and testing of new cold-weather uniforms that drew on the long-standing lessons from outdoor sports. In the immediate postwar era, these wartime developments entered civilian life via army surplus clothing and equipment. As Chapter 5 shows, veterans sold wartime goods for recreational purposes in army-navy stores around the country. Even as surplus became ubiquitous, some outdoor enthusiasts saw an opportunity both to improve on surplus and to build family businesses as community centers of outdoor culture, as Chapter 6 reveals. In 1959, the Holubar Mountaineering Company of Boulder, Colorado, which got its start as a surplus reseller, sent a sleeping bag, a tent, and climbing hardware to the American Exposition in Moscow. The American way of selling nature had become a national symbol of American democracy and capitalism. By the 1960s, outdoor recreation had become both affordable and visible in popular culture, suggesting that the outdoor identity was now within reach for many Americans.

The final chapters explore the implications of rising interest in outdoor recreation for the industry, consumers, and the environment. The expansion of backpacking in the 1970s, covered in Chapter 7, offered outdoor companies the chance to build broader communities, often coalescing around environmental politics. By the early 1970s, forty million Americans sought out the great outdoors annually, and scores of companies grew to cater to their interests. These new outdoor stores, from shops run out of family basements such as Gerry Mountaineering and Frostline to chain retailers such as Bass Pro Sports, offered new equipment designs that increased both the comfort and the cool factor of outdoor recreation. Chapter 8 looks at two gear phenomena of the 1970s: the do-it-yourself kit trend and the rise of the high-tech waterproof and breathable synthetic Gore-Tex fabric. DIY kits and technical synthetics reveal how consumers weighed their desire for effective, exclusive, and affordable gear in the era of big business. By the 1980s, large corporations had bought out scores of what had been small regional outdoor companies, such as Eddie Bauer and the North Face, and sold stylish hiking boots and puffy jackets for daily life as well as for expeditions to Everest and Antarctica. Chapter 9 examines the broadening market of outdoor-wear consumers. Company executives faced a challenge: how to cash in on the rising popularity of outdoor wear as everyday wear while maintaining an aura of authenticity that attracted American consumers to the brand in the first place. Ultimately, these chapters show the challenges and rewards of bringing outdoor goods to a mass market.

This book's examination of outdoor clothing and gear is a fresh look at the history of American outdoor leisure in the nineteenth through twenty-first centuries. Outdoor recreation has long yielded rich insights about the American past. Environmental historians have shown, for instance, why sleeping outdoors can be deeply political, and how skiing transformed western landscapes. Other scholars have highlighted the paradox of a booming consumer culture at odds with popular conceptions of nature as an escape. Pink plastic flamingos and CDs of rainforest sounds, for example, became emblems of engagement with nature, but Americans usually failed to recognize the disconnect between their purchases and the real, material rainforest they were trying to connect to. The outdoor industry and the stories it sells to Americans are rife with similar contradictions. What also distinguishes this book among works of environmental history is the way it incorporates the science and economics of product research and development, design, and marketing. The book takes seriously the outdoor world as a business that sells nature experiences to the masses.[6]

This is a history of gear and of clothing, only some of which can be clearly identified as fashion. By integrating analyses of clothing as technology and as cultural symbol, it makes a novel contribution to material culture studies. This book shows why the histories of tents, surplus jackets, and even a nearly invisible synthetic laminate ought to be traced with the same kind of rigor as that of high-heeled shoes to bring their impact on American life to light. The outdoor industry is hardly unique in drawing on particular cultural ideologies to foster consumer interest. Indeed, one historian has shown that the production and consumption of a silk dress in the colonial period just as aptly reveals a world of commodities where colonists actively fashioned national identities through the objects they exchanged. Others have argued that buying served as a way of becoming a better citizen or asserting political rights. With the outdoor identity, possession of material goods taught and granted competence with an American cultural narrative.[7]

This is not a book about one particular product, akin to commodity histories on cod, coffee, or chocolate, and it does not celebrate individual entrepreneurs as a tycoon biography of Vanderbilt or Ford might. Instead, it most closely aligns with books that encompass entire industries. Business historians, for instance, have shown how soft drinks and fast food have had an immense influence on American culture. This book also looks at companies that started as regional niches and grew to behemoths with a national economic impact, explicit political aims, and most important, cultural resonance. Many founders of outdoor companies named here have published memoirs that reflect on the origins and growth of such prominent brands as Cabela's, JanSport, and Patagonia. The book uses these valuable works but situates them in a broader context that looks beyond the internal story to industry trends.[8]

In the 150 years that stretch from the age of buckskin to army surplus to such high-tech synthetics as Gore-Tex, outdoor enthusiasts have continued to engage in a peculiar paradox. Rather than leaving the modern world behind when in nature, Americans carry it with them through their purchases of the latest outdoor gear. What had been a draw for a few thousand people a year in the 1880s has grown to encompass tens of millions of participants (and consumers) every year. Outdoor clothing, once a quirky niche market, has been transformed into a fashion statement. Packing lists evolved, too, with new inventions and investments from the U.S. military, chemical companies, and athlete-entrepreneurs. In the twenty-first century, the outdoor industry's economic and cultural impact has only grown. Americans' love of gear transcends regional boundaries and the political spectrum, even though the way people love their gear varies wildly. It includes the Patagonia-clad mountain bikers taking laps on local trails as well as the family ducking into a Cabela's tent by a reservoir. Old-timers whose outfits have acquired a cherished patina and who shun weekenders in their North Face simulacra of outdoor mastery are likewise part of this trend. Outdoor companies continue to sell their products to this varied marketplace, reaching the expert adventure athletes and lifestyle consumers who have no plans to climb a mountain, leading to more than $400 billion a year in spending on outdoor recreation in the United States by 2023. How the industry sold nature with such resounding success, and why consumers responded the way they did, is the story we now turn to.

ONE

Buckskin

The Origins of Outdoor Style

Emerson Hough, nature writer and outdoor enthusiast, opened his familiar junk closet more than a hundred years ago and looked happily on his many precious possessions: a trove of guns, rifles, rods, footwear, and more. One garment that stood out was his buckskin shirt, made of a soft, tanned deer hide. When Hough opened his gear repository—it was his wife who called it junk—he could still smell the sweet, smoky campfire when he pressed the wholly useless and wholly beloved buckskin shirt to his face. It offered a "map of the outdoor world" with each deep inhalation.[1]

For Hough, who wrote western and historical novels in addition to an "Out-of-Doors" column for the *Saturday Evening Post*, the buckskin shirt was an "impossible" garment, so out of fashion that there was no place to wear it. It was impossible, too, because "no one but an Indian" could make a worthwhile buckskin shirt, but in the outdoor world that Hough and his fellow outdoorsmen envisioned, Native peoples were more a disappearing backdrop to their outing exploits than expert craftspeople. Indeed, with every passing moment, his face buried in the buckskin shirt, Hough was likely imagining not just the smoke of camp but also an American past where white men could be caretakers of historic Native goods that still had utility in modern American life. This was a selective longing that turned masculinity into a tool of nostalgia. Hough may have believed that buckskin stood in for the pioneer man of the past, but buckskin—smoke-tanned, smooth, and pliable—was the genius of Native women. This costume of the outdoors, made famous by the likes of Davy Crockett, Kit Carson, and Teddy Roosevelt, had its origins in the strong hands and careful attention of Ojibwe, Blackfeet, and Ute women.

The buckskin that outdoorsman Hough and his contemporaries so prized could mean several different things. It could variously signal primitivism or civilization, rugged men or pitiable pansies, and a preindustrial past or a modern era. Buckskin is just one example of how clothing conveyed concepts of race, gender, and even the progress and civilization that buttressed Victorian American culture. Native dress had long been an important marker of "the other," symbolizing the wilderness and the primitive. Indeed, in kidnapping narratives from the early years of the republic—stories of settlers abducted by Natives—clothes often signified a changed identity and affiliation. At the same time, white Americans had played Indian at the Boston Tea Party. These costumes served both political and social purposes; among other things they asserted Americanness and the superiority and inevitability of white supremacy on the continent.

Outdoor recreation without playing dress-up was no recreation at all, and emerging experts on outdoor recreation—white men who claimed insider knowledge by virtue of their connections to the country's Native past—argued that dress for the outdoors should be not only functional but also conform to prevailing notions of civilization. The clothes crucially demarcated the wild as a leisure space as opposed to a work space, and it established boundaries between leisured white Americans and working and Native people. Clothing likewise elevated the act of fishing, or walking on a trail, above the mundane. Buckskin was the first of many costumes for the outdoors that became naturalized as a part of white men's frontier past, erasing the very Native histories it purported to honor. And its production, use, and symbolism in the nineteenth century established many of the themes and paradoxes that would come to define, if not set the terms of, the outdoor culture and industry in the next generations.

Many historians trace the origins of outdoor recreation to 1864, a momentous year for several reasons. This was when William H. H. Murray, or "Adirondack Murray," went camping in the Adirondack Mountains and then wrote his guidebook, *Adventures in the Wilderness; or, Camp-Life in the Adirondacks,* which described a vacation of sport and health for both men and women. The guidebook detailed where to go and stay. Within a few years, his guidebook caused a stampede to the woods. Murray-ites were urban dwellers, wealthy, and eager to experience summer camping by a lake. Key to this experience was dressing and looking the part, and acquiring the right stuff.[2]

In 1864, Congress also set aside the Mariposa Grove of redwoods and the Yosemite Valley for "public use, resort and recreation." Although it did not establish a national park—that would come in 1872, with Yellowstone—the federal government recognized with this set-aside that wild lands in the West had value beyond development, and that these places might be primarily defined by recreation. In many ways the state park effort in Yosemite, and the lobbying efforts that followed to preserve Yellowstone as a national park and pleasuring ground, was a response to the commercialization of older tourist landscapes such as Niagara Falls, overrun with hotels and hawkers. Only government legislation could simultaneously dispossess Native residents of these regions and prevent further tourist infrastructure and commercial development. Americans' notion of wild space, in other words, was framed from the start as a space outside commercial life and would retain this aura through the decades.[3]

To contextualize outdoor recreation more deeply, as we must, in 1862, Congress passed the Homestead Act, which enshrined white Americans' expectation about access to land and asserted power over Indian territory not already vanquished by federal forces or commercial interests. Also in 1864 was the Sand Creek Massacre, in which federal troops, urged on by a bloodthirsty colonel and with the blessing of Colorado territory governor John Evans, set upon a camp of Cheyenne and Arapaho people waving white flags of surrender and slaughtered hundreds. This context is crucial, as well, for understanding how Americans prepared for the outdoors and envisioned the American wilderness as a space devoid of human history, where Native cultures white men destroyed could be appropriated and poached for symbolic meaning and ironic indicators of "authentic" expertise.

In the years after 1864, these sites of brutal violence and colonial conquest became focal points for creating a tradition of outdoor recreation. Between 1870 and the turn of the century, railroad construction laid tracks to the American West. Natural resources could be shipped eastward, a national market for manufactured goods was created, and new residents and tourists had reason to move westward. By 1880, the majority surveyed in the U.S. census were not farming, and by 1890, two-thirds of Americans were wage workers. Life expectancy jumped from forty-two in 1870 to forty-seven in 1900. In industrial cities, citizens and immigrants encountered skyscrapers and new forms of communication, from telegraph to telephone to typewriter. For these harried wage workers, some rest and recuperation in the woods seemed to be in order. Between 1870 and 1900, outdoor recreation began to flourish.

These earliest participants in outdoor culture, both guidebook authors and campers themselves, could not rely on any kind of tourist infrastructure, or on a dependable source of specialized clothing or equipment. That industry did not yet exist. Nonetheless, this period was the crucible in which the ideas cultivated and sold by the future outdoor industry were developed. In it, a generation of guidebook authors, railroad marketeers, park promoters, and lodge owners first shaped conceptions of how people should go back to nature, and why they would want to, and set the stage for gear producers and manufacturers who would do the same in the twentieth century.

In this era, no one would have thought of the guides and guidebooks and general stores that provided wares and advice for the camping family as an "industry." Indeed, the provisioners of a camping vacation were nothing like the business empires of John D. Rockefeller's Standard Oil Company, Colin P. Huntington's domination of railroads, and Andrew Carnegie's steel monopoly—the associations many Americans had with modern and especially commercial life. The camping vacation's distance from this kind of business only made it more attractive.

✳

As these changes shaped and transformed the land and landscape of the West in the late 1800s, writers also began producing a robust literature that affirmed white men as the inheritors of a Native past. It was a cruel paradox, of course, given that the sale of land, or even its protection as a park, depended on the erasure of Native people from the landscape. But guides, guidebook authors, and even companies selling the outdoor experience referenced the Indigenous presence, so long as it was firmly lodged in the past, as a selling point. They believed that selling Indian ideas—outdoor crafts, in particular—gave them a deep authenticity. As the founding generation of guidebook authors embraced the ethic of woodcraft, they saw themselves as guardians and purveyors of the knowledge of a dying race. Significantly, their guidebooks shaped outdoor expectations for the decades that followed. In particular, these authors contributed two key concepts that the outdoor industry would develop: first, they endorsed the idea of crafting over buying and, therefore, nature vacations as anti-commercial; second, they presented a particular narrative of an Indian past focused on woodcraft that authenticated and came to exemplify the outdoor experience.

On the first point, the outdoor guidebook author George Washington Sears—perhaps better known by his adopted faux-Indian name, Nessmuk—recommended that "hard-worked" Americans head to the woods for a "season of rest and relaxation." But Sears had no patience for the average *Forest and Stream* vacation. He denigrated the wealthy types who spent freely to have guides introduce them to woods and water sports. He directed his tome *Woodcraft* (1884), the first of dozens on the subject from the late nineteenth century to at least World War II, to the "hundreds of thousands of practical, useful men" who were "far from being rich" and who knew better than to pay for the pleasure of communing with "the blessed woods." Sears, like the many authors who followed him, hoped to translate advice about how to survive and thrive in the woods for the white, urban man of sufficient means to take a vacation from a desk job, but not of sufficient means, or so morally bankrupt, as to hire a guide to mediate the experience for him. Indeed, Horace Kephart, the author of another epic tome on the craft of camping in the woods—*Camping and Woodcraft* (1906)—thought it all well and good for those who could afford an outfitter to take care of everything from packing to paddling the canoe, selecting the campsite, and catching, cleaning, and cooking the fish, if they "like that sort of thing." But, like Sears, he was writing for a different kind of man, one who was looking to recover his rugged masculine identity and individuality through a strenuous physical and mental test.[4]

Guidebooks described skills that distinguished the novice from the master. If a camper found himself alone in the woods, in "a struggle for his life," Kephart explained, there was hope, but only if the camper had the skills and goods to survive. He must be "not only master of himself" but also master of the woods. The landscape—"nature's storehouse"—held the real tools to survival, if only the man knew how to wrest them from nature.[5]

What these prospective outdoorsmen did—or, more to the point, did *not*—purchase would define their ethic. Guidebook authors advised that in addition to carrying only necessary equipment, travelers should relinquish any misguided desire for discomfort. Only a tourist would buy into the notion that the woods should be rough. Instead, a master would learn to make the time in woods and waters "as rest and pleasurable" as possible. Mastering the outdoors meant going out in comfort—"smoothing it" rather than "roughing it." Mastery was sleeping warm and staying dry. Mastery was keeping the bugs off. Mastery was the male head of household managing the capable but flighty women of his camping party.[6]

For nineteenth- and early twentieth-century guidebook authors, outdoor mastery was achievable if outdoorspeople adhered to a clear and practical set of rules and guidelines. According to Kephart, "a camper should know for himself how to outfit, how to select and make a camp, how to wield an axe and make proper fires, how to cook, wash, mend, how to travel without losing his course, or what to do when he has lost it; how to trail, hunt, shoot, fish, dress game, manage boat or canoe, and how to extemporize such makeshifts as may be needed in wilderness faring." He must know these things so well and deeply that they became immediate, almost natural or instinctive actions. Only then, writes Kephart, "is he truly a woodsman," resourceful, with a "doughty self-reliance."[7]

Kephart and Sears did not begrudge their reader the odd purchase or two, knowing that any worthwhile sportsman was likely to buy the finest "guns, rods, reels, and such-like" as he could afford. But Kephart did advocate for caution and care in not buying too much: Why get a silk tent when a "second-hand army one" will do just fine? Why buy fancy nested aluminum cookware when tin will do just as well? Why buy a fancy outfit of loden, a thick woolen cloth, or gabardine when a "discarded business suit" will work much the same?[8]

Although Kephart and Sears wrote in the generic, their imagined reader was male. Their guidebooks often equated outdoor mastery with the recovery of white manhood, and used two different archetypes to elaborate it: the backwoods frontiersman and the Indigenous man. The modern man aligned himself with these two towering archetypes when he knew how to *make* rather than buy what was necessary to survive and when he eschewed excessive comforts and luxuries. Horace Kephart described the first archetype plainly: "In a far way you are emulating those grim heroes of the past who man the white man's trails across this continent." Be comfortable, but not obsessed with comfort—can you imagine Daniel Boone "reclining on an air mattress" or Kit Carson "pottering over a sheet-iron stove"? Kephart and other arbiters of outdoor expertise suggested that outdoor survival skills were intimately connected with masculine identity and its proof "in a manful way" by getting "closer to nature and closer to those good old times."[9]

The Indigenous man was the other archetype of white masculinity. For Ernest Thompson Seton, founder of the Woodcraft Indians youth group, "the Ideal Indian stands for the highest type of primitive life. He was a master of woodcraft, and unsorted, clean, manly, heroic, self-controlled, reverent, truthful and picturesque always." Seton, like Kephart, Sears, and other authors, relied on an essentialized vision of Indianness that placed Indians outside of modernity, even as they appropriated Indian practices for modern ends. Their stereotyped vision of Indian manhood was keyed to a set of skills: a true master would not starve "in a land of plenty." Instead, Kephart wrote, he would "learn from the natives, who, however contemptible they might seem in other respects, were past masters of the art of going 'light but right.' " The more outdoorsmen knew, and the more they could emulate manly heroes of the American past, the less they needed to carry with them. Guidebooks often reiterated this principle: "The less a man carries in his pack, the more he must carry in his head. . . . The simpler the outfit, the more skill it takes to manage it, and the more pleasure one gets in his achievements." According to many guidebooks, the authenticity and worth of an outdoor excursion could be measured by the equipment that a man did *not* carry.[10]

The woodcraft ethic itself was a colonial appropriation of Native knowledge, and the primary modes of transmission for this ethic—magazine articles, guidebooks, and advertisements—were consequentially positioned to further appropriate Native peoples and traditions. These texts' germinal recommendations on what and what not to buy would shape generations of outdoor habits.

There were no uniforms in this era, and no brand logos, and at this time the quintessential outfit of the backwoods frontiersman and Indigenous man archetypes alike was a buckskin suit. Outdoor guides celebrated buckskin as a sartorial expression of doughty self-reliance. It was, it seemed, the height of the woodcraft ethic to make your own buckskin. But, as we will see, buckskin suits in fact laid bare the contradictions inherent in the larger craft ethic of the early outdoor culture and its tension between the commercial and the authentic; between rugged individualism and dependence: any celebration of doughty self-reliance also included a quietly purchased buckskin suit—smoked, tanned, and sold by a Native American woman.

※

Buckskin as a Native product with a history was acknowledged across a broad geographical area. James C. Allan, for example, explained in 1888 that for snowshoe trips near Manitoba, Indian-made buckskin hunting shirts and fringed leggings were an expensive but desirable investment.

Guidebook authors of the late nineteenth century bandied about the language of handcraft and self-sufficiency but agreed that only Native women could make a buckskin suit the right way. "It takes an Indian woman" to smoke and tan a hide so that it is properly soft and pliable, explained Emerson Hough in *Out of Doors* in 1915. Indeed, he wrote, though of course a skilled man *could* made his own buckskin, "it is much better to let the Indian woman . . . do all the work of making the buckskin."[11]

Guidebook authors and nature writers rarely deigned to refer to these women as real people or characters in the story. Emerson Hough, whose overflowing gear closet sparked so many memories and ruminations, invented a character called Laughing Water to explain how to brain-tan buffalo hide.[12]

It was a paradox that these men, so eager to perform outdoor masculine expertise, had to rely on women for the buckskin. The product came to symbolize the backwardness of Indigenous gender systems, because women were doing the work while, it seemed to white observers, the men were lazing about. As explained in a *Forest and Stream* article in 1899, all a man needed was a "good squaw to do the work" of tanning. White trappers, too, could descend into this category of compromised masculinity when they married Native women. J. W. Schultz wrote in a *Forest and Stream* sportsman column in 1903 that while one Beaver Bill just lay around smoking, his wife "cuts the wood, carries the water, cooks, breaks and makes camp, sews moccasins and buckskin shirts for him," and more. According to these guidebooks, when Native women made buckskin, it signaled the ignoble backwardness of their society; when white men made buckskin, it signaled their ennobling masculinity through the recovery of a vague past connoted by the archetype of the Indigenous man—even though, of course, buckskin had never been men's work.[13]

"Indian tanned" referred to a process as well as a product's origin. Ojibwe Paul Buffalo liked to watch the women tan hides, smoking and scraping until the hides were velvety and soft. The process for making buckskin mattered not just for its function but for its authenticity according to white men's criteria. The first step was to submerge the hide in running water or bury it in mud for a few days, so that the hair would slip off more easily. Then a woman would remove all traces of hair using a scraper tool. After placing the hide in a frame or on the ground, she would begin to scrape the flesh side as well, until it was left even and soft. After breaking down the fiber of the hide with twisting and pulling, she brain-tanned it. Splitting open the skull, she would rub in a thick coating of crushed brain on the hair side of the hide, allowing it to dry in a cool place. Finally, she would smoke it, stretching the hide over the fire and turning it to smoke it evenly. Depending on the market, the hide could have a number of uses. The woman and her family might use it for baby cradles, bedding, and clothes. And if she lived near white consumers, she might add a bead pattern—to make it a more attractive product to sell.[14]

Amid concerns that American men were losing touch with manual labor skills, guidebooks advised on the one hand that they should be able to make buckskin. "The ideal woodsman," explained one guidebook, "should be able to fashion at least every piece of his outer clothing, including cap and

"Indian-tanned" buckskin referred to the process by which mostly Native American women smoked and scraped skins. ("Chippewa Indians smoking and scraping buck skins," Truman W. Ingersoll Photograph Collection, c. 1900, E97.34 p9 Negative No. 11299, Minnesota Historical Society)

moccasins." On the other hand, it seemed that in practice, most men were happy to buy these items instead. Hough thought it quite foolish for a white man to take on this task. Even with two thousand dollars, he claimed, a white tailor couldn't make a real buckskin shirt to save his life. Hough had an essentialized view of Native women's capacity for labor: they were patient enough to wring and stretch and rub the buckskin, whereas "no white man" would take the pains to "do it right." Even once the hide was prepared, Hough argued, "no white man or woman" could make a buckskin shirt. Then again, a "heartless civilized squaw" might try to pass off a shirt sewn with thread—bogus—as the genuine, sinew-thread-sewn article. For Hough, a slender thread—literally—distinguished the proper buckskin artist from the fraud.[15]

Despite the recognition that Native women were the best, or even the only, real buckskin artists, authors of guides to woodcraft often presented the process of making buckskin much as they presented other recipes for outdoor equipment and supplies. By presenting a how-to guide to making buckskin, Kephart established the expectation that a woodsman should be able to follow this recipe and similar processes. The craft of the woods was so often about making various dopes and dubbings, from canvas tent treatments out of water, alum, and sugar of lead to the bug dopes to guard against "venomous little wretches."[16]

As for buckskin, it worked. It was durable, it was the right neutral color for hunting in the woods, and it kept out the wind and cold. According to Stewart Edward White, there was no better way to get through brush noiselessly. For Kephart, buckskin guarded against thorns and burs. White men who adorned themselves with buckskin rarely picked it for functionality alone, however. If anything, they invoked functionality as an alibi to obscure the otherwise suspect connection between costume, style, and manhood.[17]

Look carefully at late nineteenth-century photographs of self-styled rugged outdoorsmen, and buckskin is everywhere. Theodore Roosevelt, famous for his recommendation of "the strenuous life" to strengthen American boys into men who could handily win wars, posed in a fringed buckskin suit to promote his book *Hunting Trips of a Ranchman*, published in 1885. The outfit had been a dream since childhood, when young Theodore imagined an adventure in the American West where he "straddle[d] the Continental Divide clad in buckskin." The historian Michael Canfield writes that buckskin symbolized Roosevelt's ambition to be taken seriously as an outdoorsman. Even in his later years in Washington, D.C., Canfield explains, Roosevelt the politician dressed fashionably but plainly in a business suit, but at home, his "favorite buckskin jacket waited for him," ready for another adventure. Like the literary hero of his youth, Natty Bumppo from James Fenimore Cooper's *The Last of the Mohicans* (1826), Roosevelt wore buckskin on the trail. A buckskin shirt topped the list of clothing Roosevelt packed on a trip to the Bighorns in 1884. Roosevelt's poses helped solidify buckskin's status not just as an appropriate material for the outdoors but also as sartorial shorthand for a broad range of outdoor skills.[18]

Roosevelt did not make his own buckskin. He knew that his trip west in 1884 was "playing at frontier hunter." Acquisition of a buckskin suit was right at the top of the list for playing this part, along with bagging an antelope. The fringed buckskin shirt was, to him, "the most picturesque and distinctively national dress ever worn in America." To procure his buckskin Roosevelt visited the mud hut of a Mrs. Maddox in the North Dakota territory, known for her "first-class" buckskin attire. Roosevelt found her personality and situation as remarkable as the clothes themselves. Cornelia "Neal" Maddox lived in a mud-roofed hut on Sand Creek, and a young Roosevelt was drawn to her reputation as a sewer of buckskin. Roosevelt held her in awe, both for her sharp way with words, her apparent ease with the local Sioux who visited her, and her "terrible vigor." Maddox measured Roosevelt for her suit and then sat him and his companion down for dinner. Her manners and language were crucial for Roosevelt's sense of what buckskin symbolized: a world beyond civilization, where women were not quite ladies.[19]

Roosevelt picked up the suit later, and it's unclear whether he already planned to pose in a New York studio with that very suit. When historians describe the background of this iconic photograph, they rightly focus on the artificial stiffness with which Roosevelt represents his western experience in the eastern photography studio. But the link to Maddox so often disappears in this retelling—and, with it, the complicated certification of masculinity through buckskin, laboriously produced by colonized Indigenous women.

Using buckskin as certification of recovered white manhood was decidedly common. Roosevelt might be the most famous example, but other white men in silly costumes abound. Both the use and the idea of buckskin pervaded nineteenth-century literature on how to get back to nature. Daniel Carter Beard, founder of the youth organization Sons of Daniel Boone, suggested that buckskin hearkened back to the "good old pioneer days." He called his band of scouts the "Buckskin Men." For Beard, every archetypal outdoorsman was a "buckskin man." He took that to mean young white men who, through their play in the woods, continued the legacy of the great pioneering backwoodsmen of the early nineteenth century, like Daniel Boone and Kit Carson. For Beard, buckskin stood metonymically for both

Theodore Roosevelt posed in a buckskin suit sewn by Mrs. Maddox because to him it symbolized his serious outdoorsman credentials. ("Theodore Roosevelt in 1885," George Grantham Bain, 1885, Library of Congress, www.loc.gov/item/2009633128)

outdoor know-how and the larger ethic of mastering the land that he saw as white men's birthright. "Boys of the Open," he wrote, "pull on your buckskin leggings, give a war whoop, . . . this great Republic belongs to you."[20]

To consumers, buckskin offered a path to access the authenticity of the premodern manual laborer who worked with his hands and made real things. For Beard, buckskin belonged to a world already lost by 1900, or at least disappearing. The "romantic and picturesque plainsmen and the wild and rollicking cowboys have followed the herds of buffalo"—they are no more, just like the "whoop of the painted Indian." But Beard could revitalize American manhood and celebrate the pioneer and Indian past by donning a buckskin coat. For these men, buckskin was a material and a style that told a history of conquest.[21]

For all its functionality, there was nothing inherent in the material itself, of course, that gave buckskin the power or particular symbolism that Roosevelt imbued it with. Nowhere is this clearer than in the ways that federal officials forced Native peoples to shed buckskin to take on the mantle of civilization. For white male buckskin enthusiasts like Roosevelt, Native dress and equipment indicated authenticity and function, but the same clothes on an Indigenous person indicated savagery and backwardness, and their surrender of buckskin was a token of forcible assimilation, the process of molding Indian children into Americans through education and dress.

With military, corporate, and religious force, American imperialists banished buckskin from the wardrobes of Native children, at the same time that they colluded to dispossess Native peoples of access to the deer and other animals whose hides would make the material itself. Officials forced Native children on reservations and later in boarding schools to don western dress, to cut their hair, and to speak only English. Clothing was an important measure of a school's "success" in assimilating children into white norms. Starched collars and tight waists were the costumes of civilization for Bureau of Indian Affairs officials and schoolteachers.

The outdoor industry and its products originated in a nostalgia for a preindustrial past, conveyed by an Indian aesthetic on white frontier actors, such that a sartorial mark of recuperated masculinity on the white man became a sartorial mark of "savagery" on the Indigenous man, who was little more than a stylized archetype of masculinity for the former. Whether on the bodies of Native peoples or as an artifact appropriated by the white outdoorsman, buckskin was part of a story being crafted at the end of the nineteenth century about the American frontier. It was "rudely fashioned" when worn by Indians who served as part of a display in a sportsmen's show, but a celebrated technology and costume of masculinity on the body of white men, where it looked "frontierish" and conveyed a desirable kind of "ruffianism."[22]

Around 1897, Ah-ne-pitch and Tomas-cita sat for a family portrait in a studio in Denver. Their child, Ma-rez, lay between them in a Ute cradleboard, snug against the willow frame because of a buckskin cover. This style of cradle had been widespread since at least the 1870s. It allowed mothers to transport a child easily on their backs or on a horse. The buckskin, brain-tanned, was dyed white for a boy and yellow for a girl. This buckskin, though similarly adorned with fringe and beads, did not connote the rugged, authentic, or masculine. Instead, the cradleboard of buckskin was an example of precisely the problem with Native women, who did not adhere to white

Victorian standards of marriage and motherhood. Though cradleboards were ubiquitous and effective for carrying very young children, white reformers saw them as "evidence of poor mothering skills." Not only were they tight against the babies' bodies, the cradleboards also held children vertically on the back, a contrast to modern, scientific mothering. Though denigrated at the time as uncivilized, the design and concept behind the cradleboard would come to shape white Americans' child carriers decades later. In the nineteenth century, however, they were an important counterpoint to the power imbued in fringed buckskin jackets by white men. It's not that the buckskin itself was different but, rather, the stories men chose to tell about buckskin—offensive when used as a cradleboard by a nonwhite woman; empowering when worn as a jacket by a white man. It seems that buckskin, as a form of primitive dress, was only suitable for white men's play.[23]

Late nineteenth-century guidebook authors had two favorite ways to depict this outdoor man, and they were almost always instantly recognizable by how they wore their buckskin. The first was the "woodsman." He was an experienced white man who, like his pioneer-era brothers, could make his own clothes, hunt his dinner, and build his shelter. He relied on himself. White argued that "a superabundance of paraphernalia proves always more of a care than a satisfaction." Why carry an air mattress, he asked, when a balsam bed would do just as well *and* was in no danger of getting punctured? The woodsman knew that "when the woods offer you a thing ready made, it is the merest foolishness to transport the same thing an hundred miles for the sake of the manufacturer's trademark." Buying gear in the city, in other words, undermined the performance of manhood. However, given that Emerson Hough, Horace Kephart, and other guidebook authors often made use of the "ready made" shortcut of buying buckskin suits from Native women, the description of an anti-commercial, authentically self-reliant "woodsman" seems largely aspirational.[24]

The second stock character was the tenderfoot. He was the opposite of the woodsman: uncomfortable in his store-bought buckskin, uneasy in the woods, and hapless when it came to providing for himself. In contrast to the expert woodsman, who theoretically made what he needed from raw materials in the woods, beginners relied on store-bought equipment and clothing they did not understand. To guidebook authors, this commercial tendency indicated a deeper flaw in their masculine character. "The tenderfoot is a queer beast," wrote the chronicler of outdoor life Stewart Edward White in *The Mountains* (1904). "He makes more trouble than ants at a picnic, more work than a trespassing goat." Most important, the tenderfoot is recognizable because he "always overdoes the equipment question." For a day of shooting, for instance, he "accumulates" clothing and equipment "until he looks like a picture from a department-store catalogue." For a day in cow country, he goes all out in "Stetson hats, snake bands, red handkerchiefs, six-shooters, chaps, and huge spurs." Be kind to such an "amusing" man, White recommends, for he is "not as other men"—"he has been raised a pet." The tenderfeet "plod" where woodsmen walk. They have "corpulent duffel bags" and "air mattresses and camp chairs and oil lanterns," and they hire others to carry their equipment. They move their extravagant caravans at the slow pace of only five miles a day.[25]

As a shortcut to identifying whether a man was a woodsman or a tenderfoot, see if the man in question knows how to identify real buckskin. Kephart wrote in his guidebook that woodsmen ought to understand how to make buckskin "if for no other reason than to avoid being humbugged" when they want to purchase it. He warned that "much of the so-called buckskin used by glovers and others is a base imitation."[26]

✳

At the beginning and end of the trail, clothing also allowed people far removed from outdoor recreation to judge recreationists' adherence to gender and class norms. Off the trail, playing outdoors and dressing the part provoked two deep concerns. One was racial passing—the ability of some men (never women in this case) to play Indian based on dress and activity but reveal themselves to be white when they removed their hat or dirty buckskin jacket. The second concern was class passing: men might appear to be locals or workers, based on how they dressed and acted, but might pull out a first-class railroad ticket or good manners and reveal themselves to be respectable elites on vacation. Both of these concerns touched on identity and anxieties over the boundaries of authentic belonging in recreational nature. Whiteness and class status were malleable—to an extent. Elite white men delighted in their ability to move between categories of identity because it proved their skill in playing the outdoorsmen, but they chafed at any treatment that undermined their privilege. They wanted both to play Indian and to maintain their seat on the train, their service at a restaurant, and their ability to court a lady.

A group of white men in buckskin—hunters—went to a hotel restaurant in Sioux City to eat lunch. Meat and pie were on the menu. The plainsmen waited, none too patiently, for the Black waiter to serve them. The author who recounted this story years later, in 1902, surmised that the waiter, put off by their long hair, unshaven faces, and general unkempt appearance, decided to serve the "more respectably dressed guests" first. But these men were impatient and hungry, and one decided to pull a gun on the waiter to expedite the serving process. They were arrested when the hotel proprietor returned with the town marshal and sheriff. The men faced a hefty fine, and never did get a taste of pie, but beyond that there were no repercussions to this assertion of white power in front of a Black service worker.[27]

In their attire these men toyed with the line of social acceptability through their appearance but ultimately saw white privilege as inviolable. One white man claimed that a buckskin suit and a few invented Indian words were enough for people to mistake him for an Indian. Buckskin, as with other attire for the outdoors, reflected a broader conversation about how to be civilized in wild spaces and the danger of being mistaken for wild in the civilized ones. Considering the attire of outdoor recreation reveals not just where the recreational wild began, but also *who* had the status and control to safely don outdoor clothing *temporarily* without actually being transformed by it or compromising their privileges of race or class. Buckskin revealed these identities to be unstable but also reinforceable.[28]

Many guidebooks recommended clothes that were worn but still fashionable as an appropriate compromise for the trail. In his guide on *How to Camp Out* (1877), John Mead Gould wrote that "camping offers a fine opportunity to wear out old clothes, and to throw them away when you have done with them." The quality and appearance of even old clothes meant for sport mattered because strangers evaluated race and social status through attire. Clothing signaled which leisure-seeking woodsmen were employed, respectable men who ought to be admitted to the train car, the restaurant, or the hotel when they came off the trail. Gentlemen of the woods might return to city life seeking "juicy beefsteaks," wine, and cigars after many nights of camp dinners. Waiters would take a look at the grime on their knuckles, the dust on their shirts, and the flop of their hats and turn such customers away because "guests were not allowed to eat without coats."[29]

There were ways to guard against misrecognition of the elite white man, even when he was in old suits or buckskin costuming. In his guidebook, John Mead Gould highlighted the concern that urban elites traveling to the countryside would be mistaken for people of that area. Gould recommended that men wear a suit "sufficiently in fashion to show that you are a traveler or camper." Simple but luxurious touches like a leather hat band transformed leisure seekers from mere woodsmen to "gentlemen of the woods" in costume. These touches were crucial if outdoorsmen did not want to be mistaken for "two-dollar a day laborer[s]" because of their appearance.[30]

For white men, the ability to pass for someone else was part of the outdoor experience. Stewart Edward White, for instance, fairly delighted in instances of mistaken identity. One February, he later recounted, he stepped onto a train "clad in fur cap, vivid blanket coat, corded trousers, German stocking and moccasins," his only baggage a pair of snowshoes. In that instance, his fellow passengers looked at him "askance." The most flattering experience, though, was when a young boy, upon encountering White in a similar outfit, exclaimed, "Look mamma! . . . there's a real Indian!" For White, these encounters proved that his garments were correct for the trail and that he had performed masculinity well. This ability to pass was only flattering because White knew that with a bath and a change of clothes, it was an identity easily shed, a mistake easily rectified. In other words, it was a costume—not an identity. Overall, white men seemed to benefit from being mistaken for Native because the misdirection conferred on them expert knowledge. The guidebook author George Washington Sears—to recall, he published under the name Nessmuk—revealed his white background in the pages of his texts, but still used the name on the spine as evidence of insider status by virtue of deep association with Native peoples. As with dressing up in buckskin, this was a performance for white audiences.[31]

The rules were different for women. Guidebooks did not invite women to aspire to the status of expert woodsman, nor did they indicate there was any possibility of being mistaken for an Indian or a day laborer. While guidebooks challenged men to adhere to a rugged standard of outdoor craft, they made much narrower suggestions to women, who were presumed to be companions on group trips, never individuals alone in the woods. Guidebooks did not suggest that women learn to survive on nature's storehouse. They also regularly admonished women to give up any pretentions to finery or spare clothing on the trail. Rather than guiding women toward mastery of what authors saw as a man's wilderness, guidebooks imparted how to be appropriately feminine on the trail without burdening male companions. To do this, much like the men, women needed to wear the right clothes.

Two concerns permeated recommendations for outdoorswomen's attire. First was the notion that women would be tempted to bring formal wear with them to the woods. Charles Nordhoff, in *California for Health, Pleasure, and Residence,* his guidebook published in 1874, suggested that women should "leave all finery behind" because there was "no stand[ing] upon ceremony" in these nature parks. The second concern was the idea that women's bodies were too weak to handle clothing for outdoor activities. According to some guidebook authors, both corsets and heels had so shaped women's bodies that to discard them immediately for the recommended outdoor outfits would put women at risk. A woman's back muscles and her foot arch would not be strong enough to withstand such a rapid wardrobe change. Kathrene Pinkerton, a rare female voice in the chorus of guidebook writers, suggested in *Woodcraft for Women* (1916) that women train themselves to get used to the new clothing. Preparations for the out-of-doors life included going without a corset for a few hours each day until the aspiring outdoorswoman's back and stomach were strong enough to support her torso. For weak feet, Pinkerton recommended camp footwear and that women wear low heels before a trip to strengthen their arches. Pinkerton wanted to convince women that while the shift in clothing was dangerous, it could be manageable and worthwhile.[32]

These concerns are significant because they introduced and established tropes about women in the outdoors that would persist for decades, sometimes despite descriptions of women's very real experiences to the contrary. These guidebooks essentially "gendered" concern about fashion and style, and established the trope that they were women's preoccupations, thus implicitly rendering any man's choices—even his foolish reliance on gadgets—to be neutral by comparison. Indeed, even a man's preference for toys of the outdoors were not dismissed as finery in the same way that women's attire was, because men might (although rarely did) craft their toys by their own hands. Similarly, the suggestion not only that women's bodies were too weak for the activities of the outdoors but even that their clothes themselves were to blame contributed to the notion that women were perpetual outdoors neophytes who required coddling. While men might be freed from the strictures of civilized life with outdoor attire, women needed to train simply to be able to wear relaxed clothing, ironically, with comfort.

Finally, the focus on how fashionable women's wear was, how decent or appropriate, introduced a very different conversation than the one about white men's authenticity. While men could playfully test and trespass the boundary between gentleman and convincing Native in costume, women could not, for there was no equivalent to the buckskin suit for women, no glorious rugged past that such attire might revive. There were a few exceptions, of course—Wild West celebrities such as Calamity Jane and Annie Oakley, for whom fringed buckskin might serve as performance attire. Overall, though, women were generally exempt from guidebook insults about fakes in buckskin—but this also meant they were unable to demonstrate expertise. Bloomers were functional, but never the clothes of a true woodsman and hardly on par with buckskin for history and romance. The recovery of the past through dress, then, was not possible for all aspiring recreationists.

※

In 1915, Ruel Garnich Baldwin, a young white man in his early twenties, brought the hides of deer he had shot to a Native American woman near Ashland, Wisconsin. Baldwin sought a Bad River Chippewa woman's sewing skills for what would become his prized jacket: a tanned, scraped, and smoked leather garment that reminded him of his hunting adventures. To Baldwin, such a jacket likely felt extraordinary—a highly personal and individual garment, an emblem of a time gone by. But Baldwin's acquisition of a homemade buckskin jacket, and his reliance on a Chippewa woman to make it, reprised a paradox of white men dressing up in Native-made and women-made clothing to flaunt their masculinity, expertise, authenticity, and rugged individualism. Buckskin, as both a material garment and an idea about the American past, set the narrow and exclusionary terms of just who belonged in the world of outdoor recreation that would recur in successor generations. Far from being a quirky emblem of times past that Baldwin rarely wore but trotted out occasionally to show his children, the deer hide jacket sewn by an unnamed Ojibwe woman tacitly connected Baldwin to generations of agents of empire. And in this garment and all the contradictions and paradoxes that it mobilizes are the origins of the American outdoor industry.[33]

The buckskin era anticipated important trends in the twentieth-century outdoor industry. By relying on the association of buckskin with frontiersmen rather than the Native women who made the buckskin, guidebook authors created an outdoorsman archetype accessible only to men. By downplaying Native women's role in the making of buckskin, guidebook authors and outdoor enthusiasts similarly erased women as central actors within the industry as designers and creators as well as participants in their own right. Discussions of buckskin in outdoor guidebooks and magazines also established a trope of the outdoor industry: equipment was about function rather than fashion, which led to the conflation of men's buying habits with functionality rather than style. This was a circular kind of argument: the more people like Emerson Hough could make the case that buckskin was out of fashion, the easier it was to claim it was equipment, rather than mere costume.

Together, these trends helped to create the central paradox of the outdoors. Make, don't buy, was a central admonition of outdoor guidebooks of the late nineteenth century. This directive embedded a suspicion of consumerism, which signaled ignorance, inexperience, naivete, feminization, and overcivilization. Yet even in this early era, buying outdoor clothing and equipment—at least when men were doing the buying—was a necessary guilty pleasure.

This generation of outdoorsmen found ways to rehabilitate their purchases. Emerson Hough's overflowing gear closet became not a shameful

IS there anything you ever did in your life that made you feel any better than getting away for a few days, or even a few hours from the city, especially after a strenuously busy season?

Didn't that fishing trip bring new life to your tired brain and nerves, and doesn't it make you glow with health to get out into the country, through woods and fields?

How about the feeling when you landed that four-pound bass after a twenty-minute fight?

What is it that makes us all, young and old, long for the life out-of-doors?

Think over these questions.

Catalog images like these suggested that desk-bound urbanites could find rejuvenation in outdoor recreation. Buying the products advertised was the first step toward that escape to nature. (*Pfluegers' Tips on Tackle*, no. 139, 1919, Enterprise Manufacturing Co., Akron, Ohio, Autry Library and Archives, Autry Museum, Los Angeles, 95.121.1) artifact of his acquisitive nature, but rather a sign of his manhood. When Hough and his ilk decided that buckskin was a frontierish fashion and functional as well, they elevated it as a garment that transformed men into men. Each time they played dress-up, they helped establish and solidify the norms of an outdoor industry and modern outdoor recreation practices. Smells like history and romance, Hough would say as he lingered over the fragrant garment—the outdoor industry was one built for white men's nostalgia.

The consumer economy glumly haunted the desk-bound, effete men who went to the woods, but, White wrote, the man who knew how to procure and wear a buckskin shirt had a chance to leave behind the "world of made things" and head for "unchanging" nature. The belief that nature was an escape from modern, commercial life would remain constant through the twentieth century. New, however, was the notion that outdoor outfitters held the key to that escape. A catalog from an Akron-based fishing outfitter, Pflueger's, in 1919 makes clear the company's role as a mediator of the outdoors: A young man in a suit slouches at his roll-top desk, while industrial smokestacks darken the sky outside his office. "Is there anything you ever did in your life that made you feel better than getting away for a few days?" the copy reads. Below the text, a man sits in a canoe, landing a four-pound bass while the sun sets in orange and yellow beyond the pines on the far bank. By the early twentieth century, companies like Pflueger's sought to "bring new life" to Americans with "tired brains and nerves." These outdoor companies offered the "world of made things" as a gateway to nature. Guidebook author Kephart admonished readers to shy away from "boughten" things and to instead fashion what they needed "on the spot." Outdoorspeople, however, were quite ready to embrace buying as a part of the outdoor experience.[34]

TWO

A Green Respite

Creating the Outdoor Store

The nature writer Stewart Edward White could always sense the place where wilderness began. For the adventure and travel writer working in the early twentieth century, a physical place marked the transition from city to trail, from modern, urban existence to the primitive wilderness. He called this place "the jumping-off place." It was both a real place and symbolic of a complicated relationship to products and material objects in the back-to-nature enterprise. The comparison between the artificial "world of made things," as White described it, and the primeval and unchanging wilderness gets to the heart of what Americans sought when they went back to nature: an escape from modern life. Yet, most often, that journey began at an outdoor store.[1]

Despite White's suspicion toward the world of made things, the most important stop on his journey out of that world was a little country store he called the "aromatic shop." It had wooden counters and "dusky" aisles of goods and was like many other country stores, except that "in the dimness of these two aisles lurks the spirit of the wilds." This was the transition zone, the place to find smoke- and oil-tanned moccasins, snowshoes, and tumplines for a pack. White described the shop as aromatic because it smelled like the wild: "The reek of the camp-fires is in its buckskin, of the woods in its birch bark, . . . of the evening meal in its coffees and bacons."[2]

The shopkeeper was just as important to the transitional experience as that campfire smell. He was wise and accommodating, leaning his elbows

In Stewart Edward White's *The Forest*, two men contemplate an escape to the trail. Their business suits and indoor setting suggest they are planning a departure from the world of made things. (Stewart Edward White, *The Forest* [New York: Outlook, 1903], 1)

on the counter as "together you go over the list" of what to pack. He had the time to talk about your supplies (less coffee, more pork). And he saw you off early the next morning. He represents "the last hand-clasp of civilization" before the Long Trail. The shopkeeper, like the town and the shop, helped the wilderness lure its visitor.[3]

In the early twentieth century, stores like the one White visited changed tremendously. They were selling products such as hunting suits, canoes, and numerous other outdoor gadgets to a growing number of outdoor enthusiasts. No longer jumping-off points near the wilderness, new stores opened in big cities to cater to urbanites long before they arrived at the trailhead. These stores used a dual approach of mail order and in-store retail to reach these large markets. As stores expanded so did the outdoor literature and press, especially guidebooks and magazines, that highlighted expert advice and aligned packing lists with particular products. And as general stores moved from the frontier to the big city, they began to revise the myths about the Native past that had been so central to nineteenth-century outdoorsmen. The rise of these specialty outdoor and sporting goods stores that rivaled department stores in their grandeur, including Abercrombie & Fitch in New York City and Von Lengerke & Antoine in Chicago, also told a new story: the goods they sold were true necessities for real outdoorsmen, and those products marked not just a path to nature, but nature itself.

Historians have long homed in on the early twentieth century to explain the rising popularity of outdoor recreation in the United States. They've looked at railroads, promoters, and hotel owners to understand the messaging around back-to-nature experiences, and how the messages were entwined around a story of turning the wilderness into a consumer experience. Technology, especially, was an important part of outdoor recreation's growing popularity, including tents and stoves as well as automobiles. But the anti-consumerist woodcraft ethic for outdoor recreation that had already influenced generations of wilderness philosophers paralleled the expansion of a consumer outdoors experience. How can we reconcile these two apparently contradictory or at least conflicting phenomena, the expansion of an outdoors consumerism and an anti-consumerist outdoors ethic? We find our answer in the "dusky" aisles of the aromatic shop and in its successor: the urban outdoor store.

In the early twentieth century, outdoor stores pushed the illusion that they were non-commercial spaces for commercial transactions. Outdoor shops sold the woodcraft vision of anti-consumerism by presenting stores as both masculine and "green" (with "green" in this context meaning adjacent to the woods rather than, as in contemporary usage, environmentally friendly), thereby creating a gendered alibi for any accusations or fears of frivolous consumption. At the same time, these outdoor stores included women's departments that created a new icon—the outdoor woman—who would not threaten the masculine space the store was working to create. As enticing, delightful spaces these stores suggested that the "wild" started right there rather than on the trail. Stores promoted shopkeepers as expert outdoorsmen who could advise on purchases, in sharp contrast to the ideal of the frontiersman who learned and tried everything firsthand. Finally, outdoor stores helped make outdoor attire a hallmark of the leisured class.

Customers made two kinds of purchases in the store: the commodity itself and the stories about the goods. The latter often came in the form of a masculine, heady space where the transaction itself occurred.

※

Abercrombie & Fitch (A&F) was one of the many early twentieth-century outfitters that helped shape the look of Americans' outdoor leisure experiences. Manufacturers and retailers created and codified the category of leisure goods now known as "outdoor clothing." Rather than only looking backward to an imagined American past out on the frontier, white middle-class American consumers could self-identify as *modern* "outdoor men" and "outdoor women."

From around 1900 to the 1920s outdoor outfitters such as A&F developed a recognizable aesthetic, tried out different marketing strategies for selling experience and authenticity, and dressed many thousands of vacationers. Through store layout, conversations with customers, and goods sold, A&F and similar companies reinforced consumption as a serious and legitimate part of the American outdoor experience. To stake their claim on the outdoor recreation world was no small feat, given the truism that the *authentic* outdoorsman did not buy gadgets and, indeed, made his own equipment and clothing. A&F promotional material suggested that men and women alike could visit the boulevard en route to the trail and buy what they needed to feel comfortable, safe, and stylish.

The A&F building was alluring from the street. In 1922 visitors to this self-proclaimed "greatest sporting goods store in the world" would have found themselves at the crossroads of commerce and nature. At twelve stories, the A&F headquarters towered over its neighbors at Madison Avenue and Forty-fifth Street and announced the company name in large lettering on at least three sides. Like other dry goods houses and merchandisers at the time, A&F participated in the move toward a new aesthetic of "commercial enticements." A&F was neither as large nor as grand as the famous "marble palaces" such as Macy's and Marshall Field's. Nonetheless, A&F and other outdoor outfitters used everything from modern advertising techniques to window displays to create an "aesthetic of desire and longing" that would lure customers, predominantly male, to the store and entice them to buy.[4]

Outdoor outfitters attempted to attract men who were skeptical about consumption fitting into their anti-commercial back-to-nature fantasies. Merchant John Wanamaker could turn to heavy, Japanese-inspired draperies to frame his store's grand staircase. Marshall Field's hired a leading window display designer to create "coherent pictures of luxury" using mannequins in the latest fashions. However, to sell equipment for outdoor recreation, A&F could turn to neither and instead helped develop a new visual language for selling nature. Its floors of tents, the game adorning the walls, the miniature pond, and the log-cabin paint defied prevailing commercial design and, more specifically, the color and luxury intended to attract female consumers. In 1922 A&F presented a more muted color palette and consumer spectacle to attract men by suggesting that outdoor sports would help them recover their lost manhood.[5]

Wanamaker's had a Grand Court during the Christmas season. Macy's had a parade. A&F had a tent. The company fashioned stores as a "home camp," not just to the pastimes that we would recognize as outdoor sports today—camping, hiking, fishing, and hunting—but also to a wide range of other outdoor activities, including cycling, motoring, tennis, and golf. Deer, moose, and buffalo heads watched over the store as men (women had a separate department) in knee-length wool coats and caps leaned over the glass counter to examine an item the male salesclerk had just pulled out from a cabinet. Like other retail stores of the era, shopkeepers behind the counters mediated interactions with the goods. A&F had walls of guns and fishing rods, along with counters of golf clubs and tennis rackets. The visual look of the store and the feelings the displays generated shaped the messages that visitors received. In this light the A&F scene mattered as much as the commodities to cultivate loyal customers.[6]

In the back of the main sales floor, under the large set of windows, stood a large and fully erected tent, at least seven by ten feet. In a photograph from an A&F catalog, in 1913, two young men sit under the tent's shadow reading in two camp chairs, perhaps waiting for their father to finish up the purchase of a pair of skis that lean against the framed tent. Nearby, a camp hammock—complete with a fur blanket—beckons to the young men should they get restless. In the shoe department another male customer hikes up his pant leg so that the salesclerk can help him try on a pair of new boots.

On a different floor, A&F designers cultivated an entirely different look for the prospective sportswoman customer. The women's outing department boasted no trophy heads or counters crowded with wristwatches. Instead, sportswomen in floor-length dark skirts, fur-trimmed jackets, and

VIEWS OF RETAIL SALES DEPARTMENTS.

A&F stores boasted not just walls of guns and fishing rods but an entire floor of Camp Goods and a "Davy Crockett" cabin on the roof of the twelve-story building. These elements, A&F marketers hoped, would create a "green" respite from city life. (Abercrombie & Fitch catalog, 1913, National Museum of American History, Smithsonian Libraries and Archives) feathered hats met with their own salesclerk at a long wooden table in the center of the room while wide-brimmed and beribboned hats had pride of place on top of glass cabinets. Elsewhere, customers would have headed to the Camp Goods floor to assess the Forester tent, along with the accompanying "camp paraphernalia." Up on the roof a customer might have sat in the Davy Crockett Log Cabin and imagined himself in the woods rather than in the "heart of the greatest city in the world." Right next to the rooftop cabin was a fly-casting tank, where customers could try out their rods and flies. Commerce unified the woods and the city. In this building, catalog copywriters imagined, the "blazed trail crosses the boulevard," and this became one of their slogans.[7]

An A&F ad from 1920 in *Country Life in America* explained, "There is one spot in the metropolis which always remains green in your memory, even when you're out among the fields and the links and the lakes." Abercrombie & Fitch copywriters envisioned the store as a green respite from city life, not unlike Frederick Law Olmsted's Central Park.[8]

Nationwide, stores less wealthy or prominently situated than A&F took cues from marketing trends at larger department stores, and nowhere was this more evident than in display windows featuring nature and nature-related consumer goods. In the 1890s, many dry goods stores, sporting goods stores included, crowded as much merchandise as possible into windows facing the street. Von Lengerke & Antoine, for instance, a sporting goods firm based in Chicago, crammed tennis rackets, baseball mitts, and all kinds of balls into the front window without designing a coherent scene, perhaps to demonstrate the phenomenal breadth of its product offerings. By the turn of the century, many outfitters began to create distinctive displays that captured the store's ethos. Swanstrom and Erickson in West Duluth, Minnesota, for instance, created a nature-inspired display for its storefront in 1922. Boots and a sign that read, "Duxbak: Serviceable clothing for Life in the Outdoors," sat on a layer of artificial grass. Jackets and other clothing items were displayed above their respective brand-name signs, in front of a curtain of reeds. Other vines drooped down from above. Eddie Bauer's storefront display in 1927 stood out even more. Not content simply to depict a natural scene in the window, Bauer displayed trophies from recent trips on

This Duluth storefront in 1922 is not as dramatic as the most well-known department store window displays, yet the touches of greenery help establish the natural aesthetic as masculine by focusing on functionality. ("Neighborhoods of Duluth: West Duluth, Swanstrom and Erickson Store window display, Duluth, Minnesota," University of Minnesota Duluth, Kathryn A. Martin Library, Northeast Minnesota Historical Collections; provided courtesy of the St. Louis County Historical Society)

the sidewalk of his Seattle store. Two bucks hung from their hooves on either side of the display windows; two more occupied the sidewalk in front of the store. These animal carcasses were Bauer's "calling card," a portal for customers.[9]

Manufacturers of a wide range of goods, from Shredded Wheat to carpet sweepers, began to offer more direct advice—and even cardboard cut-out materials themselves—about how to construct a display to attract customers. Hirsch-Weis recommended that sellers create a window display with their most popular outdoor garments, including shirts, jackets, and hats. Like the Bissell Carpet Sweeper Company, Hirsch-Weis promised to provide merchants "free display materials" to create "whole window" displays.[10]

In lieu of these directives some retailers improvised their own strategies to attract customers. The Model Clothing Company of Klamath Falls, Oregon, which stocked Hirsch-Weis's waterproof garments, came up with one creative strategy. In 1929, the store took a Hirsch-Weis coat and "placed it on a frame so that the back of the coat formed a depression." Into this depression the shopkeepers poured water and two goldfish. To prove that the coat was "absolutely waterproof," they left the fish swimming in there for days, even changing the water and doing the feeding in the window to attract the attention of passers-by. While not glamorous, this window display invited customers to imagine how the jacket would withstand the worst possible weather.[11]

Through in-store displays, window displays, and imitation ponds and cabins, outfitting companies sought to present the urban store as a bridge to actual outdoor adventures, and to masculinize an environment associated with female consumers. These branding and advertising strategies suggested that a shop on the way to the woods was part of the return to nature, rather than its antithesis—even though the return itself was inspired largely by a yearning to escape from the "world of made things," commerce, and the effete realm of consumerism.

✳

Writers who described the outdoor store's products played a vital role in reconciling this otherwise paradoxical union of commercial culture with an outdoor culture cherished precisely as an escape from the world of commerce. To guidebook authors in the late nineteenth century, advertisements seemed suspect because they were less trustworthy than firsthand conversation with an expert or learning from experience. George Washington Sears, one of the leaders of the woodcraft era, had written near the turn of the century that outdoorsmen should be careful to "buy no advertised hunting coats or suits." One magazine article warned readers that "asking information from an outfitter is, as a rule, worse than useless." Outfitters were usually inexperienced, and based their suggestions "on the promiscuous conversation of [their] customers and [their] stock of goods." Among other things consumers feared overspending and over-equipping; taking city advice on a country activity; looking silly in front of the guides they might hire; and being cold, wet, and uncomfortable in the woods. Radclyffe Dunmore recommended in an article in 1907 that the outdoorsman consult a guide or friend, lest he take the "far more risky" path and "goes to a city outfitter and gathers some second-hand, and usually very unreliable information." Outfitters, who operated primarily in eastern cities, had to promote their personal expertise to neutralize such critiques. They had to sell their camping experience so a customer would trust them. Advertisements contended with the same kinds of challenges. They had to convince customers to buy new instead of continuing to use old goods and to trust shopkeepers—salesmen, that is—in lieu of their own experience or trusted guides and friends.[12]

The new consumerist ethic of the early twentieth century suggested that, ultimately, equipment—and not just enthusiasm—determined the success of an outdoors excursion. The differences between a new camper who returns "enthusiastic with the pastime" and "those who couldn't be induced to repeat their performance" even if they were paid came down to gear. It was not character, not "the men themselves," as much as it was "what they took with them in the way of an outfit and their method of using it." This was a major change in the sensibility of the authentic outdoor experience, which was now more about equipment in an urban store than mastery of "nature's storehouse." Guides described a kind of Goldilocks zone of the woods. Too little gear and the novice assumes "camp life means sleeping on a blanket-covered heap of brush leaves . . . and living on canned goods." Too much gear and the novice "loads up a freight car with everything that a sporting dealer tells him is a good idea," which would make him "pretty nearly as uncomfortable." Campers needed to trust their own "actual experience" to make the right choices, but in the early twentieth century, that sporting goods dealer gained an outsized influence over how Americans made their shopping choices for getting back to nature.[13]

To overcome Americans' fears of being oversold or upsold by city shopkeepers, outdoor companies employed a range of strategies to establish themselves as foremost experts as opposed to salesmen or merchants; they were, each of them, that rare exception to "irresponsible salesman." They claimed "practical experience" in the field, and through a network of publications positioned themselves alongside outing magazines and guidebooks as a central part of the outdoor experience.[14]

Outdoor companies advertised not just their wares but their expertise. Abercrombie & Fitch advertised in prominent half-page spreads that accompanied articles like "Some Hints for the Amateur Camper." We have "Everything to Make the Camper Comfortable and Happy," the advertisements announced. The image paired with the text features a broad range of equipment and a picturesque outdoor spot. But perhaps the most crucial part of the advertisement was the few lines that established the expertise of the A&F sales force. "We can advise you where and how to go," the ad suggested, because "We have had twenty years' experience in camping out." Abercrombie & Fitch's authority came not from years of *selling*, but from years of *doing*. The practical, hands-on experience outdoor outfitters claimed to possess points to a shift in how American consumers came to understand mastery of the outdoors: city-based sporting goods manufacturers and retailers slowly became the primary source of information about how to camp out. Advertisements alone did not account for this shift, but they did signal a larger change in how Americans learned about the outdoors.[15]

Around the turn of the century, a new set of outdoor-oriented magazines, a broader outing-focused national press, and a cooperative relationship between outing-oriented authors and outdoor companies changed the way Americans perceived outdoor expertise. Even though guidebooks had advised outdoorsmen to shun advertisement in favor of local guides and knowledge, they were part of a new outing press that published books, pamphlets, and magazines designed to teach consumers how to access expertise. These publications were commercial ventures, heavy in advertisements and pitched at a broad audience at mass-market prices. This new informal outdoors conglomerate claimed to hold the authority to define the right way to "do" the outdoors. Through their collaborations, the American nature experience became, in part, the American consumer and commercial experience—the process of buying, reading, and learning from nature books, magazines, and catalogs.[16]

The first step toward the "ideal way of seeing the mountains" by "touring afoot," a guidebook wrote, was to purchase the necessary equipment—but no more than what was necessary. The drawings and photographs that accompanied publications like this one, along with the ubiquitous packing lists and recommendations about outfitters, helped create an aesthetic of outdoor experience and consumers' expectations for it. The outing press, though not consistent in format, circulated nationally information about outdoor recreation that specifically underscored the vital importance of purchased equipment and clothing.[17]

Beginning in the last few decades of the nineteenth century, outdoorspeople subscribed to special-interest magazines for anglers and hunters, for example, where outdoor outfitters targeted them through advertisements. The most well-known ones were published in New York, Chicago, and Denver. They included *Forest and Stream, Sports Afield, Field and Stream, Outdoor Life, Outing Magazine, Outers' Recreation, Recreation, Wildwood's Magazine*, and *Country Life in America*, among many others. The list of presses that published nature-oriented books and book series included the Forest and Stream Publishing Company, the Outing Publishing Company, Recreation Publishing Company, the Outdoor News Company, Doubleday, Page and Company, the Macmillan Company, and Houghton, Mifflin and Company. The companies often published using different media. The Forest and Stream Publishing Company, for instance, had an "Outdoor Library" series in addition to *Forest and Stream* magazine. Doubleday, Page and Company published the magazine *Country Life in America* and promoted its two nature-related series: the Nature Library and the Little Nature Library.[18]

The Outing Publishing Company's Outing Handbooks series was one of the most influential nature series in the early decades of the twentieth century for shaping American outdoor recreation norms. In 1906, the company's editor announced that a series of "several high-class volumes" following the same standards as the *Outing Magazine* would appear in the spring of that year. The first book in the series was #1, *Exercise and Health*, by Dr. Woods Hutchinson, followed quickly by #2, *Camp Cookery*, by Horace Kephart, and #3, *Backwoods Surgery and Medicine*, by Charles S. Moody, M.D. Volume #6 discussed *The Automobile—Its Selection, Care and Use*, and volume #40 covered *Winter Camping*.[19]

The Outing Publishing Company published more than fifty books in its series, initially pricing each volume at eighty cents and designing them as "textbooks for outdoor work and play." The books had a uniform design, including identical flexible, light green covers and a forest graphic. The company understood its readers as "out-door enthusiasts," which included "The Fisherman, the Camper, the Poultry-raiser, the Automobilist, [and] the Horseman." The press defined "Outing" broadly and covered *Suburban Gardens* (#24) as readily as *Fishing Kits and Equipment* (#7) and *Touring Afoot* (#52). While the authors—"experts" in their fields—were mostly men, a few of the Outing Handbooks directed at women were also authored by women: Kathrene Pinkerton's *Woodcraft for Women,* for instance.[20]

The most famous of all American outdoor guidebooks was—and perhaps still is—Horace Kephart's *Camping and Woodcraft.* This tome, initially published in 1906 by the Outing Publishing Company, was republished for decades thereafter in different editions. Like the Outing Handbooks series, Kephart's how-tos are important because they helped establish American consumer habits even as they espoused an ostensibly anti-consumer woodcraft ethic. Nathaniel Nitkin was one of many thousands of city hikers who hit the trails after consulting his Kephart volume. Nitkin described his compatriots: "They crowd the train and bus stations of the metropolitan area, wearing picturesque outfits and swimming packsacks of all sorts." These "jaded office workers [who] . . . hike[d] over the rugged trails" assembled their hiking equipment drawing on "long experience" and the "rules laid down by Horace Kephart."[21]

The wide range of material produced by the outing presses helped connect readers to retail outfitters, either explicitly through advertisements or implicitly through the author's personal endorsement of particular products. A quick perusal of the pages of any outdoor magazine or newspaper reveals that readers encountered advertisements for equipment and clothing alongside articles describing camping excursions. More important, letters from customers confirm that these advertisements had an impact on consumer behavior. Henry Coons of Naples, New York, for instance, wrote of reading about Hirsch-Weis in *Hunting and Fishing* magazine and then purchasing a Hirsch-Weis coat that served him well for a 1929 trip to the Adirondacks in "snow and sleet."[22]

Even more telling than the somewhat predictable juxtaposition of ads and text is how advertisements worked in tandem with other outdoor sports publications. Outfitters, guidebook authors, and publishers symbiotically endorsed one another as outdoor experts to whom readers should turn for practical advice. Guidebooks and magazines recommended brands in columns or advertisements; in turn, catalogs printed selections from guidebooks. Abercrombie & Fitch's catalog included excerpts from Kephart's *Camping and Woodcraft*, with ruminations on "the charm of nomadic life" and "the best vacation an over-civilized man can have." The catalog also mentioned, of course, that the book was for sale for $2.50. Kephart, for his part, implicitly endorsed Abercrombie & Fitch with a couple of mentions of the company's catalog in his volume. A later edition of *Camping and Woodcraft* included an illustration of an Abercrombie & Fitch pack frame and a David T. Abercrombie sleeping bag (the company founders split after the earlier edition). An advertisement for a Kephart volume on *Camp Cookery* in the *Outing Magazine* strengthened the links between the company and the guidebook author. The copy included an endorsement from Abercrombie & Fitch president Ezra H. Fitch, stating that Kephart's "book should be in the pack of every man who goes into the woods." The Abercrombie-Kephart connection was by no means the only cross-endorsement between authors in the outing press and outfitters. For instance, within the span of a few pages in the guidebook *Camp Craft*, author Warren H. Miller refers readers to *Field and Stream* magazine (of which he was then the editor) and to David T. Abercrombie products.[23]

Editorial departments at outing-focused magazines deliberately called outdoor companies' attention to magazines as potential promoters of outfitting companies. In a letter written in 1923 from *Forest and Stream*'s New York offices to an unnamed equipment manufacturer, the magazine requested the "latest catalogue describing your full line of camp goods." Future issues, the editorial department explained, would "have an even greater section devoted exclusively to camping and camping equipment," and outfitters who kept the magazine abreast of their latest and best-selling products would be featured prominently. The new section would describe "the most practical camping equipment of the various manufacturers throughout the United States," and companies were invited to send images along with their catalog. This cross-referencing and commercial overlay reinforced for readers that a network of mostly city-based white men with desk jobs as writers, publishers, and gearmakers was the authority on how to get back to nature the "right way."[24]

The repetition of named experts helped to create an ensemble of outdoor celebrities. The names Bean, Bauer, and Abercrombie adorned storefronts and clothing tags, helping those outfitters join the likes of Kephart as outdoor experts. Leon Leonwood Bean, David T. Abercrombie, and Eddie Bauer each used his own name and reputation to promote his brand. Bean and Bauer made themselves characters in their eponymous catalogs, citing their experience. Abercrombie wrote his philosophy of celebrity expertise directly into the catalog copy: "When a man brings his experience right from the heart of the woods to his own factory, his equipment service to the camper and sportsman is bound to be good and true because it is founded on *knowledge*. Davit [*sic*] T. Abercrombie is a practical woodsman and a practical manufacturer. His broad principles of design of tents and camp goods are the evolution of seeing and living and knowing what is best and most helpful." Not just shopkeepers but Abercrombie himself tested the gear. A 1926 catalog included a drawing of the man himself in hiking breeches, a heavy coat, and a packsack with tumpline.[25]

Some authors in the outing presses were uncomfortable with the endorsements they offered, not so much because consumer goods were antithetical to the experience they wanted to create but because they did not want to play favorites with particular companies for fear of appearing biased and therefore untrustworthy. Stewart Edward White, in his *Camp and Trail* guidebook originally published by the Outing Publishing Company, wrote a preface to make explicit his choice to name brands as a part of his guidebook writing. He was tired of the many hundreds of inquiries about "where this, that, or the other thing may be had" inspired by his camping pieces in the *Outing Magazine* and his earlier book, *The Forest*. In *Camp and Trail*, White decided, he would "include the names of firms where certain supplies may be bought" to save himself time. He said, for instance, that "you will not go astray in purchasing" the Putnam's boot made by A. A. Cutter of Wisconsin, and that a particular Abercrombie & Fitch tent was "all right" though the "fly rigging is all wrong."[26]

White was conscious of the risk to his reputation should readers suspect that he recommended particular companies on the basis of personal financial gain. This boundary was difficult to patrol, but it was an important one to his authenticity as an outdoorsman. He assured readers in his preface that he "received no especial favors from" any of the companies he mentioned. "I realize that I seem to be recommending [Abercrombie & Fitch] rather extensively, but it cannot be helped," wrote White. "It is not because I know no others, for naturally I have been purchasing sporting goods and supplies in a great many places and for a good many years." Significantly, and indicating a shift over time, his discomfort was more about privileging one company over another than about tying nature experiences romanticized as anti-urban and anti-commercial to urban and commercial outfitters. Purchasing outdoor products as a consumer was no longer an indefensibly inauthentic, unmanly act, but only compromised one's status as an "expert" if one acted too much like a huckster or biased salesman.[27]

The outing press and outdoor companies grew up together: outdoor magazine editors and guidebook authors relied on the equipment and expertise of outdoor outfitters, and outfitters relied on these authors extolling their products. Through this mutual reinforcement outdoor outfitters attested to the necessity of reading Kephart, and Kephart attested to the necessity of buying an A&F tent. The underlying ethos of the early twentieth-century outdoor press was by no means an unrestrained celebration of shopping. Guidebooks insistently warned about over-equipping and missing the point of the outdoor experience. Nonetheless, the union of outdoor sports and the well-designed equipment of outdoor outfitters coalesced. Guidebooks, magazines, and outfitters all pushed Americans, in improvised concert, toward an outdoor experience in which outfitting for the trip became a necessary first step and core part of the experience.

At times, outfitters even claimed to surpass the expertise and authority of guidebook authors. The Abercrombie & Fitch catalog in 1908, for instance, suggested that the company had a broader knowledge base about outdoor experience around the globe than the narrow expertise of famed authors like Stewart Edward White. White and others "write most admirable and charming books of personal experience," the catalog explained, "but usually they write of only one country." In contrast, as a "Clearing House" for the insights and experiences of a range of "Sportsmen, Travelers and Explorers," Abercrombie & Fitch was best situated to offer advice on what to buy (and what not to buy) to access the "Silent Places of the World."[28]

Ultimately, the co-creation of outdoor recreation by the outdoor press and outfitters was a quintessentially modern experience, and one that managed in the modern style to reconcile the profound, if not unavoidable, contradictions between outdoor recreation, increasingly prized as a refuge from the emasculating modern, urban, commercial life, and a modern, urban, and commercial outfitting enterprise that had become the new "jumping off" point for the outdoor adventure. By the new logic a salesperson was an "expert" akin to guidebook authors, and consumption was not contradictory to the wilderness. The chorus of loosely affiliated sources confirmed that to venture out on the blazed trail, you *had* to start at the boulevard.

＊

The "you" of that message was almost always a man. Both the outdoor press and outfitters, however, also wanted to shape the experience of a group they deemed especially ill-equipped for what nature had to offer. Although advertisements seemed to promise great things for the "over-civilized" man looking for an escape, what nature might offer the "outdoor woman" was decidedly less clear.

In the late nineteenth century guidebook authors had various suggestions for outdoor women. Some recommended shortened skirts; others promoted custom-made bloomers. By the turn of the century, as outdoor companies began to build product offerings to respond to the intense interest in outdoor recreation, they did not entirely neglect the New Women of the outdoors. The wilderness continued to be a place to try out clothing and activities not otherwise socially acceptable in everyday life.

In the early 1920s, camping was newly accessible to middle-class families such as the Bay Area–based Strohmaiers. Erwin Strohmaier recalled that his mother relished the idea of equipping her family with specialized outfits for camping—divided skirts for women and riding pants for men. Though camping was "the thing to do in the summer," the style-conscious Mrs. Strohmaier didn't wear her outdoor clothing in the city. "Every time we came home from camping," her son later remembered, "my mother was always hoping the neighbors would not be outside and see her in her camping clothes and her sun tan." Clothing styles were changing rapidly in America during the 1920s, and yet as Erwin Strohmaier's mother recognized, a sweaty, dirty female in camping clothes was an unseemly, and uncommon, urban sight.[29]

In guidebooks, on the trail, and at home, women encountered both men and women who expected them, above all else, to fulfill the qualities of Victorian womanhood, even as those characteristics were changing rapidly. The outdoor guidebook author Edward Breck wrote in 1908 that although women had lost "just a bit of womanly tenderness" since the 1830s, modern women were much better off than their grandmothers. This New Woman "benefited even more than her brother by the 'nearer to nature' movement." Yet for Breck, outdoor women of the turn of the century needed to consider how to dress and act so that they would earn the highest praise from the men of their group: that they were "not a bit in the way." In the early twentieth century, outdoor outfitters' offerings for women of the woods reveal novel expectations about appropriate dress and behavior for women on the trail. Whereas "mannish" had once seemed a quality to be avoided by "real women," by the 1910s it was the primary, positive descriptor for much of the specialty hunting and camping attire for the outdoor woman that outfitters sold.[30]

Sports and bodies in motion, writes the historian Sarah Gordon, "provided a space in which women contested notions of 'feminine' and 'appropriate' bodies, behaviors, and appearances." Clothing is a visual and public statement. Women wearing unusual, even suspect, clothing in outdoor activities did not go unchecked, but they did get a pass to explore new options because the clothes were not for work or everyday wear, but for leisure.[31]

There were at least three options for outdoor women in the 1910s: bloomers alone, bloomers accompanied by a skirt on top, and riding breeches. Each of these options came laden with critiques of women's tendency to focus on frivolous matters like fashion even when they needed a functional jacket. The recommended jacket to go along with a divided skirt was a tailored Norfolk jacket that would "fit her figure smartly." With attention to details like tailoring, a woman could dress for the trail but, like her male companions, travel by train to get to the trail without looking "too conspicuous or bizarre." While outdoor costuming for men had to be functional to escape charges that it was womanishly fashionable, women's outdoor costumes needed to be fashionable to escape charges that it was mannishly functional.[32]

The choice between these garments—essentially, how much a woman should reveal that she had legs—often depended on the nature of the outing. The farther from civilization, the more appropriate pants became. The supervisory role of men on the trip also mattered. Kephart warned that "tight or draggy dress" would render a woman "simply hopeless." Kephart argued that women's attire should ultimately depend on the activity at hand. "For real wilderness travel," he wrote, "travel riding breeches, cut full at the knee, are far better than a skirt." *Woodcraft for Women* author Kathrene Pinkerton argued that appropriate clothing gave women, like men, "freedom of movement, resistance from snags, and proof against rain." Bifurcated garments allowed women to participate in "strenuous activities with a minimum of effort."[33]

Some guidebooks recognized both the hesitation of women to wear pants on the trail, and the limits of a society outside of wilderness spaces that looked askance at women in pants. For these reasons, some guidebook authors offered suggestions about skirts to throw on over bloomers and riding pants. Warren Miller assured readers that "the modern divided skirt is no shocking affair; it looks like the ordinary skirt with a double row of buttons fore and aft." The freedom of movement it allowed "over rough portages and mountain trails" was "essential." For places where men would not accept women in bifurcated garments, where they were "not yet civilized enough to approve common sense in a woman's costume," Horace Kephart recommended a buttoned skirt that could go over riding breeches.[34]

By the 1930s, bloomers and split skirts were no longer controversial. Women regularly wore riding pants and even shorts, reflecting an increasingly relaxed norm for women in at least some hiking areas. Grace Leach Hudowalski, a prolific hiker of the Adirondacks, grew up during these transitions. Born in Ticonderoga, New York, in 1906, she began hiking in her

SPORT CLOTHES FOR WOMEN

CAMPING,

HUNTING,

FISHING AND

ALL OUTDOOR SPORTS

THE FOREST SUIT

THE FOREST SHIRT AND SKIRT

THE SMITH   THE OUTDOORS

THE SOU WESTER   THE SURF

Abercrombie & Fitch served the needs of the outdoor woman just as much as those of men. The images of these outdoor women as well as guidebooks' recommendations worked to spread ideas about alternative forms of dress that were still appropriately feminine despite the masculine lines. (Abercrombie & Fitch catalog, 1922, National Museum of American History, Smithsonian Libraries and Archives) teens. Along with her husband, she was a peak-bagger—the first woman to become a 46er, climbing all the northeastern mountains above 4,600 feet. Hudowalski was proud of this accomplishment, which she worked toward in the 1920s and 1930s during time away from her job as a publicity writer and, later, travel promotion supervisor for the New York State Commerce Department. She did most of her walks in a plaid button-down shirt and a pair of checkered blue and white shorts. A photograph of her in her usual hiking outfit survives. In it, she is thirty-four or thirty-five, sporting her red plaid shirt and the blue checkered shorts, the 46er patch celebrating her feats ironed on near her right hip. Later articles about Hudowalski explained that this way of dressing "was not so very unusual for sportswomen" of the era. At the time, however, Grace Hudowalski and her hiking partners were mindful that even in the woods, a female body was potentially an incitement for men on their hallowed ground of the wilderness. Women were simultaneously welcome outdoor participants and suspect, sexualized bodies that threatened the masculine character of the woods.[35]

A few years before she posed for the photo on Mount Phelps, Hudowalski, along with her husband and friends—both men and women—were hiking up the Cold River in New York's Adirondacks on an August day. The women wore shorts. As a variety of newspaper and magazine articles later recounted, the group came close to "hermit" Noah John Rondeau's shack in the woods and Hudowalski's husband told the women to cover up. "You can't appear in shorts before that man who's been so long alone in the woods," he argued. Recounting the encounter decades later, Hudowalski spoke of it with "resignation." She and her friends put on the culottes—long and loose pants—they had carried "for brushy areas." Bare skin sufficiently covered, Hudowalski entered the hermit's shack. The group partook of the hermit's "signature" coffee, "thick and black and sweetened with condensed milk."[36]

This story was often recounted in articles about Hudowalski, who became a well-known leader in the Adirondack 46er club; in addition to serving as its first president, she was an active member for sixty-seven years. The culotte coverup does not seem to have challenged Hudowalski's own sense of belonging in the woods (or her sense of humor). She became friends with the hermit, Rondeau, and brought him a "decorated birthday cake every year." A younger club member remembered her as "a tenacious old broad" who loved a stiff drink and climbing mountains.[37]

Hudowalski was unusual in that she worked to preserve her hiking stories from the first half of the twentieth century. But though invisible in the conservative advertisements produced by outdoor outfitters, her experiences were not unusual. The scrutiny of her body reinforced that the wild was very much an extension of the modern world, and not a world apart, and that women needed to adapt to men's gazes to operate in a man's wilderness.

For their part, advertisers continued to suggest that while women could participate in outdoor activities, it was men—properly dressed—who had ready access to authentic experience. Authenticity as marketed by outdoor companies was, still and all, a male quest.

THREE

Buck Skein™

Trademarking the American Past

One of the most unusual marketing techniques outdoor companies used in the early twentieth century was to sell a nostalgic vision of the American past that idealized male outdoor workers to assert the authenticity of their products, as the archetypes of the woodsman or Indigenous man had earlier. This narrative had actual historical precedents. The outdoor industry really did begin by selling workwear, which in the last decades of the nineteenth century included denim jeans, cotton duck overalls, and wool or flannel work shirts. The clothing historian Daniel Delis Hill observes that these clothes were advertised as rugged and functional.[1]

Among other businesses, the evolution of the manufacturer Hirsch-Weis, based in Portland, Oregon, illustrates how outdoor companies moved from work clothing to a new kind of leisurewear that was sold on a nostalgic view of the past. Max Hirsch, a German Jewish immigrant, worked at Meier and Frank, his uncles' department store in Portland. In 1907, Hirsch and his brother purchased the Willamette Tent & Awning Company, which sold canvas goods for sailing ships, wagon covers, and tents. The Hirsch brothers brought on Harry Weis, who had worked for the company before the purchase and was an expert on canvas products, as a partner in the newly renamed Hirsch-Weis. By the 1910s, Max Hirsch began to change the company's manufacturing focus from canvas equipment to canvas clothing, effectively getting "into the work clothing business through the back door." The company made a product for Pacific Northwest loggers' wet days outdoors that became popular: tin pants.[2]

The Tin Pants line of clothes—the name referred to Hirsch-Weis's water-proofing treatment process—included jackets, hip leggings, and hats in addition to pants. The items were made of a common workwear base fabric—heavy cotton duck—but treated "by the special Hirsch-Weis process which lengthens the life of the fabric and waterproofs it." The Hirsch-Weis process was to dip the canvas into "tubs of boiling paraffin, which stiffened when it cooled." The treated garment would slowly adapt to the wearer in the field: the "paraffin itself would crack . . . and then air could get through." The result was a patterned and deeply creased fabric, every crack indicating both proper garment treatment and heavy use outdoors. Hirsch-Weis advertised tin pants, and its work shirts and bib overalls, as "purely for work, not sportswear." Nonetheless, sportsmen, who were growing in numbers and economic power, were equally interested in the tin treatment and began to seek out the specialized Hirsch-Weis clothing. "Taking advantage of this demand," Max Hirsch's son Harold later recalled, "Hirsch-Weis Manufacturing Company began to nationally advertise and thus aggressively entered the sportswear field."[3]

Hirsch-Weis touted its origins in workers' clothing as a certification of its products' authenticity and reliability. As Hirsch-Weis shifted from "working man's stores" to "high-grade" shops like Abercrombie & Fitch to sell the clothing it manufactured, its owners found that their new customers viewed the company as authentic, rugged, and masculine, as illustrated by the Stag Cruiser, a wool jacket popular in the 1920s.[4]

Hirsch-Weis's national advertising campaigns reemphasized the Stag Cruiser's putative use by timber cruisers in the Northwest woods. Co-owner Max Hirsch built the mythology, writing in one catalog, "In the Pacific Northwest there is a hardy group of outdoor men who demand the utmost in clothes—complete weather protection combined with complete body freedom." He continued, "Hirsch-Weis Stags were originally designed for the exact use of these men," timber cruisers. The timber cruiser era had passed, he explained, but he encouraged customers to see this history as proof of quality and authenticity. "Other outdoor men, impressed with the comfort, utility and appearance of the garment, have adapted it to their own use." New customers embraced the mythology. An ad booklet from

1925 shows a man in a Stetson hat and Stag Cruiser, shifting gears on a trac-
tor in a farm field. "Stags are built for outdoor work," the caption reads.
While this is an accurate explanation of the Stag Cruiser's origins, the next
panel reveals that outdoor workers are no longer the company's main target;
instead, its customers are men preparing for when "work and care are left
behind." The accompanying images show different models of the "famous
Hirsch-Weis Stag" on men of leisure, carrying golf clubs, ski poles, and a
pipe.[5]

The company published customer satisfaction letters about the Stag
Cruiser in pamphlets and company catalogs after carefully selecting and editing them. Even so, the predominance of letter-writers who were men buying for recreational purposes points to Hirsch-Weis's success in reaching this
new target market. By the late 1920s, letters and presumably many more orders reached Hirsch-Weis from around the country—the Midwest, Intermountain West, and Pacific Coast are particularly well represented,
although customers wrote in from Alaska, North Carolina, Pennsylvania,
Rhode Island, and New York as well. Most writers self-identified as "out of
door [men]," echoing the language of advertising copy from Hirsch-Weis
catalogs. The activity mentioned most often was hunting, though writers
also referred to mountaineering, hiking, and fishing. One customer wrote
of hunting pheasants "in a very hard rain" and returning "as dry as when
[he] went out" thanks to the Stag. Others wore the Stag for Dartmouth Outing Club activities, or, in another case, "on a Mazama trip to Mount St.
Helens over Memorial Day" in 1926. This customer wrote that many members of his party were asking him about the shirt, which kept him warm during two damp nights in the woods. Customers' letters saved by Hirsch-Weis
over the years reveal that recreational purchasers of Stag Cruisers valued
not just the fit and performance of the jackets but also their friends' opinions
about the garments. "I received my Stag, in hunter's bright red color, yester-
day, and I am very well pleased with it. . . . I shall show my Stag to the other
members of my Hunting Club and know they will be pleased with it," wrote
Harold Bomberger of Manheim, Pennsylvania, in 1929.[6]

Some outfitters saw old customers—"old" defined by experience more
than age—as among the best boosters of their brand for two reasons. The

longevity of the products spoke to their quality, of course, but customers with a coat that had acquired the marks and patina of age revealed how the outdoorsman might reconcile the antinomy between a wilderness valued precisely for its distance from the market and an industry where consumption of gear had become a central part of that experience. These "old-timers add to the power of advertising" by wearing hunting coats "that have been in use ten, even fifteen, seasons," explained one business analyst. The coats no longer looked new, but that only spoke to the strength of the fabric, the rugged construction: they are "delightfully shabby, yet workmanlike in appearance, and are still giving service." Catalog copy referenced the "old-timer" category of experts explicitly. The catalog of the Seattle-based Filson Company included an image of a wizened, mustachioed man sitting on a log and smoking a pipe to illustrate the claim, "Oldtimers choose Filson Waterproofed Khaki Trousers for Their Economy and Comfort . . . Young Men Profit By Their Example!" The ad makes clear that this "oldtimer" wisdom about the outdoors was accessible to the young and inexperienced through the right purchases. The long use of these coats could make them non-fungible, essentially decommodifying them. The incessant attention to age and wear with the old-timers speaks to that alluring process, where a coat molded by the wearer's individuality and experiences upholds an anti-commercial outdoor culture within a commercial outdoor industry.[7]

As the consumer market grew, outdoor clothing manufacturers and outfitters debated their advertising targets: working men or leisure seekers? Hirsch-Weis used the myth of the wise old-timer to market to leisure wearers, but then found it difficult to maintain its actual old-timer customer base. A business report in 1921 explained that for Duxbak, a company with a similar history, "efforts directed at truck men, miners, lumbermen and other workers who need wear-resisting clothes have met with but poor success." The writer guessed that though advertising "seeking to sell [to] them has been done, it has not reached them to a sufficiently large extent." Although these companies used the mystique of the old-timer to sell to the leisure outdoorsman, the link between the two groups, and classes, seemed to end there.[8]

Other gearmakers made a different decision and focused exclusively on recreational customers. In Chicago, the outfitter Von Lengerke & Antoine echoed sporting magazines of the turn of the century when it emphasized that the company was selling solely to recreationists. Its catalog in 1932 offered "Dependable Equipment for the Enjoyment of the Out-of-Doors for All Who Play the Game 'Just for Sport.' " Those who hunt or fish out of necessity or as work, the implication went, need not inquire.[9]

David Abercrombie and Ezra Fitch eventually split because of a disagreement about their ideal market, with Fitch preferring to focus on wealthy New Yorkers rather than the expanding middle-class market. Many more companies, however, learned that advertising the fact that workers had used—or might use—their clothes was valuable. In this sense, the rugged timber cruiser or the outdoor worker performed the same archetypal role as the Indigenous man or the backwoods frontiersman had earlier, with buckskin: this worker conjured a vanished past of authenticity and masculinity that could be used to market modern commodities. As an advertising technique, the suggestion that clothes were built for work but ready for play would have remarkable longevity as outfitters sold nostalgia through modern marketing.[10]

✳

Consumer culture and advertisers helped stoke desire and shape the meanings that Americans brought to their commercial interactions and their notions of the outdoors in the early twentieth century, but this does not preclude other approaches to the history of outdoor recreation. For instance, the historian Silas Chamberlin has written about the participatory, producerist ethos developed in clubs like the Mazamas and the Sierra Club around the hiking community and infrastructure. This communitarian approach to the outdoors did exist, but by looking to other sources and focusing on the cash nexus—the interactions between outfitters, advertisers, and consumers long before people arrive at a trailhead—we can see the important role played by the producers of mass consumer culture and how they affected outdoor recreation.[11]

Selling tin pants and Stag Cruisers with great success allowed Hirsch-Weis to expand further into the recreational market, even in the dire economic climate of the late 1920s and early 1930s. Harold Hirsch, Max Hirsch's son, would later take over his father's business. The younger Hirsch recalled that he grew up in a "clannish" Jewish community in Portland, Oregon, and watched his father's business grow and migrate from workwear to sportsmen's attire. Hirsch attended Dartmouth in the mid-1920s, where he pursued his interest in skiing. Although he felt profoundly out of place at Dartmouth as a westerner, a Jew, and the son of a clothing manufacturer, Hirsch did get an education in marketing: he recognized that the outerwear his father's company was selling to workers and then sportsmen was better than the ski clothing his peers wore. During his years at Dartmouth, he designed and then sold a jacket using green and black plaid wool from his family's Portland factory. He "paid a group of students to sell [the ski jacket] room-to-room in Dartmouth dormitories." It was so popular that the local businesses that had catered to this crowd, Campion's and the Dartmouth Co-op, agreed to carry a line of Hirsch-Weis ski jackets if only Hirsch would "quit competing."[12]

Hirsch, who had intended to study sociology or anthropology at Oxford after graduating from Dartmouth in 1929, returned instead to Portland after only a semester in England to work at his father's firm. He felt lucky to have that option after the stock market crash. Because of his Ivy League skiing experience, Hirsch saw a "growing market" for ski clothing that the family company—with its background in hardy worker wear and sportsmen's outfits—could fill. Until the 1930s, most American ski clothing "was either imported from the Scandinavian countries or from Switzerland or Austria and was very expensive," Hirsch recalled. Additionally, he thought, the Swiss clothes were "a little gimmicky," with embroidered edelweiss flowers—a strong aesthetic contrast to the conservative two-tone design of the Hirsch-Weis Stags. So Hirsch started to sell woolen ski jackets to customers in the West. He sold first to individual customers, such as ski jumpers and ski lift operators, and then moved on to stores that would carry the goods, such as army-navy stores in California. Later, Hirsch expanded the company's ski clothing all over the country. He traveled in an old Studebaker with another clothing salesman from Portland to sell at high-end outdoor outfitters, from Abercrombie & Fitch and Alex Taylor in New York, to Von Lengerke & Antoine in Chicago, to Campion's and the Dartmouth Co-op in New Hampshire.[13]

Hirsch changed Hirsch-Weis from a western sportsmen's company to a national skiwear and outdoor company in part through branding the outdoor sportswear as a distinct component of the business. Drawing on a course in business administration he had taken at Dartmouth, as well as the example of his clothing manufacturer colleagues at Jantzen, Hirsch developed a new brand name and logo. Hirsch was ever mindful of his status as a Jew and German-American in a country potentially hostile to "a foreign-sounding name" that "nobody knew . . . east of the Rockies, anyway." He found success in a loosely translated version of Hirsch-Weis: White Stag. Hirsch-Weis had already used a leaping white deer as a logo in advertisements and catalogs throughout the 1920s. Hirsch promoted the White Stag brand by elaborating on its origins as workmen's as well as western clothing. "Born in the West and Ready for Action," announced one ad that featured a cowboy in the mountains. Much like Levi's and Jantzen, the White Stag brand created a regional, outdoor-oriented style that built on the narrative that it was rugged western workwear, even after the company had left that market behind. To this day, Portland residents take pride in the giant illuminated White Stag sign near Burnside Bridge.[14]

The New York clothing manufacturer Bird, Jones & Kenyon Company illustrates how outfitters invoked the natural and the modern simultaneously, and harmonized the two. The company manufactured workmen's overalls in the late nineteenth century. As the Adirondack Mountains became more popular with vacationers thanks to guidebooks and newspaper reports extolling a trip to the woods, the company—located in Utica, a gateway town to the Adirondack Park—sensed an opportunity. Its owners realized that they could supply clothing similar to what they already manufactured specifically to sportsmen. To the new recreationists of the Adirondacks, the company "offered a line of strong waterproof, well-made outfits, specially designed for mountain wear by men who knew what was needed in the mountains."[15]

Like White Stag, Bird, Jones & Kenyon rebranded to market to recreational customers. As an assessment of the company's business strategy explained in 1921, Bird, Jones & Kenyon chose a brand name to represent this distinct aspect of its business that would also point to its technological innovation: Duxbak, as

The Utica-Duxbak Corporation brand
Duxbak emerged when the clothing
manufacturer Bird, Kenyon & Jones
Company sought a memorable name
for its outdoor clothing line. As this
catalog cover explains, the name
referred to the waterproof performance
of the Duxbak garments. (Duxbak,
catalog, [1939?]; courtesy of Adirondack
Experience)

in, "sheds water like a Ducks Back." Duxbak "conveys at once the story that
these were garments off which water would run as off a duck's back; also it was
good-sounding, easily remembered and attractive, for the purpose in every
way." The trademarked name allowed the firm to create a spinoff company in
1904, the Utica-Duxbak Corporation, aimed at sportsmen. The company later
added a second trademark, Kamp-It, to sell "a complete line of outdoor tog-
gery" that was lighter than Duxbak. In addition to direct advertising in outdoor
publications "from the beginning," indirect advertising, through famous outdoorsmen and expeditions, including Theodore Roosevelt on his "African expedition" and Smithsonian expeditions, also boosted Duxbak's reputation.
Bird, Jones & Kenyon advertised nationally to reach "sportsfolk." Its brand
power had remarkable success, garnering mentions in Horace Kephart's
Camping and Woodcraft as well as Edward Breck's *The Way of the Woods.*[16]

Companies could lose control of their trademark as consumers as well as
other manufacturers began to use the trademarked term as a generic feature. When Edward Breck wrote of Duxbak in his guidebook, he referred to
the product in lowercase, as in, the "duxbak shooting coat" that was not "impervious to rain," implying that "duxbak" was a type of fabric rather than a

brand. Other large corporations, such as Eastman Kodak, encountered similar problems and sought to protect their trademarks because they were "valuable business assets." In the early twentieth century, businesses registered tens of thousands of trademarks to attract attention and cement their reputations. Ironically, success could lead to the protected trademark becoming a generic word in the outdoor lexicon.[17]

The worker added a third archetype of the outdoorsman to the earlier two, which persisted in the twentieth century. Lloyd F. Nelson's design for the external frame wooden pack from 1919, the Trapper Nelson Indian Pack Board, shows that the link between contemporary outdoor recreationists and an imagined frontier and Native past survived and thrived in the early twentieth century. Nelson, who was neither a trapper nor a Native American, trademarked and branded his invention, a rigid wooden frame with soft shoulder straps that enabled hunters and other outdoorsmen to carry heavy loads more comfortably. The pack became a mainstay of scouts and the U.S. Forest Service, and a coveted object for aspiring young outdoorspeople. The pack's origin story, marketing, and rising popularity in the 1930s show how tropes of the nineteenth-century outdoors were adapted to the modern twentieth century and its consumer culture. Packboard advertising featured both white frontiersmen and Native Americans, contributing to a growing commercial mythology about who had had dominion over the outdoors. The packboard combined this reassurance of tradition with the promise of new technology to provide a level of comfort. In this way, outdoor gear in this example and others was sold paradoxically as a new-old product.

Lloyd Nelson liked to recall the pack's Native roots in his accounts of company history. Nelson, who had briefly trapped wild game as a youth in Oklahoma, was working in shipyard construction near Kodiak, Alaska, in 1920. Done with his paid work, he hoped to discover oil nearby and needed to assemble equipment to make the trip and stake a claim. He noted, "An Indian agreed to lend me his crude Indian pack board made of sealskins stretched over willow sticks, a style used by generations of his ancestors." Nelson complained that the pack was crude and "back-breaking" and soon after the trip began designing an improved version. He called his pack "scientific" and a "prototype" (signaling his intention to sell it) that was more logical and comfortable.[18]

With the help of friends Nelson improved the design. He had a wood-worker bend thin pieces of oak to the right shape. He added a pocket on the outside of the bag. With a friend, he went on test hikes in the mountains. Nelson selected Bill Horsley, of the Pacific National Advertising Agency, to advertise for him. Within a week, Horsley came up with the name "Trapper Nelson's Indian Pack Boards." Around the same time Nelson applied for a patent and began advertising to U.S. Forest Service employees and Boy Scouts.[19]

Despite these small improvements Nelson's packs did not sell well. In 1929, Nelson sold the business to Charles Trager, who had been a recent partner in the business, and by coincidence, one thousand orders arrived soon thereafter from the Forest Services in Missoula, Montana, and Salem, Oregon, both of which were besieged by fire that year. Movie newsreels covered the fire and displayed the pack. Its popularity spread. In addition to scouts and rangers, Trager found success where Nelson had not, and sporting goods and department stores such as Osborn & Ulland and Sears Roebuck stocked the packs.[20]

Customers embraced the packs because they were comfortable and sturdy, but also because they conveyed an ethos of "true grit" reminiscent of earlier pieces of equipment like the buckskin suit. For Northwest hiker Tom Swint it wasn't just that he loved his faded packboard, it was also his own "snobbery"—thinking that he was a kind of Goldilocks of the outdoors who hit the mark between the ignorant who carried too little and the "sissy campers" who carried too much. This reputation for the Trapper Nelson came from the story its branding told. Trager's branding made special use of the pack's "Indian" origins. Logos and tags from the 1930s included a man in a headdress. The pack also was vaguely frontierish. When the Trager model became popular, other companies made knockoff versions and emphasized that they were trapper-style packs. Jones Tent & Awning, Ltd., even sold an imitation pack with the confusing name of Pioneer Brand Trapper Nelson Indian Pack Board. The mishmash of historical claims mattered little to the pack's many fans, including the famed mountaineer Paul Petzoldt, who called the packboard an essential of his youth.[21]

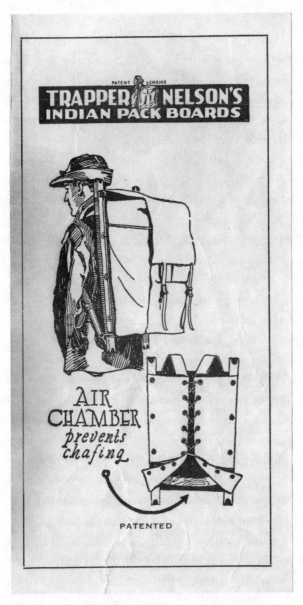

Though Lloyd F. Nelson was neither a trapper nor Native American, he had a marketing expert brand his invention the Trapper Nelson Indian Pack Board. (Charles Trager, "Advertisement for Trapper Nelson's Indian Pack Boards," c. 1930, *Jane Claire Dirks-Edmunds Documents*, Linfield University Archives)

✳

Even if other clothing was mass-produced and sold at urban outfitter emporiums and stores, there was still buckskin. Handcrafted by Native women, it was surely one authentic item of outdoor gear that would elude consumer culture and marketing—perhaps the last stand out. It could not be mass-produced. If the guidebooks of the era are any indication, talk around the campfires of early twentieth-century outdoor excursions often turned to gear and clothing. The author Stewart Edward White recommended an amply sized and fringe-less buckskin shirt, yet if a friendly campfire acquaintance had inquired about such an outfit, White would have had to respond, "I do not know where you can buy one." His answer suggested two things. First, these outdoorsmen and admirers who inquired about places to buy were not *really* planning on making a buckskin suit themselves. Second, White's answer evaded the deeper backstory, that many of the outdoor experts themselves relied on Native women to do the tanning and sewing for them. White *did* know very well where to buy a buckskin suit. Indeed, he had bought one himself. But to acknowledge Native women as the experts, and white men as mere consumers, was to break the campfire narrative of authentic outdoor life.[22]

Yet for an ever larger crowd eager to equip themselves properly for the outdoors, White's response was increasingly untenable. If buckskin was a marker of outdoor expertise, then aspiring experts wanted to be able to purchase such a garment—not make it, but buy it (just as White had). A new approach to outdoor clothing and equipment began to emerge in guidebooks and magazines that catered to Americans' recreational interests.

When White "rashly offered to send to inquirers the name of the firm making a certain kind of tent," the response, he found, was overwhelming: more than a thousand inquiries on that topic alone. White began to teach readers not just what makes a good boot, but also that A. A. Cutter of Eau Claire, Wisconsin, made the best Putnam boot. Likewise for the best soup tablets (Maggi's were better than Knorr's), best blanket (Hudson's Bay Company), and best hat (Stetson). He began to specify manufacturers. If the outdoorsman could not actually make his own garments or soup then at least he could demonstrate his mastery and expertise by having purchased the right brand of these things.[23]

But this dynamic did not apply to buckskin: good buckskin shirts and moccasins did not come recommended by brand. Instead, they came with a warning to avoid fakes created "to deceive tourists." Because of its associations with craft, because of the time and skill it took to make, and because it was not made by a company but by a person, buckskin resisted these consumer recommendations. It didn't seem possible for buckskin to make the leap into the world of outdoor publications and branded products.[24]

Buckskin, it turned out, could be branded after all. Buckskin, of the hand-stretched and dubbed with deer brains variety, was hard to come by, but one company found a way to mass-produce an approximation of the authentic product that so many sought. They called it Buck Skein.

In the 1910s, the New York–based Lustberg, Nast & Company began selling wool and cotton jackets for sportsmen and outdoor workers in catalogs and by mail order. Their brand name had echoes of nineteenth-century guidebooks' nostalgia for Native American masters of the outdoors. Buck "Skein" was a clever play on words, as it conjured a coil of thread or yarn, and the similarity was close enough for many customers seeking buckskin. Lustberg, Nast & Company registered the trademark "Buck Skein," featuring a deer's head between the two words, with the U.S. Patent Office in 1924.[25]

Buck Skein encapsulates how the outdoor industry reshaped Americans' relationship with nature through material goods. Americans used the consumer products of an expanded mass market to act out "links with an actual or imagined past," to establish "communal connections," and to develop their personal identity. Advertisements for Buck Skein succeeded because they presented the reader in search of authenticity as a discerning consumer of branded products. In their search for the always unstable and uncertain "real thing" in authentic outdoor wear, however, "Buck Skein"–branded clothing often proved disappointing.[26]

In 1938, the Federal Trade Commission (FTC) brought a case against Lustberg, Nast & Company for presenting cheap cotton and wool Buck Skein products as synonymous with the highly prized leather buckskin. Since the FTC's founding in 1914, it had been expanding its work to protect unwitting consumers from their own errors of judgment in the face of deceptive advertising. The claim against the company was that advertisements appearing in national magazines and newspapers, as well as the tags on the garments themselves, fooled consumers into thinking they were getting a garment made of real buckskin rather than the woven fabric it actually was. Such a claim would presumably protect consumers, but more important to the FTC, it would protect competitors. Real buckskin, the FTC explained, was "soft, pliable, lightweight and water-resistant" skin of a deer or elk "tanned by . . . the oil process." In a celebration of the older material that resembled an ad itself, the FTC explained that buckskin was "water-resistant without the disadvantage of being airtight."[27]

Although no one who had a chance to see or touch the garments thought they were made of buckskin, the FTC found multiple witnesses who attested that they believed the products were made of buckskin based on the advertisements. The case concluded that Lustberg, Nast & Company should cease and desist using the trademark Buck Skein, with or without the deer's head, because it misled and deceived the consuming public. At the turn of the century, outdoorspeople had prided themselves on knowing buckskin intimately and used it as a synecdoche for a broad set of outdoor skills. The FTC court case reveals that, within a few decades, American consumers no longer had the expertise to distinguish authentic buckskin from imposters. Buck Skein drew on nostalgia and the romance of the Indigenous man and the outdoor world of crafting over buying (notwithstanding the dodge that white male outdoorsmen bought buckskin from Native women) to mass produce and mass market an eponymous product in a consumer culture.[28]

Lustberg, Nast & Company continued selling Buck Skein products for at least another two decades. Although the buckskin/Buck Skein controversy died down as the focus turned to war in the 1940s, the product left another important legacy. As early as the 1920s, Buck Skein jackets were treated with a waterproofing material, Zepel, manufactured by DuPont. Zepel didn't last, but it foreshadowed a relationship between chemical companies and outdoor products that was just beginning.

✳

By the mid-twentieth century, consumption was a national ethic, replacing the nineteenth-century "ideal of a republic of producers." Advertisers promoted consumption as freedom and the public largely embraced "new visions of self, family, status, the good life" that were accessible through consumption. Outdoor recreationists were implicated in this new economic system. In the early 1900s company owners began to believe their own advertising claim that people could purchase authenticity and be modern at the same time. For example, Harold Hirsch observed, "Back in the 1920's, before we began making authentic, functional clothing for the specific purpose of skiing, the only authentic ski garments one could find were imported. Otherwise, people just wore anything that was handy and warm—wool plaid lumberjacks, canvas jackets, hiking breeches, riding breeches, and heavy wool hunting pants."[29]

The owners of these outdoor companies believed that they were producing "authentic" outdoor wear precisely because it was suited for recreation—and a specific subset of it. The assumption that any old clothes would do had mostly disappeared—specialty wear increasingly became normative for outdoor wear—and was replaced, as indicated by Hirsch's comment, by the new signifier and meaning of authentic: a product sold specifically and exclusively for one kind of outdoor recreational purpose. Authenticity, it seems, was now achieved at the point of consumption rather than, as with buckskin, production. A jacket might now convey a gestural nostalgia for the past and be authentic because it specifically and exclusively catered to a specific and exclusive outdoor recreational use. In sharp contrast to promoters of the woodcraft ethos, modern outdoor outfitters helped usher in the expectation that, properly consumed, goods could be "authentic" even if mass-produced and fungible. Authority came from recognizable brand names that spoke to outdoor expertise vicariously through the experience of the men whose names were stamped on the goods.[30]

Outdoor experiences in the early twentieth century were embedded in commercial transactions. Stores, catalogs, and companies became central, however contradictorily, to the outdoor experience cherished as a refuge from modern commercial culture. Outdoor outfitters, manufacturers of clothing and equipment, took their place alongside famous explorers as the nation's foremost experts on extreme environments and the safety, survival, and comfort of human bodies in them. Through catalogs, advertisements, and creative in-store environments, Bean, Abercrombie, Bauer, Hirsch, and other outdoor company owners established their authority, certified their authenticity, trademarked their brands, and marketed their products. Outdoor magazines and guidebooks in the thriving outing press reinforced their knowledge. The link between the blazed trail and the boulevard was firmly established.

FOUR

Feather Foam and Pocket Stoves

The Making of a Scientific Industry

Early in 1942, Eddie Bauer, an expert in making down-feather jackets, strings for tennis rackets, and badminton birdies, received an urgent phone call. The Quartermaster Corps (QMC)—the branch of the U.S. Army charged with the logistics of war—was on the line asking for Bauer's "immediate cooperation." The military needed snowshoes and sleeping bags, and Bauer's outdoor sports manufacturing experience made him the man for the job. His first task for the QMC was to purchase and assemble every available cold-weather sleeping bag in the country. Through Eddie Bauer, Inc., he called his colleagues and competitors at places such as Abercrombie & Fitch, Gokey, and Woods Sleeping Bag Company to collect what they had.[1]

At the start of World War II, America's small outdoor industry became a "war industry." The U.S. military turned to experts such as Eddie Bauer, L. L. Bean, and Harold Hirsch as consultants for the design and manufacture of cold-weather clothing and equipment. In the early 1940s, most of the best equipment for sports like climbing and mountaineering came from Europe, but by 1941 those goods were inaccessible to civilians in the United States. For its part, the military's cold-weather clothing and equipment had barely been updated since World War I and what did exist had been developed for more temperate combat zones. Interwar developments were mostly cosmetic, rather than customized to "utility and purpose." In August 1941, the QMC held cold-climate and mountain equipment conferences, designed to put chemical and clothing industry experts and leaders in con-versation with mountaineers, outdoorsmen, and the military.[2]

A few days after the attack on Pearl Harbor on December 7, President Roosevelt declared war and the QMC, although up to this point far from ready and without a meaningful production budget, went to work in ear-nest. The war became a zone of innovation not just for clothing and equip-ment but also for the fabrics and fibers out of which they were made. The military had the funds, motivation, and connections to produce what it wanted on a vast scale. The QMC's research on exceptional climates in-cluded cold weather, desert, and jungle warfare. Of these, cold-weather clothing and equipment most closely aligned with outdoor recreationists and industry experts and had the biggest postwar influence on the outdoor industry.[3]

The QMC had reached out to industry men like Eddie Bauer for help, but the military ended up having a much larger impact on industry. Eddie Bauer's regional hunting and fishing shop became nationally prominent when the military used outdoor experts for the war cause. Bauer had opened his first business, a Seattle tennis shop, in 1920. From stringing rackets, Bauer expanded into fishing tackle and firearms. He was dedicated to main-taining his sporting cred, and every Labor Day posted a sign by his work bench—"Eddie Bauer has gone hunting. Back Feb. 1." By the late 1920s, Bauer had moved Eddie Bauer's Sporting Goods into a larger store and sold equipment for a range of sports including hunting, fishing, tennis, golf, and badminton. It was Bauer's design of down clothing after 1935 that attracted the military's attention. His contract work with the army changed not only military design but also the civilian market in the decades that followed.[4]

Historians have argued that American business—with factories as "free-dom's forge"—helped construct the planes and weaponry that won the war, and in turn paved the way for the postwar economic prosperity. The manu-facturers who researched, consulted, produced, and popularized American-made clothes and equipment did so for the entire military. Pup tents, windproof jackets, and down sleeping bags marked the start of a more dem-ocratically accessible national culture of outdoor-oriented consumption. Even if bureaucratic inefficiencies and hampered production prevented many goods from reaching the front lines, the work of Bauer, Bean, Hirsch, and famous mountaineers and explorers indisputably raised the profile of the outdoor industry, turned its leaders into national experts, spread brand awareness, and created the manufacturing infrastructure and technical expertise to sustain decades of subsequent expanding production.[5]

The outdoor industry, like many other industries during the war, both shaped and was shaped by wartime. The industry changed the U.S. military by infusing new ideas about design and dress. The war, in turn, gave a prominent platform to gear manufacturers, increasing the political salience of both industry professionals and outdoor enthusiasts themselves. It brought the notion that dress was a science to the industry. It reshaped consumer expectations about products, constructing a new ideal and aesthetic of "authenticity" around army green and khaki rather than brand names, built the infrastructure for chemical companies to produce and apply new synthetic fibers in recreational applications, and tacitly promised that the freedom to consume these new goods was part of what American soldiers were fighting for.

※

There were two categories of experts: gearmakers and gear users. The gearmakers were manufacturers with clear ideas about design. Gear users climbed for fun, their hobby suddenly assuming national importance. Mountaineer and QMC officer Bestor Robinson explained in 1943 that the most generative source of ideas came from civilians whose recreational activities put them in unusual situations.[6]

In 1942, just a few months after the phone rang in Eddie Bauer's office, Leon Leonwood Bean also received a phone call from the Office of the Quartermaster General. Bean owned the eponymous hunting equipment and clothing mail-order company in Freeport, Maine. The company had a reputation as a purveyor of rugged-weather equipment, sending catalogs to nearly three hundred thousand people by 1940, including a fair share of famous Americans. Franklin Delano Roosevelt carried a Bean knife. Babe Ruth was known to wear Bean hunting boots. Bean was asked to apply his experience on a special cold-weather committee in Washington, advising the Quartermaster Corps on clothing essentials for soldiers to survive cold-weather combat.[7]

Like his outdoor industry colleagues, Harold Hirsch, owner of Hirsch-Weis/White Stag in Portland, Oregon, headed to Washington as a special consultant to the quartermaster general, a civil service position. Hirsch worked on tents and clothing, while his peers specialized in skis, boots, and bags. Hirsch later recalled that wartime urgency and requirements made this work a new kind of challenge. "This was no longer recreational sport," Hirsch said. "You had to invent a ski boot that you also could march miles in." Their designs "had to serve a lot of purposes." L. L. Bean didn't just know how to make rubber-bottomed, leather-topped boots for cold weather. He also had emphatic ideas about why a ten-inch-high boot was far preferable for a day of walking than sixteen- or eighteen-inch boots.[8]

The other experts—the gear users—put products to the test. Civilian mountaineers and military officers brought equipment to the mountains of Alaska to make recommendations and design adjustments for the upcoming winter fighting season. These product comparisons included L. L. Bean, Eddie Bauer, Hirsch-Weis Manufacturing Company, Strand Ski Company, G. H. Bass and Company, and the Coleman Lamp and Stove Company. Along with American Alpine Club members such as Robert Bates and Terris Moore, who had climbed together in the Harvard Mountaineering Club, explorers such as Hubert Wilkins and Vilhjalmur Stefansson also offered expertise on cold-weather clothing and equipment. Together, these practitioners brought outdoor products to the military and, over time, the military to recreational outdoor products, in a design symbiosis sparked by World War II.[9]

✳

The military first transformed wartime production and later the outdoor industry by instituting scientific testing of clothing and equipment. In the 1930s, the gold standard of clothing tests was an individual expert, military or civilian, out in the field trying out all the options in boots or jackets. Outdoor companies highlighted their own field testing in advertising. A profile of L. L. Bean in *Life* magazine in 1941, for example, presented field testing as unquestionably the best demonstration of quality. "Scientific laboratory tests may be good enough for city slickers," the reporter explained, "but Mr. Bean prefers the endorsement of a Freeport resident who has given tough wear to a short, sock, mit [sic] or machete." In this spirit Bean invited

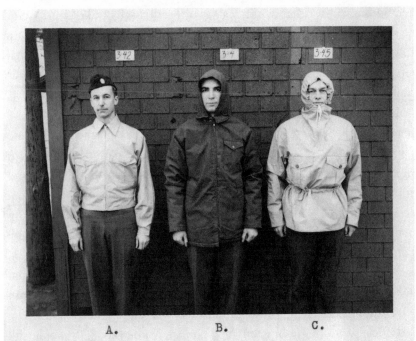

A.   B.   C.

Parka and Jackets

A. L. L. Bean, Inc. "Cossack Model Ski Blouse"

B. L. L. Bean, Inc. "Utility Parka"

C. L. L. Bean, Inc. "Featherweight Ski Parka"

Military test expeditions compared civilian garments with military uniforms. The testers, often expert outdoorsmen themselves, believed their personal opinion about effective clothing outdoors was more useful than any artificial test. (Report on Winter Warfare Equipment by Infantry Test Officer of the War Department, 1941, plate 124, 10th Mountain Division Collection, The Denver Public Library, Western History Collection, TMD1)

customers at the Freeport store to try out new equipment themselves by wading into a nearby pond.[10]

Civilian mountaineers in conversation—and often debate—with military officers generated thick reports filled with photos and test summaries that helped the Quartermaster team back in Washington make immediate decisions about whether Utility Parkas or Featherweight Ski Parkas would be warmer for winter combat. This might seem like a simple choice—is the L. L. Bean jacket warmer than the Brooks Brothers one?—but in fact civilian experts and their jacket preferences inspired the army to revamp both its uniforms and accepted principles about how to keep warm.[11]

Even as they embarked on test expeditions, some testers' bravado betrayed their belief that outdoor knowledge couldn't be gleaned from something as artificial as testing. Although they agreed to participate in the test expedition out of patriotism and a sense of duty, many did so with prefigured conclusions. Bradford Washburn, an experienced Alpine climber who had accompanied the National Geographic Society as a photographer and mapper for multiple expeditions in the 1930s, felt skeptical about the test expedition requirements. "To be honest," Washburn later told a friend, "we didn't need to test a damn thing on the trip to Mount McKinley in 1942. We all knew what would work and what wouldn't." Washburn's attitude was common among both civilian outdoor manufacturers and military men.[12]

Officials back in Washington, for their part, worried about the applicability of such narrow field tests. Although fieldwork on the Alaska expedition was a fast and relatively inexpensive method for testing the efficacy of clothing and equipment, Quartermaster General Edmund Gregory worried that the subjective focus on individual experiences of cold or wet conditions was too unscientific to guide the provisioning of an army of millions. Expedition participants affirmed that concern: the set of four books filled with reports about equipment from the Alaska expedition was, in the end, "just the product of our own likes and dislikes," explained William House, QMC tester and former Harvard classmate of Brad Washburn. "Past experience" was useful, but yielded "few actual scientific data."[13]

An ideal of scientific tests seemed more reliable than personal experience, which was subjective and "an art rather than science." So the QMC created a Research and Development Branch to improve clothing and equipment for a variety of climates based on an understanding of how to equip soldiers scientifically. This program would leave a legacy on the outdoor industry and its concepts of doing nature "the right way" in the next decade.[14]

The new head of the Research and Development Branch, Harvard Business School professor Georges Doriot, best represents the scientific approach to dress and equipment in the military. A naturalized U.S. citizen, Doriot had served in the French Army in World War I. After coming to the United States Doriot lectured at the Army Industrial College, so he was familiar with military-industrial management when he entered the army in 1941. Quartermaster General Gregory had taken classes with Doriot at Harvard in the 1920s and thought he would be the best person to assemble a team of scientists, industry men, and testers to lead the branch. Following a stint in the manufacturing industry, Doriot taught industrial management at Harvard Business School.[15]

Georges Doriot and his research laboratories transformed the testing regimen by applying industrial manufacturing logic to human bodies. Unlike L. L. Bean with his test-stomp pond behind the Freeport store, Doriot had no qualms about heading indoors to learn about the outdoors and thought that with numbers and data they would make men safer, warmer, and more comfortable. As they created a new cold-weather uniform, QMC reshaped who counted as an outdoor "expert." Even if outdoor industry professionals involved in the new testing technologies during the war found them frustrating, they would adopt these approaches in the decades that followed, along with assumptions about scientific testing of products that came with them.[16]

To test uniforms scientifically, Doriot's team first built an insulated and temperature-controlled room called the Cold Chamber. Originally used for wool-processing at a Massachusetts mill, the room was a sixteen-by-thirty-two-foot chamber insulated with sixteen inches of pressed cork and a two-inch-thick concrete floor. In the Cold Chamber, the research team divided weather variables into small, measurable units such as temperature or precipitation, each of which they adjusted incrementally to measure the physiological effects on human bodies. The soldiers who volunteered as test subjects withstood extreme cold and heat, simulated rain, and heavy packs to help the military and the civilian consultants understand what did and didn't work in extreme conditions. Soldiers walked one behind the other clad in anything from furs and mukluks to nothing but underwear while military scientists peered in through a large glass window. As scientists decreased the chamber's temperature or increased the windchill factor, they checked soldiers' skin temperature measurements transmitted via thermocouples attached to parts of their bodies.[17]

Researchers sometimes viewed testing with human subjects even under these conditions as too subjective a process, so they devised other ways to test comfort and durability without pesky humans. Machines with mechanical feet and arms tested the wear and tear on boot soles or pant legs from long-term repetitive motion that it would have taken a soldier many miles outdoors to achieve. Even more striking was the nearly life-sized "ideal soldier," a hunk of metal that the researchers called Copper Man. Researchers touted Copper Man as a revolutionary replacement for "subjective testing" with humans. The five-foot-tall model contained internal heating elements to mimic a heat-producing human body. Thermocouples attached to the copper shell measured skin temperature so scientists could track how clothes kept in or let out body heat. Measurements could chart Copper Man's decreasing skin temperature as scientists removed one layer of clothing at a time. The Copper Man was the "most accurate means yet devised for measuring insulate values" of clothes. The outdoor expert was evolving from the frontiersman or Indigenous man to the old-timer expert with invaluable firsthand knowledge to a mechanical, simulated human.[18]

The work of the Climatic Research Laboratory ramped up too slowly to be applied extensively during the war and had an uneven influence initially on the outdoor industry. Research with the cold room and Copper Man required numerous rounds of tests, which the civilian adviser Harold Hirsch saw as too slow and bureaucratic. Troops in the field agreed, reporting that long underwear or jackets were not available when they were most needed. L. L. Bean likely never came around to these scientific methods, preferring stomping through his pond to the end. Nonetheless, the testing infrastructure did overturn the older standard of personal endorsement and individual testing, and it created new variables to be tested, including windchill. With the creation of jobs in these new fields of scientific expertise, the art of dress was becoming a science.[19]

✳

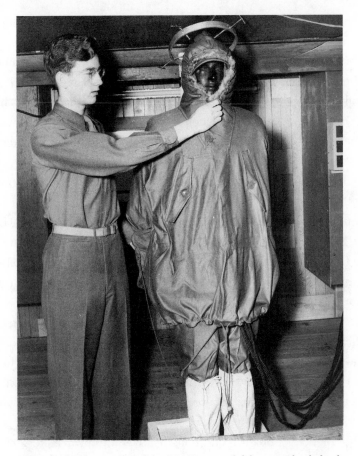

The Copper Man was part of the QMC's research laboratory that helped
make how to dress a science. ("Chauncey testing cold weather ensemble
with researcher adjusting clothing, U.S. Army Quartermaster Research
Command, Climatic Research Laboratory, Lawrence, Massachusetts,
1947" [Chauncey 004], OHA 329.8 Thermal Manikin Collection, Otis
Historical Archives, National Museum of Health and Medicine)

Whereas civilian consultants Hirsch and Bean remained skeptical of these
changes, Eddie Bauer manufactured many of the products to be tested and
then sent to the front lines, and his story played out differently. Much like the
Quartermaster's research laboratories, Bauer spent the war discovering new designs and integrating new kinds of materials into products like jackets and sleeping bags. Material shortages forced Eddie Bauer to change how he ran his

business. Like other manufacturers, Bauer was subject to War Production Board material requisition orders as well as guidelines for how to make products for the Quartermaster Corps. As Bauer came up against the limits of natural materials, he improvised so that he could continue making products for war. Like other innovations popularized because of wartime, his products shaped military and, later, civilian conceptions of new technologies and designs.

When the Quartermaster Corps called him up in 1942, Eddie Bauer held a handful of patents for goose down insulated clothing. His Skyliner Jacket, especially, helped to popularize the use of down in visibly quilted garments, rather than wool or cotton, for outdoor apparel. At the start of the war Bauer continued to operate his sport shop, as well as a mail-order business, Eddie Bauer Expedition Outfitter, and a subsidiary called Arctic Feather and Down Company, which imported the down used in the parka and pant designs sold by mail. The War Production Board wanted all of this material—the fabric, zippers, snaps, and especially the down.

The major concern of the military was having enough raw material—specifically the down—to produce enough clothing for soldiers. The supply had previously come from China and Europe, and when those foreign sources were no longer available, the QMC looked for substitutes. In the research section, the QMC experimented with milkweed fiber and kinked acetate fiber, but nothing really measured up.[20]

War Production Board requisitions nearly shut down Bauer's civilian production. He could continue producing civilian equipment and clothing as long as he didn't use the domestic duck and goose down supply frozen by the War Production Board. So, Bauer looked to worldwide supplies of down and landed on eiderdown, the small, soft feathers of an eider duck. He was able to sell eiderdown clothing to civilians who certified in a mail-order postcard that they were in a profession that exposed them to the cold, such as ranchers and veterinarians.

Bauer's Arctic Feather and Down Company produced sleeping bags twenty-four hours a day. In one year of production, he produced 220,000 single sleeping bags, assembled in units of two—inner plus outer bag. Bauer, who had contracts worth $63,000 for packboards and more than $2 million for sleeping bags by the end of 1942, had two methods for resolving the limits on sourcing down. First, he embarked on a feather-collecting campaign in partnership with the hunting conservation organization Ducks Unlimited. The Gathering Campaign publicized the military's need for feathers in the popular press and asked hunters to do their part to contribute. Eddie Bauer, Inc., collected the feathers and sent them out for processing and then to contractors. Newspaper articles, a few of which mentioned Eddie Bauer's role, urged hunters to eat ducks and save the down to dress aviators. That campaign collected thousands of pounds of down in 1942 and 1943. This was partly to ease production, but also an effective advertisement of Eddie Bauer's role in the war effort.

Bauer's second method involved figuring out how to make use of chicken feathers in sleeping bags. The United States had an abundance of chicken feathers, and curled chicken feathers approximated goose down. Bauer's new subsidiary, Feathers, Inc., processed, cleaned, and dried tons of chicken feathers a day to create Feather Foam. The military saw chicken feathers as "satisfactory" as long as they were still mixed with down and waterfowl feathers, but no one thought they were as good as goose down. Although Bauer shared the steps for making curled chicken feathers publicly, no other company sought a contract to do so.[21]

The most important part of a Bauer Feather Foam sleeping bag was the tag sewn inside it. Though most manufacturers were not permitted by war specifications to include company names, Bauer could and did. When Feather Foam and mummy design and envelope-like hoods worked, soldiers would remember the Bauer brand name.

There might not have been a true substitute for goose down, but a new material from DuPont promised to replace silk and cotton. At the testing facilities of the Quartermaster Corps, Hirsch got a first look at a synthetic fiber called nylon, which didn't mildew like cotton canvas in humid conditions. This modern wonder was mostly known as a substitute for silk in women's stockings, but wartime exigencies revealed many other applications, including nylon shoelaces, boots, and ponchos and rain suits. The possibilities were tantalizing for the Quartermaster Corps and its research and development laboratories, but largely out of reach. The U.S. Air Force had consumed nearly all nylon at the start of the war. The QMC only got access years later, as rejected parachutes were made available via surplus.[22]

By 1943, the Quartermaster Corps, and the civilian outdoor industry experts it employed, was finally able to get the nylon it wanted. In July 1944 DuPont shipped a new high of 2,657,384 pounds of nylon yarn to the Corps of Engineers and the Quartermaster Corps. Nylon's characteristics made it valuable in a wide variety of climatic conditions, from sticky, hot Southeast Asia to northern Europe's dry cold. Unlike cotton, nylon was hydrophilic so it could handle the damp and wet. Nylon laces didn't rip in soldiers' hands as they tied their boots, not even after a hundred loops. Manufacturers also used the synthetic material as a netting for bug protection, as a waterproof fabric for ponchos and tents, and as material for mildew-resistant hammocks for jungle use. From August 1943 to August 1945, DuPont shipped 948,042 pounds of nylon yarn to be made into shoe and boot laces. By August 1945, DuPont had shipped 716,760 pounds of yarn for jungle hammocks and a whopping 1,390,669 pounds for insect netting. Other smaller fields of application included nylon mountain tent cloth (516,240 pounds), ripstop ponchos (4,244,666 pounds), head nets (238,431 pounds), and sleeping bags (213,347).[23]

The promise of nylon, and its integration into research facilities more than government issue itself, changed the material's postwar trajectory as manufacturers involved in testing, like Harold Hirsch, saw its capabilities. In the Quartermaster facilities, researchers had posed questions such as, Could acetate fiber replace down? Could nylon replace cotton? They did not definitively answer these questions during the war, but their research set the stage for the introduction of materials that could indeed purport to replace cotton or down with something better than nature.

Individual soldiers' experiences can sometimes get lost in stories of wartime technology. But at least some soldiers snuggled into down bags and pulled their nylon laces taut by the thousands every day, especially by the last year of the war. More guinea pigs than consumers, these soldiers became familiar with new designs and materials. The QMC's education and indoctrination programs to teach soldiers about dress and equipment mattered nearly as much as the goods themselves. The ideologies of dress, based on new technologies and scientific approaches to testing, transmitted certain new ideas about the right way to dress for extreme weather to millions of soldiers and civilians. And these concepts would shape future leaders of the outdoor industry as well.

✳

Quartermaster Corps consultant Harold Hirsch had been an avid skier in his college days. He had customized a rugged, thick wool coat in plaid for the ski slopes, because, observed Hirsch, "we all thought that heavy wool would keep us warm." Hirsch equated heavier with warmer.[24]

During the war, however, Hirsch learned from other outdoor industry professionals and practitioners a different philosophy about dress, one that transformed his notion of the right way to dress and equip for the cold. Thousands during the war, and hundreds of thousands thereafter, shared Hirsch's newfound belief in the "layering theory."

The military did not invent layering. In the nineteenth century, home economists published research on managing body temperature that itself drew on centuries of precedent. In just one example of nascent clothing science, Charlotte Gibbs argued in 1917 that "several layers of lightweight material are better than one layer of thick material." Although it didn't create the concept, the Quartermaster Corps embraced it.[25]

Georges Doriot considered the layers of his new uniform to be as important as weapons and battle tactics. "The greatest enemy, besides what we normally call the enemy, is nature," he explained during a congressional hearing in 1946. Layering is one example of how the Doriot labs took the experiential common-sense knowledge of outdoorsmen and converted it into a science. In 1943, the Quartermaster Corps introduced the M-43, its experimental new uniform kit. The ensemble included a woolen undershirt, a long-sleeved flannel shirt, and a sweater. But the star of the kit was a new field jacket, which was (somewhat confusingly) also called the M-43—a nine-ounce, tightly woven cotton sateen garment, drab olive, sporting big pockets on the chest and at the hips. The designers intended the jacket to be used as an outer shell in different climates around the world—a global outerwear for global war. In extreme cold, a soldier would pair it with multiple thin layers underneath. In warmer climates, he could keep the outer shell but peel off other layers.

The concept of layering was precisely the kind of concept that mountaineers boasted they didn't need to test on the Alaska expedition. Many outdoor manufacturers likewise already knew about layering. They were hunters, fishermen, and outdoorspeople themselves, after all. But for those who didn't know it well, like Hirsch, the layering theory was central to the QMC's work.

Military research reports confirmed that the M-43 jacket and its accompanying layers kept soldiers warm in weather as cold as zero degrees Fahrenheit and that the jacket system worked well in the rain. Moreover, the tight weave of its cotton fabric meant that it kept out cold blasts of air on windy days. But convincing other officials and soldiers of its benefits required a concerted effort. For the M-43 layering system to work, soldiers had to know how to use it, and this was how layering went mainstream. It had come from the outdoor world and encountered quite a bit of resistance from the older guard in the military. Ultimately, it was the military's size and capacity for education that spread and democratized the layering idea.

Military experts developed a layering education program. One ninety-minute class, for example, required that soldiers listen to a lecture on how to stay alive in the cold and watch a demonstration of how to wear and adjust each item in the M-43 uniform assembly. By the middle of 1945, Doriot sent Quartermaster officers to instruct more than a million American troops in the Pacific in the science of layering. A wartime announcement explained that the clothing course was "[d]esigned on the 'layer,' or 'storm-window' principle of insulation against cold." The course taught that clothing could insulate the body's heat while keeping water and wind out. Students sat in tank tops and t-shirts under the paltry shade of palm trees to listen to Quartermaster officers explaining how to layer the M-43 jacket for extreme cold.[26]

Harold Hirsch never went to the South Pacific and never sat in on an indoctrination course on layering, but he learned the same lessons from his time with the QMC research team. Even decades later, Hirsch recalled the olive drab jacket fondly as a versatile and technically sophisticated replacement for the older woolen army greatcoats. Hirsch, like many other wartime manufacturers, was eager to show off these lessons to potential consumers rather than soldiers.

✳

Outdoor industry professionals were proud of their patriotic involvement in the war effort and planned to advertise it. Just as the outdoor industry worked closely with the military during the war, so too did advertisers maintain tight postwar connections with the federal government. The War Ad Council promoted the idea that the appropriate and patriotic way to advertise was not to brag or emphasize brands alone, but rather to focus on how a company contributed to the war effort or how consumers could benefit from its innovations. The outdoor industry comported with these trends.

Ads for clothing and equipment released during the war show that companies conceived of the conflict as good for business during eventual peacetime. The ads partly show how military designs transferred to civilian life, and how companies applied those designs and specifications to consumer goods. Even as stoves or sleeping bags were flying off the production line for the war, companies were already envisioning the postwar recreational market. At a time when civilian recreation was curtailed by wartime restrictions, including a loss of climbing partners, gasoline rations, and diminished club infrastructure, both companies and their target consumers looked forward to a lighter, more leisurely time. The ads also reflect how companies built brand awareness and invested in soldiers as brand ambassadors. These wartime insiders became an important community that mattered in the surplus era to come.

Through his work in the war industry, Harold Hirsch was able to travel between his job in Portland and his work as a special consultant and pollinate its design innovations across the country. As early as 1943, White Stag manufactured civilian jackets modeled after the distinctive M-43 field jacket. White Stag used the military origins of the "4-Season 'Off-Duty' Jacket" in advertising campaigns. "The leisure jacket gone military!" the catalog explained. The hand-drawn image in the White Stag catalog has detailing similar to the M-43. It is "a civilian garment inspired by the famous Army Field Jacket," reads the catalog copy, "made of the same government-specification" materials and waterproofing treatment. As a consultant, Hirsch had access to the new military designs and studies, and he was able to integrate the principles of those designs, if not their exact specifications, into his products. These jackets were not made for military contracts, but instead helped bring the new designs to a broader American public. In this way, military origins in outerwear became a persuasive new form of outdoor authenticity.[27]

Advertisements also highlighted the general role of the company as a supplier of wartime goods. Showing patriotism through business mattered to Hirsch, who came from a German Jewish family and who had wanted to join the military but was rejected because of his eyesight. Ski togs for ski troopers meant high-quality goods, tested in extreme conditions, and therefore appropriate for later recreational use. White Stag had a particular interest in dressing women who were wartime defense workers. As with the advertisements for men, the company line often suggested that what worked for war would work for recreation following reconversion. "Wear for war work now," a mock-up of an ad suggested—and, after the war, garden or fish in the same attire.[28]

Another outdoor company with an eye to both military contracts in war and civilian sales postwar was Coleman Lamp and Stove Company. Originally founded by W. C. Coleman at the turn of the century, the company began as a supplier of lamps for home lighting and expanded to heaters and furnaces by the 1920s. In the early 1940s, Coleman, based in Wichita, Kansas, enacted a transition similar to Eddie Bauer's toward manufacturing for the war. W. C. Coleman, the company's president, served on the advisory board to the Quartermaster Research and Development Branch. One of Coleman's most well-known products was the G.I. Pocket Stove. Model 520 was lauded as innovative because it operated in all kinds of conditions with multiple types of fuel. The stove design, created at the request of the QMC in 1941, was simple. It was a metal cylinder that weighed three pounds and measured eight and a half by four and a half inches. The lid flipped over and became the pot to cook in or boil water for coffee. The military had ordered more than $400,000 in stoves by the end of 1942. The war reporter Ernie Pyle called the stove effective, simple, and useful. He explained that the "practical little device" made life on the front just a little more comfortable, with hot coffee or warm water for a shave. By 1945, production of the little stoves numbered more than one million and soldiers had used them in every theater of war.[29]

Coleman made more than one million pocket stoves for military contracts and used wartime ads to speak to the promise of the civilian market after the war. (*Popular Mechanics*, August 1945, p. 159)

Coleman advertised the Pocket Stove during the war, even though it was unavailable to civilian campers. Nor were ski togs readily available. Many times, companies were advertising brand names and not actual products. Significantly, ads from Coleman and Hirsch-Weis focused narrowly on government objectives—the war effort—which meant they might have conformed to War Production Board and IRS regulations that made such advertising tax deductible. Businesses used wartime advertisements to link often unlabeled goods made for military contracts to their brand names, and to inspire visions of a postwar recreational world.

Like Hirsch-Weis, Coleman envisioned women as a future market. A Coleman Pocket Stove ad suggested that although ski troopers were currently drinking hot coffee in snow caves with a Coleman stove, the stove was "For YOU Tomorrow," with a far more domestic image of a couple using the same stove. The advertising council made the case that ads themselves were emblematic of the freedom America was fighting for: the fact that companies could advertise during the war showed that Americans were free people with freedom of choice.[30]

Like advertisements for manufacturers of everything from war planes to screws, outdoor industry ads portrayed hope for a future oriented toward American consumption as freedom. According to Coleman, G.I.s regularly sent the message to keep on making the Pocket Stove, because they wanted it "for fun when we come home."[31]

✳

Eddie Bauer's companies had produced hundreds of thousands of pieces of equipment for American soldiers by the end of the war, and that production had taken a very personal toll on his companies, financial health, and body. Stressed from war production and plagued by ill health, Bauer promised his doctor he'd step away from business. That was easier said than done for a man like him, who knew that despite his precarious status with the banks, he had new patents and newfound fame because of his involvement in the war effort. Feathers, Inc., shut down, as did the Arctic Feather and Down Company. The sleeping bags and down suits that had been the source of so much stress pointed a way forward in the postwar period. Bauer remained wary of the layering theory so popular at QMC headquarters. He believed it worked but wasn't sure what the concept would do for down garments that were so central to his product line. Unlike synthetics, down had no clear role in the layering assemblies developed by the military.[32]

Individual soldiers' work in the years that followed also show the spread of military ideas in the commercial realm. Paul Petzoldt founded the National Outdoor Leadership School. Bill Bowerman co-founded Nike (with Phil Knight). Gerry Cunningham, who had joined the 10th Mountain Division ski troops as an eighteen-year-old with an enthusiasm for gear, went on to start an outdoor equipment company. The textbook military approach to layering and dress as a science infused their professional and popular writing in the years that followed.

The QMC's research programs paved the way for even greater expansions of scientific authority in Cold War military programs. In the years after World War II the army pursued even more physiological, climatological, and geographical research. By the early 1950s, wary of increasing Cold War tensions and the demands of winter warfare in Korea, the QMC turned its rushed experimental laboratories of World War II into a permanent research facility near the original Climatic Research Laboratory in Massachusetts. Doriot, former director of the Quartermaster Research and Development Branch, argued passionately for the establishment of Natick, or the U.S. Army Natick Soldier Research, Development and Engineering Center. The Doriot Climatic Chambers remain a "centerpiece" of the Natick facility, where researchers continue to study the layering principle using descendants of the Copper Man.[33]

Like Eddie Bauer, Harold Hirsch and L. L. Bean returned to civilian markets. Their work utilized the new designs, approach to testing, and measurements for fabrics and waterproofing developed in wartime QMC labs. Company founders were often idiosyncratic and hands-on participants in their business, so the new approach to testing was especially consequential, and slowly made appearances in outdoor manufacturing facilities. Scientific testing became more mainstream in the decades that followed. Outdoor companies made ready use of nylon, and many more synthetic materials were in the pipeline. Outdoor companies even relied on the military laboratory's research variables when advertising the efficacy of new materials.

The long-term effects of all of these factors that shaped the outdoor industry were not yet visible, of course, to American consumers who in 1946 simply wanted to return to leisure mountain trips. They were thinking about the bounty of new technology already in production: Eddie Bauer's down sleeping bags (or even his Feather Foam ones) and Coleman's lightweight Pocket Stove promised nights outdoors with hot food and a warm bed. How consumers got these items is the story of surplus.

FIVE

Pup Tents and Mummy Bags

Spreading Surplus to the Masses

The Surplus Property Act of 1944 defined surplus as anything beyond the "needs and responsibilities of the owning agency." In other words, scrap, or waste. But to veteran Nelson Bryant, surplus was treasure. In a nostalgic account years later, he recalled two beloved items from surplus stores acquired just after the war. One was a simple army pup tent consisting of two pieces of fabric, called shelter halves, that campers strung between two poles to hold it up. Bryant's other government-issue purchase was a rucksack, little more than a canvas sack attached to a metal frame. The army had paid a premium for such equipment just months before, but V-E Day made these items nearly worthless. Bryant, however, took pride in them as "the best the Army had produced." Bryant, who grew up fishing near his family's home on Martha's Vineyard, developed a special expertise in recreational equipment as the *New York Times* outdoors columnist, but his attitude was otherwise typical of the postwar period.[1]

When President Roosevelt signed the Surplus Property Act, camping was far from his mind. The act was designed to organize the distribution of war property such as tanks, planes, and bases more than socks, jackets, and tents. Through the surplus objects handled by the War Assets Administration, the vast wartime bureaucracy and scale of wartime industrial production became visible to Americans, and public perceptions mattered.

In the popular press, barely worn military boots sounded useful. But what about 18,577 mate-less boots when few stores could move that kind of merchandise? Starting in 1946, new army surplus stores around the nation answered this question. After World War II the unprecedented scale of goods made surplus a part of everyday life as hadn't been seen with the smaller quantity of goods on the civilian market after the Civil War and World War I. Savvy veterans, many of them outdoor enthusiasts themselves, bought up huge lots of military waste and turned them into consumer treasures. Surplus stores appeared as TV and radio sitcom punchlines. Highbrow climbing journals and pocket guides to equipment recommended which surplus sleeping bags to buy and how to identify the genuine article — a postwar iteration of the persistent quest for authenticity in outdoor recreation commerce.[2]

But there was one major problem with this wealth of military surplus: it was *terrible*. Surplus was often used and in need of repair. Pup tents like the one Nelson Bryant acquired were no good in the cold. Rucksacks like the one he carried were heavy and uncomfortable — a "kidney-killer," one equipment expert called them. Looking back, Bryant realized this equipment "wasn't much," but it remained central to his outdoor experience for the simple fact that he could afford it. That was a big part of what made surplus a national phenomenon. Surplus spread around the country because it was cheap. It fit almost no one, but hunters, campers, backpackers, and fishermen all wanted it. Americans nationwide went to army surplus stores, also called army-navy stores, to browse and buy. They loved the thrill of searching, the cheap products, and came to appreciate the distinctive smell, even when individual tents or rucksacks failed to live up to expectations.[3]

The culture around military surplus clothing and equipment reveals something important about how the outdoor identity evolved in the mid-twentieth century. World War II veterans in the immediate post-1945 years brought their intimate knowledge of brands, equipment, and how to use it with them to their recreational activities. There was no single reason why so many millions of Americans chose conquering the outdoors as their activity of choice in the postwar years. For some, the nostalgia for the brotherhood and sense of purpose men felt during the war might have motivated it. For others, the stultifying cookie-cutter suburbs and a desire to escape capitalist modern life might have offered an incentive. Finally, many embraced camping and outdoor activities as an affordable family-oriented vacation. Whatever the reason, army surplus offered an accessible way into the outdoor experiences so many sought.

Presidents and pundits—and, later, historians—argued that American business had won the war. The country's capacity to radically expand industrial production brought the boys home. Surplus stores brought the goods that had supposedly won the war into American homes. Nowhere was this material and cultural influence more evident than on the trail. Climbers and skiers encountered the goods of war each time they roped up or clipped in. Yet the postwar increase in sales of leftover military pup tents and down sleeping bags went beyond these sports. Americans who never climbed up a mountain or skied down one also began to access new equipment and clothing. In the 1940s and 1950s, surplus democratized access to the products that supported outdoor experience. Surplus also began to turn outdoor gear from something simply used in the outdoors, by outdoorspeople, into a larger aesthetic. It became a fashion disconnected from value.[4]

✳

Military waste was a problem of piles and perception. The matériel of war sat near the front and on military bases waiting to be shipped. Piles of goods also sat in factories; some objects had never been used at all before production specifications changed and they became obsolete. Many military officers remembered the ill-planned release of surplus goods following World War I, and the ensuing depression. As they planned for peace they often used metaphors of surplus products "clogging" or "choking" the "industrial bloodstream." Government officials worried about the nation's economic security urged President Roosevelt to sign the Surplus Property Act. The act defined surplus and the purpose of its resale.[5]

One problem was how to calculate the value of military waste. One measure might be the price the government paid for it, as set by the War Production Board or wartime contracts. Another measure might be how much the government would get for its resale—usually, a small percentage of the original cost. A report in 1944 warned that the government should expect substantial losses since wartime costs did not accord with peacetime value and even specialized, costly tools might only have value as scrap.

Some estimates put the property value at $34 billion or $60 billion, others at $100 billion. Land, buildings, aircraft, and machine tools comprised the bulk of the surplus material. Nonetheless, one category loomed much larger in the popular imagination: consumer goods. That textiles, apparel, and footwear were valued at just $1.1 billion and accounted for only one-fifteenth of the surplus to be resold mattered little.[6]

Outdoorspeople—often veterans and their families—eagerly waited at the front of the line for these goods. Popular articles primed consumers to anticipate them. News reports suggested there would be "veritable mountains" of consumer goods at "cut-rate prices." The reports made the surplus products sound inevitable and just around the corner. "Congress Trying Now to Decide What to Do with War Leftovers," one article reported. "A Mile of Jeeps," announced another. In the service, or in popular magazines and newspapers back home, Americans read about the vast system of military innovations. *Stars and Stripes* magazine, *Life*, and the *New York Times* all ran articles about the new cold-weather equipment developed in the Quartermaster Corps to serve the ski troopers at Camp Hale. Stateside, civilians watched news reports that explained just how the Quartermaster Corps invented and tested this magnificent new equipment—in fact, two military leaders from the Quartermaster Corps were appointed heads of the new War Assets Administration (WAA) in 1946. (Who better than experts on war matériel to field complaints when there was a mismatch between consumer expectations and reality?)[7]

Veterans themselves set some of these high expectations. Even if uniforms had not served them well during war, soldiers wrote appreciatively about the possibilities of newly designed ones. "I only look toward the finish of the war so that I can get outdoors and wear [the] garb," wrote one officer who was a fan of Georges Doriot's wartime research laboratories. "It will be ideal for what I have in mind—after the war." Veterans who had been active outdoorspeople before the war were among the first to recognize the potential for both fun and profit in integrating military equipment and clothing into outdoor recreation. For example, mountaineer and Quartermaster consultant H. Adams Carter predicted that the improvements made in clothing and equipment would be a boon to outdoor sports following the war. Much like soldiers who tasted K-rations and returned home with a taste for American industrialized food, so too did soldiers' uniforms and equipment teach them what materials worked, with what layers, and in what weather. The material of war—from weaponry to mundane soda pop and undershirts—had imprinted itself on the minds of sixteen million American G.I.s.[8]

Outdoor enthusiasts were also excited about the surplus equipment boom. Since 1943 or 1944, rationing had removed much of the traditional gear from catalogs and stores. The Recreational Equipment Cooperative (which would later become REI) and L. L. Bean were among the many companies that had to tell potential customers that their stocks were slowly disappearing. The Seattle-based Co-op had been unable to stock air mattresses and down sleeping bags since 1942, and expected that it would not restock anything with wool or metal as supplies disappeared. Even the established outfitter Abercrombie & Fitch had not sold a single lightweight tent since the war started. Overseas imports from Europe also ceased during wartime. Piles of military goods adapted for leisure use would address Americans' deferred demand for outdoor gear.[9]

Outdoor magazines and club reports heralded wartime innovations as part of the larger victory of government science and technology. The American Alpine Club published a special issue of its journal on wartime developments in equipment and clothing in the mountains. One War Department photograph in the publication showed a rucksack, boots, one-burner stove, plywood backboard, bear paw snowshoes, and a mountain sleeping bag with the model's nose just barely peeking out from the head of the bag, all framed by a nylon mountain tent. The photograph captured a vision of the new "right way" to do the outdoors, with wartime-tested and -inspired American science and technology.[10]

Although war products were not necessarily suited for civilian life, the link between wartime equipment and the outdoor recreation industry was not accidental. After all, outdoor industry professionals had helped design nylon mountain tents. Mountaineers tested the latest design of mummy sleeping bags. Eddie Bauer and L. L. Bean knew how to integrate wartime innovations into their businesses. Likewise, ordinary soldiers sensed they could profit from giving surplus goods a second life.

With high expectations generated by media reports and word of mouth, there was clearly a market waiting for surplus outdoor goods. The challenge was getting, literally, tons of apparel and equipment from government facilities into the homes of American consumers. In reaction to this public demand, American military veterans—who were granted special access to the WAA's surplus auctions—began to search for stock to sell.

In 1946, thirty-year-old Ed Orkney was looking to make some money quickly, not to start a surplus empire, per se. Orkney, who had been a B-52 bomber pilot, first attempted, unsuccessfully, to put his wartime skills to use by finding work as a pilot. He had attended the University of Washington for a year, but college life didn't suit him. He saw more value in building a business, so he borrowed money from his mother and drove from Oregon to Fort Lewis, Washington. There, he could buy large lots of military-issue surplus products that were not for sale anywhere else.

Orkney purchased two thousand down mummy-shaped sleeping bags for $1.50 each. This was a new way of doing business. Back in Oregon, he quickly resold them next to a fruit stand for $12 to $15 each ($180 to $228 in 2022). The quick profit appealed to him. For the next two years, he worked ad hoc, buying surplus lots at Fort Lewis, and later at McChord Air Force Base in Tacoma and Pier 91 in Seattle, and reselling items to customers on street corners as well as to dealers up and down the West Coast. The trunk of Orkney's car was his "warehouse," and a table he carried his "showroom." Scores of other entrepreneurial veterans who saw American consumers' excitement for the innovations of war joined Orkney. These men bought government-manufactured goods at auctions, sometimes camping out overnight to wait for sales, and then resold those goods on street corners and in makeshift shops. They transformed G.I. trash into treasures for the masses.[11]

What counted as "salable" often relied on the purchaser's imagination. Larger property was adapted to new uses by businesses, universities, and individuals. For example, the amphibious DUKW trucks saw a new life as tourist vehicles—"Ducks"—in the Wisconsin Dells, and as water-bound school buses in New Jersey. Universities appropriated Quonset huts as classrooms on college campuses brimming with new students on the G.I. Bill. Hollywood producers bought war planes to use in movies.[12]

Consumer products often proved more eclectic and available in inconveniently large numbers. To some, 166,000 two-ounce bottles of insect repellant originally intended for soldiers in the South Pacific might seem like a challenge—this was too many bottles to resell and each bottle alone was too small to be of much use. But to a buyer like Orkney, who knew the wrath that hunters and fishermen directed at mosquitoes as well as the premium they placed on lightweight equipment, these goods could be turned into a windfall. Orkney and his contemporaries gathered at army bases and storage facilities around the country to participate in bidding. At times, the government announced the auctions with specific products—"Tent Frames on Sale"—at the center. In other cases, bidders would bid blindly on a lot and hope to discover salable goods in it. Veterans like Orkney received priority in the bidding process, often purchasing up to 40 percent of surplus products from government lots before they were even available to the general public.[13]

In 1948, Orkney joined with five partners to open a shop. A canvas hospital tent—government issue, of course—gave the retail store a distinctive look. The partners named the store G.I. Joe's. Orkney's son David later explained, "All he sold was government issue, and G.I. Joe's, he felt, was a name that everyone would instantly know what it was all about." When the store opened an ad instructed customers to "follow the searchlight" to its location—David speculated that it was probably a war surplus searchlight—as if a store of rucksacks were as glamorous as a Hollywood premiere. For consumers, "government issue" could denote two things: military specifications that determined how the product was manufactured, and more generally, authenticity by a new definition. A pup tent stamped "G.I." signified that it really had been built for war.[14]

The guidebook author Harvey Manning called the immediate postwar years "the epic era of war-surplus stores," as tons of products moved nationwide from government warehouses to auctions to army surplus shops in places like Sioux Falls, South Dakota; Ashtabula, Ohio; Pinellas Park, Florida; and Ogden, Utah. In 1946 and 1947, as these stores opened, the flood of surplus materials entering the civilian market was so voluminous that a single successful auction bid was enough to stock an entire shop.[15]

The scale of war surplus in 1946 was unprecedented, but not its existence. Americans had actually used army shops to equip leisure-time activities since the Civil War. The most well-known surplus reseller of the
nineteenth century was Bannerman's, based in New York. After World War
I, many more companies joined Bannerman's. Cal Hirsch & Sons, of
St. Louis, Missouri, sold tents and riding breeches. Russell's of New York
sold both military surplus and non-military equipment manufactured specifically for outdoor recreation. In 1922, the company offered haversacks,
army breeches, and even women's outdoor clothing, including breeches,
skirts, and bloomers. These military surplus company catalogs made clear
that their primary customer base was sportsmen and women. The cover of
the Cal Hirsch catalog featured a soldier and sailor, flanked by their leisure-
time alter egos: two young men by a campfire.[16]

Outdoorsman Paul M. Fink, on his backpacking trips in the southern
Appalachian Mountains in the 1920s, regularly turned to army-issued clothing and equipment for its "ability to take hard punishment" on the trail.
Army goods also were stylish, although at this time only within the outdoor
realm. Men and women alike wore riding breeches almost exclusively in
the 1920s to go hiking. After World War II, the use of surplus for leisure
seemed even more important because, in the spring of 1947, the outdoor life
was calling but camping equipment was hard to find. Even smaller items
like Coleman Pocket Stoves and lanterns were "virtually unobtainable."
Finding a tent was as hard as finding an apartment, one reporter complained. Specialty outdoor stores were still relatively rare, and those that had
camping equipment in stock at affordable prices were rarer still. Outdoor
enthusiasts could visit high-end outdoor shops like Abercrombie & Fitch if
they lived in New York and could afford the high prices. A few scattered
niche operations run by families out of their basements focused on importing mountaineering equipment from Europe. But for most Americans,
these stores remained obscure and out of reach. Instead, army surplus
stores, in strip malls and main streets of cities large and small, became the
first place to look for equipment and clothing for outdoor sports. By 1947,
surplus resellers had moved clothing valued at $150 million, and the WAA
estimated that almost that much was still left to auction off.[17]

The key to moving the seemingly endless quantity of surplus was reaching the vast market of G.I. "converts," who had learned to love the outdoor life while in the military. But most surplus store owners knew veterans were only the start. The sleeping bags, cots, and other products with outdoor recreation uses were what "really pulled people in the door." The products previewed what would soon be available commercially as manufacturers shifted toward a civilian market.[18]

In 1952, Ed Orkney bought G.I. Joe's outright and moved from his plywood and hospital-tent showroom to a permanent location in North Portland. As a newspaper story later reported, from those modest beginnings "it didn't take long . . . to recognize the tremendous demand for all sorts of outdoor sporting equipment." The products varied and the stock constantly rotated. Treasures included standbys like sleeping bags, canteens, cots, tents, and also empty ammunition boxes, bins of insect repellent, mess kits, sewing kits, and tarps. "Customers never knew what wonderful new items they would find," recalled Ed's daughter Janna Orkney. The unpredictability was part of the experience. Unlike the consumer standard for authenticity of earlier years, tied to a specific style or store, Orkney's shop was notable because it offered the same standard, mass-produced, and interchangeable products as so many other surplus stores around the country.[19]

Popular media sometimes played up surplus shop oddities. The popular radio sitcom *Fibber McGee and Molly* painted the war surplus auction as both a trap and a treasure trove. In one episode, Molly warns her flighty husband that they have no use for products like a rubber life raft. Inattentiveness leads them to buy thirty weather balloons rather than the ten gallons of house paint they wanted. In an episode of *The Mickey Rooney Show* from 1955, the host and his friend planned to buy a war surplus shop. Rooney saw the store as "a gold mine," but going through the inventory yielded unexpected—and unwanted—surprises. The store boasted twelve dozen infantry boots, all in excellent condition. The catch was that they were all size 15, width DDD, and to top it off, there were only left feet. In addition to skis, packs, and even knight's armor, the store stock included six gross of army sunglasses with unbreakable lenses—all broken. The implication was that this was all worthless junk; at best it was unclear if a customer would find any real treasures.[20]

One thing was predictable, though: the smell. Army surplus was distinctive for its immediate sensorial assault. Much like buckskin beside the campfire had been the olfactory certification of authenticity in the late nineteenth century, military supply served that purpose after World War II. Although its source was elusive, one possible culprit was canvas, musty from sitting in government warehouses. Cosmoline, an oily rust-preventative slathered on metal goods, was another likely offender. Whatever its source, customers came to associate the scent with genuine government issue. David Orkney recalled, "it was Army stuff and it was greasy and it smelled like Army stuff."[21]

G.I. Joe's was a family endeavor. The older child, Janna, remembered the "piles of army knapsacks, canteens with holders and belts, stacks of inflatable rubber rafts," and more in the basement. All you had to do was open the door and "the fragrance of army surplus would waft up from the basement and surround you," Janna recalled. Janna and David played in the backyard in a G.I. pup tent. A yellow rubber raft, government issue, became the kids' wading pool when Charmian, their mother, filled it with water. When the children were very small, Orkney would let them nap in the sleeping bags in the store windows. When the children were older, they both worked at the store. G.I. Joe's even affected the family dog. After hearing from their father about a sale of tarpaulins, the waterproof covers also known as tarps, at the shop, David and Janna decided to name the family dog Tarpsy.[22]

Beyond family, a buying group called Worldwide Distributors helped Orkney's surplus business grow. The group was made up of more than twenty owners of surplus goods stores in the Pacific Northwest and Alaska, and Orkney joined it in the 1950s. Orkney learned that his experience was part of a much larger trend. The proprietors of Swain's General Store in Port Angeles, Washington, Tri-State Distributors in Moscow, Idaho, and Big Ray's in Alaska had important lessons for him. The group taught him about the benefits of advertising when he was reluctant to do so. The organization also gave small stores like G.I. Joe's the chance to order larger lots than they could otherwise afford. Many of the original members of the buying group had a similar background to Orkney's. They were also veterans, and that went a long way toward building "trusting relationships with other retailers" who had parallel interests but were not competitors since the surplus market was always local. The collective power of this buying group would become even more important to Orkney when government auctions began to dry up.[23]

When the outdoor guidebook author Harvey Manning looked around the mountains near his home in Washington, he saw a blur of khaki. To Manning, these men—and a few women—dressed in an array of army clothes and using army mess kits, hammocks, and field rations, were essentially a "vaudeville version of the Mountain Troops." He called them the Khaki Gang, and outdoorspeople of his generation would have recognized the term. The Khaki Gang was not a formal group, and it was more than a style. The name suggested those who found similar spirits on the trail. They connected over their aesthetic uniformity, the leisure activities they shared, and the values their purchases represented; in a word, they were "cheapskates." Through their visits to stores like Ed Orkney's, these outdoorspeople not only disseminated the matériel of war into everyday life but also changed the value system associated with outdoor recreation.[24]

When outdoorsmen visited local surplus stores, they left with "the appearance of soldiers equipped for field duty." These products *could* have connoted American military success or been valued because they reenacted soldiers' expertise and experience. But surplus ended up with very different connotations than those it had carried in wartime. Surplus was grubby. Uniforms had been sharp. Surplus was cheap—it came already used, already rejected by the military. War matériel embodied technical expertise and equality. And during the war, civilians had devoured reports of military goods as innovative and modern. In contrast, at an army-navy store, buyers had to be selective to find treasures amid the junk. This was true because, above all else, the surplus that outdoorspeople wore and used was terrible. Hence the curious contradiction of surplus: it was coveted, but people complained about it. It was cheap, but not always useful. It was modern technology and it was used and discarded, all at once.[25]

Three characteristics of the surplus experience that the Khaki Gang brought to the outdoor world help explain these contradictions and reveal the evolving values linked to the outdoor identity. The first principle, according to a Khaki Gang adherent, was that being grubby was a trait to aspire to. To young, impressionable outdoorspeople, the khaki-clad outdoorsmen seemed to own the trail and slopes with their style and dress. Charles Williams, for instance, was a spindly teen with a confidence problem when his father enrolled him in climbing school in the Seattle area. Like many newcomers, Williams pored over climbing guidebooks so he would know what to do—and how to act—as he traveled through the Pacific Northwest and Canada to climb and ski. After a few nightmarish beginners' trips filled with blisters and cold due to lack of equipment, Williams decided he needed to imitate the veterans who were drab but comfortable. To the young climber, the Khaki Gang members were the outdoor experts, more than Horace Kephart and his guidebook or a salesman presented as an expert in a sleek urban outdoor store, or even the trope of the frontiersman or Indigenous man. The men in khaki and olive drab espoused a snobbish pride about using war surplus, so Williams also learned to express (ironically elitist) aesthetic gratification in being drab. This shabby-chic authenticity reconciled in its own way, and for a new postwar generation, commercialism and the enduring anti-consumerist ideal of outdoor culture.[26]

Frugality was a second value of Khaki Gang aspirants. Peacetime seemed to promise all Americans access to more and better consumer goods. Surplus was a sign of doing without, and less expensive goods were prized status symbols rather than the most expensive. The uniform of the outdoorsperson was accessible even to non-veterans with little disposable income. A Recreational Equipment Co-op price list from 1952 listed the cost of a new parka at $10.95 (about $120 in 2022), almost ten times as expensive as the olive drab army surplus parka. The Co-op resold rucksacks, both new and used, with prices in the $2 to $4 range ($22 to $44 in 2022). Khaki Gang members bragged about the cheapest finds. Betty Nelson, a Seattle resident and outdoorswoman, recalled that her family's clothes included old woolen shirts, socks, and underwear as well as army surplus boots. Alexandra Pye, who hiked and climbed with the Seattle Mountaineers in the 1950s, remembered that for hiking clothes, her family would "buy them at Goodwill and other places where you could get army surplus pants . . . you could get good stuff." To Nelson and Pye, surplus seemed like a good compromise if they were going to buy what they had once made at home or done without. Guidebooks also directed young campers to surplus stores, where "pup tents can be purchased at little cost."[27]

The third value of the Khaki Gang was selectivity. Surplus buyers re-membered picking through piles of clothes, barely organized or labeled, in hopes of a find. The haphazardly organized makeshift stores, in car trunks and tents and eventually storefronts, contrasted sharply to the modern, brightly lit, and well-organized outdoor outfitters of the early twentieth cen-tury. Whereas Abercrombie & Fitch had carefully arranged window scenes and modern shelving, these new stores were chaotic. At Doughboy's Sur-plus in Rosemead, California, it was common to "see piles of old Army gas cans, shovels, bunk beds, trash cans, or just about anything on the sidewalk in front of the store to lure customers inside." The piles inside were not just a result of too much inventory in too little space. Janna Orkney recalled that she took on the task of neatening the insect repellent bin. After wiping all the stock clean and organizing it, she learned the secret behind her father's haphazard store appearance. He told Janna to "mess [the bottles] up again" because a messy bin looked picked through, and more full, and that would attract customers. The extra effort to sort through these kinds of piles was often worth it. For example, Charles Williams, the Seattle climber, "quickly learned to comb the local surplus stores for wool pants, gloves, sleeping bags, Coleman stoves and tents." A Khaki Gang practice, sifting through surplus, was added to the list of requisite skills for the outdoors.[28]

Treasure-hunting skills were important because stocks of surplus rotated quickly. Often advertisements correctly urged that new stock should be pur-chased as fast as possible. Ed Orkney sold out of his initial lot of down sleep-ing bags in Portland in three days. "You'll never see buys like these," claimed Vermont-based Wilson Sports Equipment Company. The firm advertised surplus goods to the seven hundred thousand readers of *Sports Afield* maga-zine, boasting of the equipment "Made to Uncle Sam's Rigid Wartime Re-quirements." The ad itself proved a success, as sportsmen sent in $500,000 in orders for the surplus equipment.[29]

Despite this rush to purchase stock, outdoorspeople quickly realized that army surplus was mostly "terrible equipment." It was rugged, to be sure, and attractive in a drab sort of way, but often heavy, bulky, and barely warm enough for cold nights in the mountains. Charles Williams remembered that his "rough" surplus equipment provided little more warmth than lining his blankets with newspaper. Even years later, backpackers recalled sagging government-issue rucksacks that just about "broke [their] backs." On the whole, army surplus clothing and equipment, from nylon ponchos to pup tents, left people unsatisfied and uncomfortable when they used it.[30]

The basic problem was that "the peculiar needs of the Services," explained an outdoor guide soon after the war, "do not necessarily produce an optimum item for the going-light tramper." One gear reviewer joked that given the size and weight of surplus goods, military equipment designers must have assumed the typical soldier was "as strong as a muskox and addicted to driving tanks over his equipment or throwing it off high cliffs." Reports from the ski troopers of 130-pound men carrying packs weighing up to ninety pounds illustrate the intense strain on both bodies and equipment. Soldiers often could not adjust equipment in the moment of battle—they had to listen to orders about what to wear and discard, and when. But hikers had the flexibility and independence to choose where they hiked and to add or subtract from their pack based on conditions and experience. Surplus packs that could support ninety pounds were both too big and too heavy for less ambitious postwar outings. Further, both limited available materials such as nylon and the necessity of designing clothing that would not be cared for meant that clothing designed for war was considerably heavier than that designed for prewar outdoorspeople.[31]

Although surplus stocks did at times include women's clothes, the vast majority of the products produced for war, and therefore the majority of the products resold afterward, were made for men. Women shopped surplus but they also had to modify their purchases to make them work. For them, frugality superseded imperatives of fit and comfort. Both Betty Nelson and Alexandra Pye, who recalled buying surplus clothes for themselves and their families, would have struggled to find surplus pants that matched their body shape and size. Mary Lowry remembered the khaki era with distaste, especially when she thought of her husband Ed's surplus wool pants. She was glad to have forced him to throw them out when she purposefully shrunk them in hot water. Attitudes about surplus were partly generational: climber Ruth Dyar Mendenhall "luxuriated" in surplus clothing's toughness and generous cut, while a few years later her teenage daughter Valerie found the same clothes "a source of unspeakable embarrassment."[32]

Surplus quality was also terrible because so much of it after the initial flood of goods was in used or even bad condition. Surplus resellers like the Orkneys in Portland, the Andersons in Seattle, and the Holubars in Boulder acquired what products they thought would sell, and labeled them according to quality, which was consistently inconsistent. There were duffel bags in good condition to be found searching through a pile, but most were shot through with bullet holes or burned by cigarettes. Hunters looking for surplus military arms learned that a seemingly inexpensive find could have an ultimate cost much higher than a new gun, with repair work. The Mickey Rooney television episode was accurate when it described every one of the store's canteens as leaky. Customers *knew* these products were worn, even well-worn. But a new mountain tent, when it came without poles or stakes, did not represent the triumph of new technology they had been promised.[33]

The beloved and simultaneously hated army tent illustrates the contradictions of these purchases. The most popular of these was the pup tent, also called a shelter half. Some guidebooks halfheartedly endorsed pup tents, while others suggested that pup tents were adequate only for "boys and backpackers" since adults needed to be able to sit up inside a tent to be comfortable. The more prized acquisition was harder to find: the two-man mountain tent, a newer military design. This was the "prince charming of the pup-tent family." The two-man mountain tent was one piece, so it had no zippers or other fasteners that could malfunction. It was made of waterproof balloon cloth, or nylon, in the newest models, and was reversible — white on one side, olive drab on the other. In addition to a tunnel entrance that could be pulled shut for warmth, it also had ventilators on both ends to ensure airflow. As with other wartime innovations, outdoorspeople expressed interest in the new technology, especially in the waterproof quality provided by nylon.[34]

Although it was the best the army had to offer, expert mountaineers suggested the mountain tent was nowhere close to perfected. Indeed, "had this tent been put up for civilian consumption, the complaints about it would have put the manufacturer out of business," claimed William House, a mountaineer and civilian consultant to the Quartermaster Corps in 1946. The fabrics either caused excessive condensation inside the tent, or were too heavy. Still, these complaints were only academic for ordinary surplus seekers because few two-man mountain tents were available. Some were lucky enough to find the army's latest model, but many more had to make do with dysfunctional but ubiquitous pup tents. Some department stores sold twenty thousand pup tents in a week. The popular press extolled the mountain tent, but surplus stores mostly stocked pup tents. In both cases, "cheapness" made them popular. The best one canoeist could say about the mountain tent was that it was "serviceable."[35]

Equipment experts warned in popular articles that buyers should be wary of the "lure of a surplus bargain." Quality equipment matters, one article explained, and surplus buyers might learn that "the bargain is only in the price." Using the language of temptation, customers sometimes said they could not resist a purchase despite having no use for a product, because it was "too good a bargain to pass up." Government-issue products might have been a bargain—"This cost the government $4,000 and it can be yours for $4.99!"—but customers often bought the $4.99 weather balloon or windshield defroster that they had no need for.[36]

How did all these conflicting values play out for someone actually buying army surplus for a trip outdoors? In early April of 1948, Earl Shaffer donned a plaid shirt and army surplus pants, and put his equipment in a pack from a surplus store. Inside, he had packed a "Marine Corp poncho, one blanket, a small tent, a mountain troop cookkit, one spare set of clothing, toilet articles and a few misc[ellaneous] items." With a hand on his hip belt to steady the forty-pound pack, Shaffer took his first steps on the Appalachian Trail, a two-thousand-mile-long walk from Georgia to Maine. As boys, Earl Shaffer and his "once in life" friend Walter Winemiller had shared an "abiding love of all outdoors" and dreamed of hiking the soon-to-be-completed Appalachian Trail together. But Shaffer returned to York County, Pennsylvania, after four and a half years of army service alone. Winemiller

Earl Shaffer equipped himself with army surplus clothing and
equipment for his Appalachian Trail thru-hike in 1948. In the
years that followed, he shared his experiences and gear
preferences via slides like this one. (Earl Shaffer Papers,
Archives Center, National Museum of American History,
Smithsonian Institution)

had died at Iwo Jima. Two years after the war, twenty-nine-year-old Earl
Shaffer was "nervous and unhappy," distraught over the death of his friend.
Paging through *Outdoor Life* magazine, Shaffer read an article about the
Appalachian Trail. The physical training of wartime had left his body strong,
and as a memorial to Winemiller and to "walk the Army out of [his] system,"
Shaffer decided he would make the trek from Georgia to Maine alone.[37]

In 1947, equipping for the trail was not a straightforward process unless a hiker had the means to visit a one-stop shop like Abercrombie & Fitch. Yet Shaffer was rightly confident about the equipment, albeit "meagre," that he had assembled. As a teenager, he had hiked with his brother and learned the art of woodcraft from his friend Walter. From his years of military service he knew what clothing worked and how to customize it. Shaffer had trained in ju-jitsu for months, but the surplus pack full of gear still weighed heavy on his back. Its silhouette was low and squat, the ends jutting out past his trim body. Like Boy Scouts, families planning vacations, and outdoor club members whose interests matched his own, Shaffer sought functional and cheap gear. His load represented the best rugged, inexpensive clothes and equipment available to ordinary people like him who wanted to go backpacking. With his surplus pack loaded, Shaffer left Oglethorpe, Georgia, in April 1948.[38]

In the years that followed the trip, now recognized as the first Appalachian Trail thru-hike, Shaffer found an audience for his stories, slides, and gear practices. He lectured at hiking clubs and schools and wrote articles for outdoor and popular magazines, drawing anecdotes from his trail-worn black diary. Aspiring outdoor enthusiasts attended Shaffer's talks. They listened politely to his nature poetry and narrations of his slides, but really craved to know details about his training, equipment, and logistics. "What did you wear? Did you carry a tent? How did you get supplies? How many pairs of shoes did you wear out?" Audiences, consisting of veterans like Shaffer but also an increasing number of families, learned in this way how to make use of imperfect surplus products.[39]

Shaffer warned that a feat like hiking the Appalachian Trail could be made only by sacrificing "much of the present day highly touted equipment" for the long-practiced lore of the woods promoted by earlier generations of outdoorsmen. Yet Shaffer was more complicated than this straightforward philosophy. Modern gear, which for him meant military surplus, could also be appropriate if modified. Shaffer sent his tent home during the trip, lopped extra straps off his pack, and even cut his blanket down to the bare minimum size, yet he kept his aluminum-frame surplus pack. In the end, he did not sacrifice too much: Guidebooks of the 1940s recommended pack weights of between twenty and forty-five pounds. Shaffer's forty pounds put him at the upper end of that spectrum. Despite his older woodsman philosophy, Shaffer's practices on the Appalachian Trail made him the epitome of the modern outdoor consumer.[40]

Shaffer's audiences had increased buying power and wanted to use it the right way, and they devoured his advice. Shaffer spoke to audiences' anxieties about how to be modern consumers while still respecting an outdoor tradition that deemed consumption feminine, enfeebling, and at odds with nature. For Shaffer, and for the first generation of outdoorspeople after World War II, surplus and the Khaki Gang seemed to link the old lore and the new.

For a few years, army-navy stores were the prime source of gear and clothing for outdoorspeople like Shaffer and his admirers. A varied group that included aspiring Boulder, Colorado, climbers and columnists writing for the New York Times turned to surplus because the products were both available and cheap. But by 1950 few of these items were still available.[41]

Surplus's success was also its undoing. Hiker Jim Beebe remembered that in the early 1940s, canteens and tents were far too heavy to add to the ubiquitous Trapper Nelson packboards. No one carried a stove, either. Margaret Dyar's first hike in the mid-1930s did not include a backpack. Instead, she carried only a sack of food, a pail of lemonade, and a blanket that failed to keep her warm. The idea that the "authentic" outdoor experience began at the urban outdoor retailer was essentially an upper-class standard. After the war, once unthinkable luxuries or frivolous gadgets—lighter Coleman stoves, warmer sleeping bags, and drier mountain tents—became democratized as the new baseline for what was needed for the outdoors, for the masses as well as the wealthy urbanite.[42]

Before the war, for example, bedding for sleeping outdoors usually consisted of one or two wool blankets, "amply warm" for most climates, a guidebook reassured. Those who did want sleeping bags, and could afford them, could purchase them from L. L. Bean or Abercrombie & Fitch at high prices. The cost of down sleeping bags meant they were rare and suited to "princes and magnates" more than ordinary consumers.[43]

But thanks to the resale of government-issued military sleeping bags in surplus stores, by the early 1950s consumers welcomed sleeping bags as a standard item on their packing lists. Abercrombie & Fitch sold a 100 percent down sleeping bag at $36.50 (about $410 in 2022) that weighed five pounds. Camp & Trail Outfitters sold a down-filled bag weighing only four pounds for $42.50. However, the army surplus down sleeping bag, designed for ski-trooper use, knocked these commercially available bags off the mountain. Called a mummy bag because of its tapered foot box and because it was "shaped to fit the body," the bag was sewn with a new technique according to military specifications. Rather than baffles stitched all the way through, partial stitches kept the cold out. In surplus outlets the bag sold in two parts—the inner semi-mummy-shaped bag that weighed five pounds, and a six-pound rectangular outer bag. Single bags were $17.95 at Blackburn's 3rd Street Army Store in Los Angeles—half the cost or less of the non-surplus options. A hiking club guide to equipment praised surplus bags as "phenomenal" because of their "fine design." The surplus bag offered value beyond cost because it was warmer, just as light, and made with finer materials than many other commercially produced bags. Despite complaints of an oppressive smell (perhaps creosote) and feathers that "poked the sleeper," guidebooks extolled the mummy bag as "the nearest approach to the ideal bag."[44]

These cheap sleeping bags were a short-lived luxury. Like other surplus goods, they became scarce within a few years. Even as postwar guidebooks insisted on the necessity of army surplus for packing lists, the sources for the same were drying up. As early as 1950, an equipment guide warned that few bags that were "really surplus" were still available. Some companies could not keep up with consumer demand for army clothing and equipment. Within a few years of the surplus flood "the vast stock of superior genuine surplus items [was] a thing of the past." Manufacturers watched as mountain tents and sleeping bags flew off the shelves (although there was no apparent end to pup tents and wool blankets) and recognized that the WAA was bound to run out of goods to auction off.[45]

In response to overwhelming interest, manufacturers resorted to making their own clothing and equipment that imitated the style, colors, and materials of surplus. In essence, and quite remarkably, they made fake surplus. The intentional manufacture of imitation surplus, which was precisely defined as cast-off waste by the military, shows just how powerful military labeling had become as a sign of authenticity and a certain outdoor aesthetic and ideal.

The irony of imitation surplus was widespread enough that guidebooks noted it. One guide warned, "Terms such as 'Army Type' and 'Navy Style' appearing more frequently these days should cause immediate suspicion since they usually mark an item decidedly inferior to the one they pretend to copy." The faux-surplus problem was not entirely new—some companies had sold imitation surplus after World War I—but it grew in scale apace with the surplus market itself. The "military surplus" label itself became a kind of brand, a marker of both quality manufacturing and identity.[46]

In 1954, the Federal Trade Commission decided that one company was benefiting unfairly from an unearned association with military surplus. The government brought a case against All American Sportswear Company, a New York City manufacturer that sold jackets and parkas. In advertisements, the company regularly claimed that its heavy outerwear was made for the U.S. Armed Forces, according to military specifications. The FTC argued that All American Sportswear was deceiving the consuming public into thinking they were getting the real thing. Through replicating the color and markings of surplus clothing, as well as using phrases like "Specification No. 1872FS" and "Stock No. 754-28937" on its labels and tags, the company sold its products as imitation surplus. The advertisements did specify Army Air Forces *Type* or Army Air Forces *Style*, but, the FTC argued, this claim, along with the use of U.S. Air Force insignia, would and did fool consumers. American consumers deserved to know that what they were buying was not authentic—authentic military waste, that is. The FTC ordered the All American Sportswear Company to cease and desist marking or branding its clothing as military. If the American public was going to buy surplus junk, it needed to be *real* junk.[47]

The FTC's case echoed the earlier court case on the authenticity of buckskin as a material compared with Buck Skein. In 1954, the issue was also about authenticity and the genuine, but with a different focus. The buckskin case concerned a company that was trying to pass off wool and cotton blends as deerskin, effectively trying to replace a non-industrial product with an imitation that could pass for genuine on paper if not in actual use. Surplus was definitely not a brand, but in many ways it operated *like* a brand. Those who adopted it aligned themselves with the values, aesthetics, and consumer products of the outdoor identity. And the arrival of fake surplus demonstrated the democratization of the consumer-outdoor nexus. No longer was a relationship with outdoor products reserved for the patrons of Abercrombie & Fitch.

By 1960, the flood of surplus goods had long since slowed to a trickle, but the flood of customers "into the fields and forests and waters" was just beginning. When Ed Orkney decided to focus more heavily on outdoor products, G.I. Joe's move from surplus to camping goods was the ultimate test of the government-issue "brand" he had helped to develop. Worldwide Distributors, Orkney's buying group, helped make the transition away from surplus goods by enabling relatively small retail stores like G.I. Joe's to buy brand-name merchandise wholesale from vendors who otherwise would ignore smaller shops. Orkney doubled the store's size only a few years later, building an eclectic mix of non-surplus products that included not just hunting and fishing merchandise but also automotive parts.[48]

Surplus stores around the country made a similar transition. Store owners shifted to outdoor sports as stock dwindled. At Bill Jackson's near Tampa, Florida, outdoor sporting goods replaced army surplus completely. A similar thing happened at Champaign Surplus in Illinois: surplus roots gave way to a focus on outdoor products. When surplus military products, or even faux surplus, were no longer readily available, these goods still had a substantial impact on packing lists because manufacturers working in the recreation industry drew both capital and inspiration from the surplus market. The product offerings, and even consumers' notions of what was necessary for a camping trip, were profoundly shaped by surplus.[49]

Within a few years of the release of surplus goods at government auctions the outdoors was "Big Business," whereas in the 1930s and earlier it had been niche, specialized, and a bit of an oddity. Surplus stores were ubiquitous, with more than twenty thousand retailers or wholesalers around the country. In 1957, total sales for surplus dealers topped $500 million. Even with all their problems, pup tents and mummy bags had beckoned a new generation of outdoorspeople to the woods. In 1961, more than forty million Americans participated in some form of outdoor recreation, in a "mass migration to fresh air."[50]

＊

By the 1960s, G.I. Joe's in Portland had expanded from army tents to a fif-teen-thousand-square-foot building. The larger footprint allowed the com-pany to stock a broader inventory that included not just surplus but also automotive merchandise, tools, and sporting goods. G.I. Joe's became a first stop for Pacific Northwesterners, from joggers to fishermen, headed out-doors in droves. By 1973, the company had sales of $4 million a year. The store no longer reeked; the products were now name-brand merchandise carefully arranged in the spacious and well-lit interior. The place had "an airy outdoors feeling," right down to the paint colors. The atmosphere of the store, according to contemporary accounts, remained "primarily mascu-line," which referred both to the goods for sale and the fact that the writers saw the outdoors as a man's world that women were "invading." The Khaki Gang's exclusive hold on authentic outdoor identity was no more.[51]

The half-life of surplus continued, taking on new meanings neither sol-diers nor grubby Khaki Gang members could have predicted. By the 1970s, army surplus clothing became associated with counterculture and Vietnam War protests. As a journalist wrote in the late 1960s, the "surplus market shifted gears" from the workingman and outdoor recreationist to eighteen- to thirty-five-year-olds who sought "military garb [that] suddenly became stylish." Youth protesters were likely less concerned about or conversant in the vocabulary of "real" or "genuine" surplus—for them, the *aesthetic* of surplus gave it power, not the function. The field jackets that became an icon of 1970s counterculture were nearly the same as those soldiers had worn in 1943 and civilians had purchased in surplus stores in 1946. More re-cently, as a mainstay of fashion runways and the Gap, the army-inspired field jacket retains the same visual iconography. But at the Gap, the jacket isn't grubby, cheap, or rare.[52]

Analysts of surplus resale suggested in 1947 that the disposal of consumer goods did not have a big impact on the postwar economy. The scale of the products was too small—surplus goods represented only "one half of 1 per-cent of consumer expenditures." In the American imagination, however, surplus goods loomed large. Many war surplus stores that opened in 1946 became specialty outdoor stores that betrayed little, if any, vestige of their military past. Customers of Fontana in Madison, Wisconsin, or Bill Jackson's in Pinellas Park, Florida, likely do not recognize the legacy of military surplus on the design of their goods or the items on their packing lists.[53]

The profit from reselling surplus military equipment and clothing gave these business owners the means and motivation to develop better equipment. War research and development hinted at new technologies, like a partially coated fabric that "may realize the dream" of all outdoorspeople of a material that would let body moisture escape but keep rain out. The new scientific approach to product design only awaited "interpretation by progressive manufacturers to make the load of the outdoorsman lighter and more efficient." Military technology trickled down slowly. In many cases, it took more than a decade for the increasingly rare but innovative designs like down mummy bags to change how contemporary manufacturers operated.[54]

These companies had to deal anew with a recurrent and immanent paradox of the American outdoor industry: the reconciliation of consumerism with the governing perception of the outdoors as a "non-commercial" world and a "man's world"—indeed, a refuge from consumer culture and its emasculating associations.[55]

SIX

Lederhosen and Tyrolean Hats

Forging Community with Brands

Just as army surplus stores began to pop up nationwide, a different trend emerged: mountaineering and climbing shops flourished in cities that recreationists considered gateways to the mountains. Many of the new stores were family affairs, with women designing, sewing, packaging, and mailing the equipment and clothing. Because women participated as gearmakers, these companies were more attuned to selling to women and children, and expanded their product offerings as a result (although outdoor companies in general still conveyed the idea of a non-commercial man's world). These small shops shared an important feature with much larger industry players: they helped consumers cultivate a sense of belonging.

The rise of Holubar Mountaineering, a store in Boulder, Colorado, run by Alice Holubar and her husband, LeRoy, illustrates how some Americans turned to outdoor products as part of their identity. Alice Holubar, a gearmaking "genius" and climber, based her business on community and connection. These commercial transactions, in other words, were much more than that. Like similar business owners, the Holubars started by reselling war surplus. Eventually, they turned to European imports and the use of wartime technologies like nylon to develop and manufacture their own superior products.

Although the population of climbers and mountaineers was minuscule in comparison to car campers and fishermen, Holubar Mountaineering's cultural impact reached beyond a cadre of elite climbers. Holubar Mountaineering created an outdoor cognoscenti. Holubar customers saw themselves as the chosen few who had access to the best equipment as well as an insider community. Their identity as climbers was shaped not just by the mountains they climbed, or even the jackets they bought, but also by *where* they bought their jackets. People acquired ideas about community or wilderness politics based on their connection to the Holubars of the world. Holubar products were a shorthand for being yourself, a remarkable shift toward the rise of a world where brands created loyal followings of customers who proudly wore logo-emblazoned clothing.

The rise of Holubar Mountaineering tracked the larger national rise in outdoor industry brands as well as the trend of businesses using promotional materials to cultivate a sense of community among users. During World War II, outdoor companies such as Hirsch-Weis and Coleman had promised American consumers that victory meant access to modern consumer products in peacetime. When army surplus inventory dried up, companies like the Holubars' grew in that space, and with a similar appeal. Outdoor styles remained hybrids of recreational, military, and overseas influences. Like other communities who bonded over the consumption of Tupperware at home parties or responded to a ringing doorbell to make a purchase of Avon lipstick, white suburban Holubar aficionados connected over their shared enthusiasm for outdoor activities. For these consumers, buying particular brands of outdoor goods became a way of defining community, identity, and a distinct subculture.[1]

✳

The house at 1215 Grandview Avenue in Boulder, Colorado, a few blocks from Boulder High School, was conspicuously busy in the early 1950s. LeRoy Holubar, known as Roy, left for work as a university math instructor every weekday morning. Alice Holubar's schedule was less predictable. A housewife and occasional German teacher and tutor, Holubar also managed the couple's growing mountaineering equipment and clothing business from the family basement, where every step of the process, from gear production to packing, took place. As Roy taught classes, Alice raised their daughter Linda and fed the cadre of young men who moved into and out of the basement while working for the company.

At the end of World War II, Roy resold surplus army equipment. Alice had ideas and a contempt for badly made things. She didn't think much of the surplus items that her husband sold and knew she "could make things better than anyone else had ever done." Over the course of her career, Holubar imported and sold mountaineering equipment and clothing from northern and central Europe and developed and manufactured new designs for sleeping bags and jackets. She built an international network of gear-makers and invited customers into a community space she cultivated one meal and conversation at a time. From 1947 to 1968, Alice Holubar helped to reshape the American market for custom-made, high-end equipment. Her timing could not have been better.[2]

Holubar Mountaineering customers and Alice's husband considered her a creative genius. She would wake up from a dream about patterns and sewing and realize she knew how to make the parka or sleeping bag design that had eluded her. Holubar could fix a customer's Primus stove, take an order over the phone, and measure and sew a rush-order parka even as she worked as a mother, cook, tutor, and neighbor.[3]

The Holubar home did not *look* like an industry-defining outdoor goods design center. And at first glance, the Holubars seemed to adhere to the era's gender norms: Roy's $150 monthly salary supported his family, while Alice managed their daughter and house. After earning a master's degree in German, Alice taught at Boulder High School and at the university, at times also tutoring Ph.D. candidates in German. "With the male partner making the decisions," one newspaper article explained, "the female member of the Holubar household [was] able to give her time to cutting and sewing." But the newspaper article got it wrong: most accounts of the couple's years building Holubar Mountaineering feature Alice as "the real spark plug" of the business. Moreover, her role in the business made space for women and children in the "man's world" of the outdoors.[4]

Alice Freudenberg was born in Suchteln, Germany, in 1911. Her father had a "fondness for the West" that shaped young Alice. After he died during World War I, Alice's mother moved her and three brothers to the United States. They settled on a ranch in "a large meadow across from high red cliffs" in Left Hand Canyon, a fair distance from Boulder, Colorado. She learned English quickly but still spoke "funny," according to some contemporaries. One friend later wondered if the years isolated with her family in Left Hand Canyon shaped her "remarkable verve and warmth for people."[5]

Alice met Roy, a Boulder native, in high school. Roy had "always liked the mountains," but it was Alice who talked him into going on his first Colorado Mountain Club trip. She was class salutatorian of their high school, while Roy was valedictorian, and both graduated a few years later from the University of Colorado. After marrying in 1937 they spent their honeymoon "on the trail." It would be more than two decades before they could take that much time just for themselves again.[6]

During World War II, Roy continued to teach at the university while the men who would later become his colleagues and competitors in the outdoor industry joined the ski troops. The ranks of the Colorado Mountain Club dwindled during those years, but together, the Holubars kept the club going. Even with the challenge of limited gasoline ration stamps and few experienced volunteers to lead the groups, Alice Holubar stood determined to serve Boulder by leading the organization for the city.[7]

Mobilization for World War II transformed Colorado. It changed Denver and the surrounding areas, creating jobs and linking residents' fate to government contracts. The 10th Mountain Division training facility at Camp Hale brought world-renowned skiers and climbers to the area. The postwar era brought new residents, wealth, and developments. Roy Holubar, who had grown up in Boulder, recalled that in the early years of his company thirty thousand new homes dotted the prairie on the hills near Boulder. The growth made sense to him, in a way, because the nearby mountains were as inviting as ever.

Boulder residents, including a growing university population, looked to the mountains as a place of freedom, as did Americans across the country. They saw travel as a way to affirm their individuality, status, and leisure time. For many, a national park road trip fulfilled a desire for authentic experiences that eluded them in everyday life. For some in the postwar era, the new enemy of authenticity was conformity—in particular, suburban life. Equipped with more leisure time and discretionary income, Americans could be most themselves, and their authentic selves, on the open road, based on where and how they traveled.[8]

Airlines and automobile clubs marketed Colorado's high country as a wonderland and iconic escape. "Vacationland," tourist boosters called it, hoping to lure both visitors and residents. New ski resorts at Aspen and Snowmass contributed to this draw, as did the Rocky Mountain National Park. Climbing and mountaineering were part of this larger trend.[9]

After the war the Holubars supported the arrival of Gerry Cunningham, who, like them, was part of the first wave of outdoor entrepreneurs to improve on army surplus. Cunningham had joined the 10th Mountain Division just out of high school. He had designed a teardrop-shaped backpack during high school to take on outdoor activities, and was interested in the ski troopers because of his love for the outdoors and especially outdoor equipment. Cunningham found the army brutal. The innovative equipment he had expected as a ski trooper never materialized. Instead, he spent many cold nights at Camp Hale, near Leadville, Colorado, making line drawings of tents and backpacks that would outperform his army equipment. Cunningham's miserable wartime experience at Camp Hale convinced him that the best place to start a business would be somewhere in the West, with easy access to mountains. Cunningham wanted to be the "L. L. Bean of the West." He likely couldn't afford the company's products, but he knew how Bean wrote catalog copy and liked its goods for hunting and skiing.[10]

In 1946, as Gerry and his wife, Ann, were driving west toward California, they stopped near Ward, Colorado, for lunch. The "pretty little meadow" across the way, 120 acres, was for sale. They spent their $600 savings to buy the place because "they knew they wanted to live somewhere out in the wilderness." After he settled in, Cunningham sought out Roy and Alice Holubar, whom he heard "were both very active in the Colorado Mountain Club." Roy later remembered that the Cunninghams lived in an "Indian tepee" that summer as Gerry built the family home. On the weekends, the Holubars helped the Cunninghams build. Thus the Holubars' community involvement paved the way for two outdoor companies.[11]

Cunningham had come to Colorado determined to improve on the army's terrible equipment and to become the foremost outfitter of the intermountain West. It was a leap to assume there would be sufficient mountaineers for such a business. Roy recalled that there were perhaps only fifteen thousand mountain climbers nationwide in 1946, by his count. Going into the outdoor equipment business full time "looked awful risky and speculative." Mountain tourism might have been taking off in Colorado, but it was more leisure drives to national parks than actual climbs up mountains. So Roy was more temperate in his ambitions. He kept his "bread and butter" teaching job while Alice and Gerry embarked down the speculative entrepreneurial path, to make new and improved equipment for their climbing peers.[12]

Cunningham used his military connections to send potential customers a catalog of mountaineering equipment and, later, clothing. His former sergeant Art Draper asked Cunningham to write a column for the National Ski Patrol newsletter. In return, Cunningham asked for the Ski Patrol's mailing list. In that way, Cunningham accessed a network of elite athletes most likely to purchase high-end camping and hiking gear. Cunningham's mailing list grew to include climbing clubs around the country, including the Mazamas of Oregon, the American Alpine Club of Colorado, and the Iowa Mountaineers. From a small mailing list in 1946, Cunningham's readership expanded to thousands who might have otherwise had access only to army surplus equipment. Encouraged by Cunningham, who said "there's room for both of us" in this industry, Roy Holubar procured a sales license in 1947. Gerry Cunningham supplied the names for the Holubars' first mailing list.[13]

Together, Cunningham and the Holubars helped make Boulder, Colorado, one of the hubs of innovation for outdoor equipment in the postwar era, along with Los Angeles and Seattle. These three cities shared some common characteristics. They were all growing western cities that had benefited from the wartime economy and continued to benefit from postwar federal investment in the aerospace industry. The cities were all close to military bases that resold surplus, which meant veterans and their business partners could establish surplus resale shops nearby, so they had experience in retail. They all had strong outdoor club histories dating back decades, and were home to mountaineers and climbers.

Together, a set of new companies—all connected through personal networks—tapped the market of new outdoor consumers. They shaped a postwar outdoor identity, quite distinct from the East Coast, hunting and fishing and woodcraft identity of Abercrombie & Fitch and L. L. Bean. These new companies served a narrow swath of outdoorspeople—climbing and mountaineering and backpacking were nowhere near as popular as fishing, hunting, and camping. But they were important nonetheless because they changed the culture of the outdoors, creating a distinct outdoor subcultural community. The companies imported modern European products rather than selling the American products of the woodcraft aesthetic. Furthermore, Holubar Mountaineering conveyed certain novel visions of outdoor manhood to a broad range of customers, even those who didn't buy their products. And Holubar Mountaineering and its competitors were the precursor to some of the most well-known brands of the 1970s and 1980s, such as Patagonia, the North Face, and JanSport.

✳

The Holubars and Cunningham did not have much in the way of new American products to sell. Climbers and mountaineers wanted specialized products not manufactured in the United States: German boots, Swiss pants, Austrian hats, French packs, and Norwegian long underwear. The Holubars resold surplus and later made their own equipment designs, but the American outdoor industry of the early postwar period was at first primarily an import business. Alice and Roy Holubar sold the best gear and clothing, and that meant northern and central European products.

In their first years of business, the Holubars owed their success not just to Gerry Cunningham and their Colorado Mountain Club connections but also to Alice's family. Alice's distant cousin, Karl Blodig, was a famous Austrian mountaineer. He helped connect Alice with company representatives, and she began importing goods in 1947. As a native German speaker, she could communicate easily with Swiss, Austrian, and German companies. Business with firms across the Atlantic was rarely smooth. Business slowed due to missed letters, slow and heavily taxed imports, and the challenges of maintaining distributor exclusivity deals against American competitors. But the effort yielded a distinctive product line and the allure of the European mountain climbing tradition.

As in America, mountain climbing Europeans imagined the Alpine landscape as a place of Romantic escape from modern life. As the growing population of Alpine skiers in these years embraced speed, mastery, and, above all, modernity, Alpinists—the summer tourists who hiked and climbed—retained aspects of the older tradition. They sought an "aesthetic, spiritual practice." The culture of the outdoors in the Alps, particularly Austria, Bavaria, and Switzerland, had surprising effects on American outdoor culture.[14]

European goods were popular in the United States because American audiences often encountered outdoor sports through a European lens. Armchair mountaineers read about the exploits of European climbers and learned of the Alps as the site of adventure, and authentic experience. The historian Maurice Isserman recounts that James Ramsey Ullman's mountaineering book, *The White Tower*, was popular with readers "who had never climbed a mountain" or visited Switzerland. Though equipment and clothing were never the focus of popular accounts like Ullman's, writers invariably included gear descriptions as an introduction to the journey. Together, European climbing publications and the presence of European athletes in the United States suggested that northern and central Europe were the world's hub for high-end equipment manufacturing.[15]

In this context, the Holubars sent out their first "catalog"—a simple list of prices and little more—in 1947. The product offerings fit on ten tiny pages no larger than business cards, held together with a couple of staples. They announced their expertise on the first page, with little of the slick bravado characteristic of companies like Abercrombie & Fitch: "We like mountaineering; do it ourselves." At that time, equipment included two-man mountain tents for $12 ($160 in 2022 dollars) or used versions for $6.50 to $9.00. By some accounts, European imports amounted to 70 percent of goods in the early years of their business. Other products included Norwegian fishnet underwear, Austrian boots, French backpacks, and German pants. As revealed in their advertisements for foreign products, the Holubars taught American customers that the mountaineering experts often hailed from the longer tradition of equipment production in the Alps.[16]

Gear catalogs show that the Rocky Mountain West operated as the Alps of the United States. The most striking products were lederhosen and felt hats. Lederhosen—leather shorts with leather straps, often with detailed embroidery—are known in America for their association with Bavaria and Austria and the Oktoberfest holiday. From the late 1940s through the early 1970s, lederhosen, complemented by the similarly stereotypical Austrian hats, were popular hiking and climbing attire sold by the Holubars and other outdoor stores in the United States, such as Gerry Mountain Sports and the Recreational Equipment Co-op, inviting American hikers to dress like the "gay peasants" of Austria.[7]

Like any form of dress, this peasant-work style of the nineteenth century has a social and political history that influenced its two decades of popularity in the United States. In the early twentieth century, urban Germans donned lederhosen as a self-conscious statement of connection to their imagined rural working past. Alpinists throughout World War II rarely donned such attire, however, as it was more ceremonial dress than activewear. The sweaters and nailed boots that defined the climber's uniform were sourced from outdoor retailers such as Sporthaus Schuster in Munich, which dated back to 1913. After World War II, lederhosen resurged in Europe, which led directly to the arrival of lederhosen in the United States. This resurgence was an anti-modernist statement: Lederhosen could represent a benign, "folk" version of German history that more recent horrific events had eclipsed.

In the United States lederhosen did not carry the same meaning. For Americans these items connoted European sophistication, a kind of quintessential whiteness that linked the Rocky Mountains to the Alps. The Alps were a Romantic icon and travel destination for Americans. They were also a symbol of expertise, both in mountain climbing and manufacturing—and they were connected to the U.S. West through American retailers' personal networks. By 1962, according to *Family Camping* magazine, Holubar Mountaineering was known for its lederhosen and Tyrolean hats.

The Holubars sold lederhosen as a "traditional Bavarian style" and emphasized the "workmanship" that went into the goods. Gerry Mountain Sports advertised its imported lederhosen as "genuine," with "fancy native trim," and promised that men who donned the matching hats would pull off the "rakish Austrian look." The Recreational Equipment Co-op co-founder Mary Anderson, also a fluent German speaker, arranged to import lederhosen and hats from Austria and Germany as well. Along with "traditional alpine dress," the Co-op catalog sold knee-high socks with an edelweiss design and fourteen different feathered hat ornaments for the Austrian and Swiss mountain hats.[18]

Lederhosen and kindred styles from the Alps, such as Austrian hats and edelweiss pins, grew in popularity in the United States because of an influence far off the trail. The hit Broadway musical *The Sound of Music* opened on Broadway in 1959 and remained there for four years. The play, set in Salzburg, Austria, in 1938, portrayed the country romantically, complete with traditional dress such as lederhosen and dirndls. The film version of *The Sound of Music* was released in 1965, and though some critics dismissed the story as saccharine, the movie won the Oscar for Best Picture. The movie garnered international publicity, much to the dismay of German and Austrian audiences, and the von Trapp family wardrobe is one of the strongest American associations with lederhosen, even decades later. In the 1960s, Holubar Mountaineering, Gerry Mountain Sports, REI, and other companies that already sold lederhosen, feathered caps, and edelweiss pins increased their offerings, likely as a response to this national media attention on Alpine styles.[19]

Consumers also connected emotionally with the Alps through their clothing and equipment. For example, longtime Adirondack Mountain Club member Katie Germond had a Tyrolean-style hat made of green wool felt with a green twisted cord hatband and a fur decoration. Germond did not have a direct connection to Germany or Austria—she was born in Newton, North Carolina, and worked at the New York Telephone Company for twenty-five years. She and her husband, Hank, began joining outings to the Adirondack Mountains in 1948 and became so committed to mountaineering that by 1952 they were spending weekends and vacations alike mountain hiking. Both served in leadership positions for outdoor clubs.[20]

Germond sewed patches on her felt hat that commemorated club trips to the Canadian Rockies in the late 1950s and early 1960s, enabling her to adopt an outdoor identity that brought the romance of the Alps to the United States. Likewise, her red nylon parka from White Stag had cloth patches commemorating the hiking trips she and her husband took in Switzerland. Together they also hiked in the Canadian Rockies, Norway,

For nearly two decades, traditional Alpine dress was a mainstay in American outdoor company catalogs. Holubar Mountaineering and Gerry Mountain Sports sold imported lederhosen, *ledertrager*, and Seppl hats to Americans who looked to European climbing traditions as a source of authenticity. (Gerry catalog, 1966, Boulder Public Library; by permission of the Gerry Cunningham estate)

Austria, Scotland, Wales, England, Wyoming, and Iceland. Germond's and her husband's hiking clothes signaled the transition from World War II military surplus to the new high-tech equipment that was beginning to emerge. The attire they purchased was not a mere symbol of escape to nature, given all these travels. Instead, it was part of a trend, brought to the United States by just a few retailers, that soon became a national phenomenon. Germond's hat, and the others like it nationwide, represented a shared sensibility among climbers who welcomed the emotional connection between the Alps and American mountaineering.[21]

On business trips to Europe, the Holubars forged connections and learned the stories behind companies that allowed them to sell Austrian, Swiss, or Norwegian expertise along with merchandise in their catalogs. By 1952, the Holubar Mountaineering equipment catalogs had expanded in size and product offerings, and reflected Roy and Alice's European business contacts.

Pants - Knickers - Lederhosen

[A] Austrian Loden Knickers. Made from 100% wool with a double seat. There are five pockets, two on the side, two hip pockets, all zipper closing, and one large pocket on the right leg flap, closing with a button. Austrian Loden-cloth is known for its long wear and toughness. Grey color. Men's sizes from 26-40 waist. Ladies' sizes: 24-30 waist.

F010A3 .... 30.95

English Tweed Knickers. Made from all wool grey herringbone tweed with a double seat and zipper closing side and hip pockets. Men's even sizes 28-40. Ladies' sizes 24-28.

F042A4 .... 17.95

English Corduroy Knickers. Made from heavy brown English corduroy, with a double seat and zipper closing side and hip pockets, with wide belt tunnels. Men's and Ladies' sizes.

F042A5 .... 17.50

English Gabardine Knickers. Similar in style to the other English knickers, but made from 17 oz. grey wool gabardine cloth. With a single seat, zipper closing side and hip pockets, they are ideal for skiing. Men's and Ladies' sizes.

F042A6 .... 21.95

English Tweed Climbing Pants. Made from all wool grey herringbone tweed, these fine pants have two zipper closing side pockets, one zipper closing hip pocket, and an 8"x10" pocket on the right leg. The seat is double and there are no cuffs on the legs. Belt tunnels are used instead of loops. The excellent British fabric will stand much wear. Waist, even sizes: 28-38; lengths, 31, 33, 35.

F042A1 .... 17.95

[B] English Gabardine Climbing Pants. These pants are identical to the tweed trousers above, except for the 17 oz. wool gabardine material used. Men's sizes even: 28"-38"; lengths, 31", 33", 35". Grey color.

F042A2 .... 23.95

[C] Bavarian Shorts. An absolute must for warm summer hikes, these smart looking shorts are made from 9 oz. Klondike cloth, 50% cotton, 50% Fortrel, and feature tunnel loops for the belt, zipper fly and 6 generous pockets, two of which go all the way to the knees. Colors: Beige or Forest Green in Men's and Ladies' sizes.

F612A8 .... 6.95

Surplus All-Wool Pants. Near new condition, or in good used with no repairs, O.D. or A.F. blue wool serge, available in most lengths and waists.

F711A11 .... 6.95

Army Mountain Pants. New condition surplus pants of lightweight pima nylon with a cargo pocket on each leg, one rear pocket, two side slits with snaps. The long crotch can be worn over other pants. Two sizes only: ML, waist adjustable between 31 and 37 with length about 29"; SL, waist adjusts between 27 and 32, length about 29".

F711A12 .... 4.95

[D] Lederhosen. These popular leather shorts are made of supple, grey leather with decorative green piping. Buttons are included that attach to ledertrager (leather suspenders).

[D] Ledertrager. Ledertrager are the colorful leather suspenders worn with the lederhosen described above. They are available in grey or green leather with an artificial horn ornament across the front. Also the grey leather comes with a pressed horn ornament and the green is available with an embroidered front. **Mail Order,** specify color and type of ornament.

[D]

LEDERHOSEN				LEDERTRAGER		
Order	Style	Age	Waist	Price	Order	Length	Price
FO15B1	Boys'	2-8	23"-26"	8.85	Grey: Pressed or Horn Ornament		
FO15B2	Boys'	10-14	26½"-28"	11.85	FO15B9	20", 24", 27½" - 33½"	1.95
FO15B3	Men's		29"-33"	14.85	FO15B10	35½" - 43½"	2.50
FO15B4	Men's		34½"-45"	17.85	Green: Embroidered or horn ornament		
FO15B5	Girls'	2-6	19"-21"	7.85	FO15B11	20", 24", 27½" - 33½"	2.25
FO15B6	Girls'	8-14	22"-24"	10.85	FO15B12	35½" - 43½"	2.75
FO15B7	Ladies'		25"-28"	14.85			

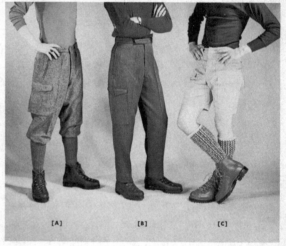

[A]   [B]   [C]

INDEX ON PAGE NINE — 5

In this REI catalog from 1968, nearly every knicker and pant on sale was imported from Europe. The main exceptions were the military surplus products. (REI Catalog, 1968, University of Washington Libraries, Special Collections, Lloyd Anderson Papers, Accession 2648-001, UW41656)

The carefully designed and illustrated catalogs were many times the size of the first booklet. There were still surplus products for sale, such as nylon rope and U.S. Army plywood packboards, but the catalogs also offered Molitor boots, bearing the name of Swiss guide and skier Karl Molitor and utilizing the new Bramani sole. The boots, for which demand far exceeded the output of its "Swiss craftsmen," sold for $45.50 (or $508 in 2022). The Holubars' European trips included visits to Sporthaus Schuster in Munich, Blacks and Nixon in London, Kronhofer in Innsbruck, and more stops in Vienna, Zurich, Bern, and elsewhere. Though Alice and Roy were able to spend a few days hiking or mountaineering and visiting relatives, the bulk of the trip was dedicated to finding "Good Alpine hats" and cord knickers to import.[22]

Consequentially, the European influence and the American response to it inaugurated a new subculture of American sporting style, one very distinct from that of the woodcraft adventurers of the eastern United States. This set the stage for the continuing popularity and brand cachet of northern European outdoor products, albeit specifically among backpackers and mountaineers—the Alpine sensibility did not extend to hunters, fishers, or RV campers. For many Americans, European goods were not just of high quality but also a "power symbol." The Alpine trend of these decades was part of a larger trend in which American consumers associated certain brands and products with the cachet to certify belonging in a subculture. Despite changes in style and function, the fact remained that the first stop on the way to nature was the gear store, either in person or via the catalog.[23]

✳

Earlier in the twentieth century, many outdoorspeople's sense of belonging was shaped by their membership in outdoor clubs. Katie Germond, for instance, saw the Adirondack Mountain Club as her main form of community engagement. In the early postwar period, the Holubars began to reinvent the American outdoor identity: in addition to region, sport, and club, outdoorspeople began defining themselves by their relationship to gearmakers. Being a mountaineer became intimately linked to going shopping in the Holubar family basement. Having the right ornament for a green Seppl hat was a way to fit in with the small set of climbing and mountaineering enthusiasts catered to by the Holubars and Gerry Cunningham.

The catalog in 1952 explained how the Holubars talked with "out-door enthusiasts from all over" to shape their product list. They also saw gear as serving a higher, non-commercial purpose: it was an entry point for "mountain recreation as a constructive force in our time." The catalog made a case for a special kind of commercial interaction, one that promised an intimate connection with the gearmakers. "Come see us when you are in town!" the catalog invited — and they meant it, because the store was still located in the Holubar family basement. The catalogs, retail experience, and products themselves worked together to create a feeling among customers that they were the chosen few.[24]

In Boulder, customers knocked on the door at the Holubars' Grandview Avenue home at all hours to get their hands on the latest parka or sleeping bag sewn by Alice Holubar — a dynamic evocative of Native women's meticulous preparation of buckskin in their domestic spaces in the 1800s. Women were at the center of these communities. As gearmakers, they created new designs and saw them through; as everyday salespeople, they knew customers personally. As mail sorters and package shippers, they ensured the business ran smoothly. Part of their appeal as company owners was that the gear they sold was also a ticket to their expertise. The connections consumers built with companies like Holubar Mountaineering suggest a transformation, rather than a decline, in the outdoor community. The success of these companies initially depended on owners' outdoor club connections and participation, and the businesses themselves slowly became hubs of knowledge-sharing. Alice and Roy's house became a meeting place that replaced the club as the primary zone of interaction. At their home "climbers met to exchange information about climbs and to learn about improvements in equipment." Before identifying with Holubar Mountaineering, before brand logos adorned jackets and sleeping bags, customers identified with Alice Holubar herself.[25]

Women's roles as gearmakers were crucial to cultivating a feeling of belonging, just as they had been with Indigenous women in the buckskin era. Mary Anderson, co-founder of the Seattle-based Recreational Equipment Co-op, for example, had been sewing the tents, parkas, and sleeping bags that the store sold for years. Like Holubar, Anderson was the hub of a community of climbers and mountaineers that grew up around the store. The Co-op began when Lloyd and Mary Anderson imported Austrian ice axes for themselves and their friends in 1938. They ran the business as a shop in their basement for years, and Anderson remained involved in sewing equipment. Co-op member and customer Jean Tokareff remembered meeting her at a Girl Scout leadership session and being impressed that Anderson sewed tents and parkas. Jean met her husband Tom on an outing suggested by Anderson, and built a friendship during climbs together in the early 1950s.[26]

Outdoor clubs had long recognized the power of a club pin or patch to create a sense of belonging, community, and connection between members. The pin might spark a conversation at a high mountain hut. The "46er" patch, like the one the climber Grace Hudowalski wore on her blue shorts, connected mountaineering community members who shared the goal of climbing the 4,600-foot mountains. Yet the pride that developed for Co-op gear that customer Mary Lowry described was different, almost snobbish. Having Co-op equipment was the in thing, Lowry remembered, adding that she almost pitied those who didn't know that. Lowry took pleasure in belonging—in having the mountain tent, parka, and Mount Rainier jacket made by Mary Anderson. Co-op customers took pride in their association with a company whose values they respected and in a shared ethic to the mountains espoused by the Co-op and gearmaker Mary Anderson, in particular. Likewise, Co-op customer Elvin Johnson recalled the Co-op's importance as a community for other veterans of the 10th Mountain Division in the early postwar years. It wasn't the gear that was important to Johnson, but rather that the Co-op customers became long-term friends.[27]

Not all customers accepted Alice Holubar or Mary Anderson as the center of their outdoor communities. Young men often looked for more macho role models. For the climber Charles Williams, shopkeepers served that role. Entering the Co-op after it moved from Anderson's basement to a makeshift store, Williams felt that the young men who worked the counters at the Co-op accepted him into an insider group. The Co-op's makeshift store was in a closet at the back of an accountant's office in downtown Seattle. It was a cramped space, and by most descriptions the accountant who rented it and facilitated purchases for a percentage of sales was grumpy. Nonetheless, Williams spoke of the Co-op glowingly. Although he couldn't afford its equipment as a teenager, the Co-op was his dream space to browse. It was a sanctuary that gave him shivers thinking about the shelves to the ceilings crammed with treasures he could not afford. Williams cited mountaineering guide Lou Whittaker (and brother of Co-op manager Jim Whittaker) as a manly role model, specifically recalling how Whittaker rejected fashion and chastised young climbers by calling them pansies. This strain of bravado and Holubar's and Anderson's rise as outdoor experts were contemporaneous: the family wilderness welcomed women and children, but remained a proving ground for manhood.[28]

Young men flowed in and out of the Grandview house, blurring the lines between customer and friend. Karl Gustafson, for instance, worked in the Holubar basement in his teens "in exchange for a few pitons or even an ice axe." Dave Robertson, who knew the Holubars from the Colorado Mountain Club climbing school, both lived and worked in that basement in the summer of 1954. It was a time, he recounted, when "the distinction between employee and family was pretty indistinct." Robertson remembered fondly working in the basement while Holubar cooked upstairs. He met his future wife, Janet, on a Colorado Mountain Club climbing trip, where the Holubars were also both active. As a wedding gift, Alice sewed Jan and Dave a double down sleeping bag. Dale Johnson went to college in Boulder in 1949, when "the major outlet for climbing equipment was LeRoy and Alice Holubar's basement." He remembered one summer when they imported "the first down jacket anybody had ever seen." It was "so soft and so sensuous," he recalled, that he and his rock-climbing friends would go down to the basement just to stroke the gossamer nylon fabric. These customers/employees/friends were all young men whom the Holubars might have encountered first in local climbing clubs or at the university. Alice and Roy encouraged an intimate familiarity, giving them warm meals, a bed if needed, part-time work, and access to the latest outdoor equipment. These men came to see their gear as an intimate extension of the gearmaker's expertise.[29]

Customers in Boulder and beyond felt connected to Holubar, writing her letters about their experience with gear, offering thanks or recommendations for improvements, or requesting custom gear. In one of the many letters Holubar received, Lee Tidball wrote from Madison, Wisconsin, in 1958 to make recommendations about where Alice Holubar should advertise her famous sleeping bags. Had she considered the *New Yorker*?, Tidball wanted to know. A young Robert Redford was inspired to attend the University of Colorado in the mid-1950s in part because of the catalogs he saw that advertised the Holubars' near-mythical basement, overflowing with mountaineering equipment. Gil Roberts, who went on to join the Everest Expedition of 1963, heard that Holubar had made a custom parka for his friend and wanted one, too.[30]

The community events extended beyond commercial interactions. The Holubars helped organize the local Colorado Mountain Club and Rocky Mountain Rescue, and they organized and hosted speakers who came through Boulder. In 1950, Bradford Washburn, a former member of the Harvard Five, came to Boulder to talk about his experience climbing Mount McKinley twice (the first time while testing equipment and clothing for the Quartermaster Corps during World War II). Washburn had published photographs from "Operation White Tower" in the *American Alpine Journal*, the prominent climbing journal connected with the American Alpine Club. Alice and Roy Holubar hosted the reception for Washburn after his lecture, complete with Alice's homemade chocolate cake. Roy served more than once as chair of the Boulder Group of the Colorado Mountain Club and maintained leadership positions for almost twenty years. Roy and Alice also invested in these kinds of community events as business owners. They supplied both the Boulder Group and the Rocky Mountain Rescue with equipment.[31]

While business progressed in 1955, Alice Holubar was as busy as she had ever been. She hustled to tutor German, bake pies, welcome neighbors, all the while sewing custom jackets and sleeping bags and tents, and writing to business contacts in England and Germany to manage imports. In October of that year, Holubar wrote to an outdoor industry colleague that she found little time to dedicate to climbing or other enjoyable activities given how much her business had grown. Occasionally Holubar made her work skills into recreation, such as when she sewed an orange ripstop nylon gown for a night at the symphony. Generally, it would be a good many years before Holubar had time to take a breath. Roy later recalled that while he helped with "design and production . . . the business was mostly Alice."[32]

Holubar presented herself as personable and a knowledgeable mountaineer as well as seamstress. The photo most often used by the couple in the catalogs and advertisements in local papers depicts them after fifteen years in the "family business" and illustrates how they tied their public personas to the brand. They both sit facing the camera, which shows them from the waist up, bodies angled toward each other. Roy is nearly bald and covers his head with a felt Austrian cap with a feather in the brim of the same kind the catalog sold. He has a thick rope slung over his shoulder, denoting his membership in various climbing organizations. Alice has her hair pulled back and she is smiling broadly. She wears a down jacket with a diagonal quilted pattern that she likely sewed herself. They were, according to a short, whimsical poem they penned for the fifteenth annual catalog, still a "mountain-loving couple / Who want their friends and customers to keep their muscles supple." To help the community of outdoorspeople "camp dryly [and] walk spryly," the Holubars maintained their informal setup: "our Avenue's not Madison . . . it's only Grandview!" They did not have the fancy advertising know-how of the famed Manhattan street, the Holubars acknowledged, but they were more connected to their customers because of it. Like buckskin maker and buckskin purchaser in the late nineteenth century, Holubar and her customers shared an intimate bond; in both instances, customers called in at quirky domestic spaces and purchased status goods of quality labored over by women in obscure corners of the home. By playing up their distance from Madison Avenue, the Holubars also rejected big-city mass culture while highlighting their own quasi-counterculture aesthetic. The outdoor identity, they seemed to suggest, was anti-commercial, even as it also centered around buying.[33]

Buying meant belonging in stores like the Co-op and the Holubars'. Of course, it was possible to take belonging "too seriously," to say that "if you don't carry the So-and-so Little Gem, you really aren't a properly equipped member of the band." There were capital-H "Hikers," a guidebook published in 1948 explained, who believed in the One Right Way: "one pack design . . . only one correct boot." The good stuff was "obtainable at some obscure little store in northern Maine, or perhaps Norway." This zeal was not just an East Coast problem: there were near-religious adherents to the Co-op and Holubar brands as well. These "snobs of the woods" spoke "in a sort of lofty and intimate manner of L. L. Bean." The limited availability of Kronhofer boots, and their high prices, or the Holubar custom-sewn jackets, were all part of the brand's status. The quality of the boots mattered, but so too the feeling and mystique associated with acquiring them.[34]

As this elitist identity was developing, and as the Holubars built a community around commercial interactions, the company participated in an event that built their reputation at home and abroad as a leading outdoor outfitter.

✳

In April 1959, "a bright red 2 ½-pound Holubar two-man tent and [a] sky blue 3-pound down sleeping bag" left Boulder for Moscow, one U.S. entry among seven hundred on an international stage that both the Soviet Union and the United States saw as an opportunity to compare "their nation's scientific and technological performance." The American exhibit in the 1959 American National Exhibition in Moscow centered on consumer goods, rather than military, space, or nuclear technologies. Exhibition organizers assigned Holubar Mountaineering gear to the "Skiing" section of the first floor of the exhibition hall. Flanked by bikes, bowling equipment, and chess sets, the ski and mountain climbing equipment exhibit and its kindred leisure products "announced that consumerism was no longer a side show of production and military technologies." Of course, few knew better than former resellers of army surplus the intimacy between wartime military and postwar consumer products. As both the Holubars and the American press saw it, the goods epitomized U.S. family leisure practices, craftsmanship, and the possibilities of small family business success under the American dream. A Boulder newspaper reported, "each article at the exhibit interprets [the] American way of life."[35]

The Holubars chose to display their in-house designs rather than their imports in Moscow. One of those was the Royalight sleeping bag, named for Roy and Alice and its light weight. Made with French nylon balloon cloth, the Royalight sleeping bag featured baffles in a mummy shape that fluffed up to a generous three inches, and kept users warm to negative five degrees

Fahrenheit although it weighed only three pounds. The semicustom bags came at a cost: $88, or nearly $900 in 2022. Holubar Mountaineering sold few American-made products in comparison to European imports, so it was important for them to show that their company could compete with better-known Austrian boots or Norwegian rucksacks. A Holubar sleeping bag on display in Moscow could attest powerfully to the quality of their handcrafted merchandise and boost their international reputation.

In a letter of "warm western greetings" posted as part of the exhibit, the Holubars wrote that they hoped the blue sleeping bag and red tent would "provide a small insight into the relatively new sport of back-packing and mountaineering in the United States." For the Holubars, the defining feature of wilderness was roadlessness—"hiking into areas where no car can go." Significantly, the Holubars' definition reflects the retailers' engagement with national conversations about conservation.

Their beloved Colorado Mountain Club, which had maintained a recreational focus for most of its history, began participating in wilderness activism in 1958, when Congress began debating a wilderness bill. The Holubars would have witnessed the debates around the proposed dam in Dinosaur National Monument in northern Colorado. They would have seen Wilderness Society efforts to advocate for protecting wild lands already owned by the federal government, given how much acreage there was in their home state. The bill eventually established a national network of federally designated areas through the Wilderness Act of 1964. A key aspect of the act's definition of wilderness was its "roadlessness," namely, that nationally protected landscapes should preserve a backcountry where no cars or other mechanized vehicles would go. The Holubars, conversant in these discussions, mentioned roadlessness in their exhibit letter. The club's support for the wilderness bill is one example of a growing conviction that outdoor consumers could and should participate in environmental activism. (It would be another decade before companies themselves articulated an environmental politic.) The Holubars' outdoors as presented in Moscow was also a family wilderness—presumably to contrast it with the crumbling communist family structure. They mentioned that when they "walk into areas where there are no roads," they "go as a family."[36]

The Holubars' letter also suggested an implicit critique of the U.S. culture of mass consumption. The exhibition is best remembered in the United States for the "kitchen debate" that transpired between Vice President Richard Nixon and Soviet Premier Nikita Khrushchev. The historian Elaine Tyler May explains that Nixon's defense of the American kitchen with its dishwasher represented not only the "essence of American freedom" but also the ideal family structure, with a "male breadwinner and a full-time female homemaker." The exhibit's larger narrative of cheap, mass-produced goods as constitutive of the American way of life did not resonate with the Holubars, who told a different story. Technical equipment offered "examples of fine American craftsmanship," not mass production. Their business, they explained, "started as a hobby," and they continued to "make many of the articles [themselves]." "[E]very piton and hammer we make is truly hand-forged on the old-fashioned blacksmith's forge," the Holubars proclaimed. "This is no mass production" but a proud "small American business." The Holubars' narrative actually contrasted with the national narrative about the promise of cheap, mass-produced goods. By underscoring the craft of their products, the Holubars implicitly critiqued American mass culture as inauthentic.[37]

The American homemaker in her modern kitchen became the most memorable display of the American National Exhibition. But place a Royalight down sleeping bag next to the refrigerator or washing machine and we see a different story. Although the public presentation erased Alice Holubar's central role as gearmaker and the international exhibit simplified the family business narrative (also hiding its meager financial rewards at this time), it glorified a small family business making craft products, which contrasted with the dominant narrative of mass production as the epitome of the American dream. With their display, the Holubars tried to explain their understanding of wilderness and confront sweeping claims about the American economic system by offering a personal interpretation of a successful business. The exhibit provides insight into how the Holubars and their customers construed their products in an international context, and the deepening alliance of American consumption with wilderness politics.

Back in Boulder, the display was of intense local interest. So, in early August of that year, Roy and Alice put similar "standard Boulder products" on display in their front yard at Grandview for three days (late enough in the evening so that Roy would be home from his teaching job). Tellingly, the Holubars chose to capture American wilderness not with an image of a stand of trees or a climber on a mountaintop but with gear, and the American exhibition committee presumably had solicited them for precisely this reason. A red tent and blue sleeping bag *were* American nature, for exhibition purposes.[38]

The Holubars last saw the goods they contributed to the exhibition when they packed them up at home for Moscow's Sokolniki Park in April 1959. When American organizers went to retrieve these goods that represented the American way of life after six weeks on display, "every one of the articles had disappeared," according to an American exhibition representative. Months later they remained missing. The Holubars calculated the total loss to be $184.40, around $1,880 in 2022 dollars. An American representative for the exhibition wrote to them in January 1960, stating that his office was "reasonably certain that they were stolen." Whether an American closing the exhibit had been lured by shiny nylon fabric and Alice Holubar's careful stitching, or a Russian visitor had been entranced by the blossoming American sport, the letter does not speculate.[39]

By 1962, when Holubar Mountaineering had been in business in the family basement for fifteen years and supported customers among the twenty-six million American families who camped, the company incorporated. It made the move from the Grandview Avenue basement to a local Boulder storefront and then expanded to a second location in Denver. Under Alice and Roy Holubar's leadership, the company grew to more than twenty-three employees, doing the work of sewing, packing, mailing, invoicing, and sourcing materials. The Holubars continued to serve local climbing clubs, but they gained a much bigger reputation after Moscow. In 1962, even given the inroads Alice Holubar had made with the Royalight and other designs, the company's image was definitively linked—still—to central Europe. *Family Camping* magazine described the outdoor store and said the American company, which outfitted American families for the outdoors, was best known for its lederhosen and Tyrolean hats.

✳

For outdoor gear companies, moving out of family basements and accountants' closets in the 1950s and 1960s signaled the beginning of the end of the founders' participation in their own businesses. Often this change proved for the better, as gear company founders sought to return to the mountains that had inspired their businesses in the first place. On losing control of Gerry Mountain Sports to a conglomerate of Colorado Outdoor Sport Industries, Gerry Cunningham said, "I never did want to be a businessman. I wanted to be a designer. I became a businessman by default to get product into the public's hands." Alice Holubar's basement and the industry she and Roy built epitomizes the transformation in outdoor equipment manufacturing from family and friends affairs to larger national corporations.[40]

The Holubars had a similar impulse to return to the mountains. By 1968, the Holubar company was bringing in $200,000 annually in business, around $1.7 million in 2022 dollars. Dale Johnson, who as a college student had spent time investigating new fabrics in Roy and Alice's basement, had long since graduated, left, and returned to start his own outdoor company. George Lamb started Alp Sport. Gary Neptune opened Neptune Mountaineering. Alice Holubar was diagnosed with cancer in 1964, and after years of fighting for both her health and the family business, she and Roy sought a buyer for Holubar Mountaineering so they could make the most of their remaining time together. Roy had left his teaching job a couple of years earlier to help her run the business, although he would have preferred to continue teaching. Roy remembered that the doctor recommended they get out of the business for Alice's sake, because she "felt responsible" for the business and its vicissitudes. They found Jim Kack, a freshly minted MBA with little outdoor experience, to buy the business. Kack remembered that they told him, "We want to get rid of the business, because we want to take some time off and do a little traveling while we still can."[41]

Kack represented a new kind of gearmaker whose expertise lay in business acumen rather than outdoor skill. Kack himself acknowledged that when the Holubars "handed me the keys and left, . . . I truly didn't know a sleeping bag from a woodpecker." Kack joined a number of MBAs heading outdoor companies in Colorado and elsewhere that already had strong reputations and customer bases. These men, too young to have lived through the surplus era, grew up knowing about brands like Holubar and Gerry if they were outdoorspeople. As some of the oldest American outdoor companies, like Eddie Bauer, L. L. Bean, and Abercrombie & Fitch, were expanding their offerings to match new consumer interests, newer companies remained specialized in just a few extreme sports.[42]

When Colorado Mountain Club member Jan Robertson visited Holubar in February 1967, Holubar's illness was apparent. But ever the host, Holubar drew in Jan's shy young son with a lively tale about a bobcat. One last time, the Holubar house became a space of community and friendship. It had only been free of the bustling basement business for six years at that point, but the influence of Holubar's decades of cutting and sewing fabric was by then international. Mike Brady wrote to her in May 1968, informing her that her pack and sleeping bag designs were copied in shops from Norway to Germany. Holubar died in November 1968, just months after selling the family business. For years afterward, people would ring the doorbell or address a letter to 1215 Grandview Avenue, just to see if the company was still going.[43]

The outdoor identity that Holubar contributed to breathed new life into anti-commercialist ideals that were still tightly linked to American capitalism and consumption. Holubar acolytes were far from their Khaki Gang predecessors. They embraced expensive, often custom, and high-end equipment where surplus aficionados had emphasized thrift and scruffiness. Despite these differences, both built communities around outdoor activities and the specialized purchases they made. Both also cultivated an insider group that linked knowledge about outdoor gear to belonging.

As the business imperative of many outdoor companies grew stronger in the 1960s and 1970s, the local community spirit that Alice Holubar had helped create was no longer possible. A new generation of gearmakers began to imagine a new model for business, keeping in mind that they had little in the way of Alice Holubar's authentic, charismatic mastery of the outdoors to offer. The question was how to provide a similar feeling of belonging that consumers had experienced in the Grandview basement, but at scale.

Above all, the lesson for retailers of the next generation was that Holubar customers linked their *identity* to the brand, and the company. This would prove a powerful lesson as outdoor brands expanded into the clothing of everyday life toward the end of the 1960s.

SEVEN

Rucksack Revolution

The Supermarket of the Outdoors

In the 1970s, wrote one Pacific Northwest journalist in 1987, the popularity of hiking "exploded like an overheated camp stove." Outdoor recreation had been getting more popular since World War II, but this appeal grew exponentially in the late 1960s. Outdoor enthusiasts described the 1970s as a time when "an entire nation began carrying rucksacks." Government studies quantified anecdotal evidence. In 1962, nine million Americans went camping. Only ten years later, that number had increased to forty million. Retail sales increased, too: in 1972, Americans purchased four million camping vehicles and spent $3 billion on trips and outdoor equipment; in 1974, six million backpackers spent around $400 million on outdoor clothing and equipment. New gear increased comfort: closed cell foam pads made sleeping on the ground warmer and more comfortable, domed tents afforded more headspace, and backpacks with internal frames rested comfortably on the hips. There were more outdoor stores than ever before, and in more cities.[1]

Gearmakers, guidebook authors, and outdoor lovers (often one and the same) recognized that this growth was a problem. The designer J. Baldwin, observing his tent designs move from outdoor enthusiasts to the broader marketplace, commented on the adverse effect of his work on nature: "too many people trampling around." Insiders like Harvey Manning worried that with advancements in outdoor gear technology, *his* wilderness would be threatened by masses of newcomers. "Where did all these damn hikers come from?" Manning asked in an article in the outdoor magazine *Back-packer* in 1975. In the illustration accompanying the article, the bearded and experienced hiker is outside the frame, alongside a bear and "nature," while the masses remain unaware of nature's presence in their rush to get back to it. They have ample gear but no faces, making it easy to vilify them and their consumer choices. Ironically, this question came from Manning, the guidebook author affiliated with REI, whose work inspired so many to buy the gear to get back to nature.[2]

Although popular retrospectives often celebrate the 1970s as a golden age of outdoor entrepreneurship and democratic access, this period was fraught from the beginning, and more corporate than these idealized views would suggest. The newly widespread popularity of both outdoor activities and the consumer goods that went with them provoked almost immediate hand-wringing within the outdoor industry and among outdoor recreationists. Columnists at outdoor magazines, guidebook authors, self-described old-timers, and outdoor company founders all grappled once again with how to reconcile the culture of consumption with nature as an anti-commercial escape from it. Since the nineteenth century, outdoor companies and consumers alike had worried that buying gadgets rather than crafting them would undermine the authenticity of the outdoor experience. Though the concerns were hardly new, the industry's response was. It began to address these concerns, first at the level of individual businesses and then systematically, with quasi-political involvement at the corporate level. The industry also responded with a new self-awareness and recognition of the outdoor industry's ironic position as the producers and marketers of high-tech commercial goods designed to equip an escape from the commercial world.[3]

The changes in one Seattle-based outdoor company reveal some of the larger, fundamental issues at stake for the outdoor industry in the 1970s. Between the immediate postwar period and the mid-1970s, the Co-op, later known as Recreational Equipment, Incorporated (REI), changed from an odd gathering space for climbers into what one reporter called the "Neiman-Marcus of the outdoor world." Like so many other outdoor shops in the early postwar period, Lloyd and Mary Anderson's had started by reselling surplus as part of their business, and then slowly replaced that dwindling inventory with goods manufactured in-house. The Co-op offered a small dividend each year to members who had made purchases, and evolved from a side-project to a full-time job for the Andersons. It leapt from a "help-yourself operation" in an accountant's back office to a succession of stores with expanded floor and display space near downtown Seattle. Co-op members often pointed with pride to membership and sales growth during the 1960s. The Co-op started with twelve founding members, grew to 12,000 in 1958, 79,000 in 1968, and 292,408 in 1972. In 1972 it had nearly $12 million in sales.[4]

General manager Jim Whittaker, a renowned mountaineer in his own right, saw REI's growth and reputation as the "Sears and Roebuck of the outdoors" as positive, not just for REI itself, but for outdoor recreation and Americans' ability to access it more broadly. "My thrust has always been to get more people off their butts and into the woods," he said. "If you promote that through a supermarket of the outdoors, well that's OK by me." The concept of the supermarket of the outdoors suggested anonymity, a lack of experts to help customers in the store, and a scarcity of specialty goods, all of which were ultimately problems of doing business at scale. Whittaker himself would have readily noticed, and perhaps critiqued, REI's inflection away from the sense of community that the entrepreneurial Holubars had fostered and toward a corporate ethos and a diminished focus on climbing and mountaineering in favor of less intense outdoor experiences.[5]

But for Whittaker the benefits outweighed the losses: cheaper goods relative to the 1960s because of scale; more accessible goods because of expanded mail-order catalog business and the opening of REI stores in new cities; a more family-friendly environment, both in terms of products, such as kid carriers, and the store's aesthetic; the addition of classes and travel services; and a huge REI membership, which led to both a solid business platform and one for environmental activism. That activism was always threaded through the notion that Americans should buy their way to a better outdoors — buying the right stuff to leave a smaller footprint in the woods. The right logo and t-shirt could become a proxy for activism.

The wondrous new equipment of the 1970s is so often cited as the cause that brought people to the woods and waters. And new gear did encourage new participants. But the technology was less revolutionary than the change to outdoor culture itself. For better or, as many would eventually argue, for worse, the supermarket era fundamentally changed outdoor recreation in the United States.[6]

✳

For George Appleton's forty-seventh Christmas, his wife Dottie bought him his first real backpack. Though Appleton had long been a car camper, he was excited for the end of the school year, so he could leave behind his role as a teacher and spend more time in Death Valley, Zion National Park, and other locales close to his Las Vegas home. Appleton attributed his newfound enthusiasm for backpacking—and by extension, his desire for a real back-pack—in part to Harvey Manning's guidebook *Backpacking: One Step at a Time*. The manual prompted readers to get outside, he wrote in a thankful letter to the author. Appleton's experience of being motivated to buy gear and participate in a new outdoor sport because of a guidebook was common. Guidebooks, magazines, and other outdoor texts inspired people to get out but also to get out and shop.[7]

Several other factors fed the outdoor recreation boom of the late 1960s and early 1970s, including new federal approaches to environmental policy, cultural movements, and educational structures. A casual enthusiast like George Appleton would not have cited federal policy as a motivator for his backpacking trips, but these changes did create the conditions for people to access the outdoors. Projects of the New Deal era, including infrastructure projects led by the Civilian Conservation Corps and promotional posters created by the Works Progress Administration, created the infrastructure for tourists and spread awareness about America's leisure landscapes. The National Park Service built modern campgrounds focused on automobile traffic that organized and regulated visiting campers. Overwhelming numbers of visitors to public land in the first fifteen years after the war prompted the government to organize a comprehensive study of the outdoor recreation phenomenon to plan for future growth. In 1962, the Outdoor Recreation Resources Review Commission published findings that shaped governmental approaches for years afterward. The study resulted in support for trail-building, specifically long-distance trails that inspired a thru-hiker surge. Similarly, in 1964 the Wilderness Act codified both land set-asides and a definition of the value of the wild, and new interstate highways helped direct American tourists to these spaces. The creation of long-distance trails also provided newspaper-worthy coverage of outdoor activity.[8] Together, these changes intertwined American national identity and the outdoors and increased camping's accessibility.

The rising profile of environmental politics also shaped Americans' recreational practices. Activists and young people who grew up in suburban neighborhoods and enjoyed outdoor-oriented vacations wanted to protect the wild they loved. Nature was a source of authenticity for those on the new left, and the counterculture called attention to contemporary ills such as war, pollution, and urban life. It's safe to assume that many of the twenty million participants in the first Earth Day in 1970 shared a love for outdoor leisure. All these changes at the national and state level also created a problem that Harvey Manning and many others grumpily articulated: outdoor recreation seemed to be too accessible, and the newcomers to the woods did not understand how to behave appropriately.[9]

Popular publications helped sell the allure of the outdoors as escape, balm, or proving ground. Many people drew inspiration from Gary Snyder's *The Back Country* (1967) and Jack Kerouac's *The Dharma Bums* (1958) for the simple and natural way of life. The anti-capitalist aesthetic embodied by these counterculture works connected to the anti-commercialism espoused by the Holubars and other gearmakers in the postwar period. In *Dharma Bums*, Kerouac envisioned a "rucksack revolution"—a bunch of "wanderers" who rejected American consumer society. For Kerouac, "wandering around with rucksacks" was a decidedly political act designed to challenge the imprisoning system of "work, produce, consume, work, produce, consume." While Kerouac was more interested in the implications of what wandering around would do, backpacks—manufactured and sold by outdoor companies—play an important symbolic role in this vision.[10]

As for guidebooks, a work destined to become the bible of the outdoors, Colin Fletcher's *The Complete Walker*, was published in 1968 and written with a beginner in mind. The broader trend in outdoor publishing, although offerings varied, was hefty tomes that were comprehensive buying guides, like Harvey Manning's *One Step at a Time*, and slim volumes that were more philosophical musings on the outdoor experience, such as Albert Saijo's *The Backpacker*, for the minimalist hippie. In the important world of outdoor magazines, *Outdoor Life* and *Field and Stream* were joined by *Climbing* in 1970; *Backpacker* magazine, founded by a backpacking enthusiast, in 1973; and *Outside* magazine in 1977. Magazine publishers, supported by outdoor companies through advertisements, understood that the magazines, like the gear, were a response to a boom in outdoor sports rather than the cause of it.

More formal educational courses for the outdoors, as with the magazines, did not alone *cause* an increase in participation, but they did invite beginners into discussions, a structure in which to learn new skills, a cohort, and a shared set of experiences. Many boys and girls learned about outdoor skills and equipment from scouting, including everyday troop activities and summer camps. In the 1970s, outdoor clubs and outing clubs on college campuses were founded or expanded. Colleges began teaching environmental education classes. Two wilderness experience organizations, Outward Bound and the National Outdoor Leadership School, blossomed as well.

Finally, evolving cultural attitudes toward fitness and exercise affected outdoor recreation habits. Exercise and fitness culture were, essentially, commercialized and brought into a market system. Like Kenneth Cooper, who promoted running in his book *Aerobics* in 1968, or Jim Fixx with his writing on jogging, fans of outdoor recreation touted its physical benefits. Strenuous activities like hiking, especially over long distances, became aligned with the virtue of intense physical activity.[11]

Outdoor recreation participants themselves, of course, had various introductions to the outdoors, motivations, goals, and experiences. In New Jersey, Paul Friedlander, no big fan of nature, decided to try out camping with an RV to see what all the fuss was about. In Ontario, Canada, Beverley Foss, who had car-camped as a child, was a novice backpacker and ardent conservationist worried about the risks of misguided approaches to the outdoors. In Michigan, fifteen-year-old Jim Forgie coveted backpacking gear he could not yet afford. Rick Hoffman of Lake Stevens, Washington, embarked on the 2,653-mile-long Pacific Crest Trail.[12]

For the Las Vegas teacher George Appleton, as with most other outdoor enthusiasts of the early 1970s, no single factor sparked his initial interest. New publications, new classes, new political movements, and new industry approaches all boosted the popularity of outdoor recreation and by extension outdoor goods. Some accounts of this era suggest that new lightweight equipment was by itself responsible for the outdoor sports expansion—as though Appleton would not have gone backpacking had his wife not given him a backpack. Undoubtedly, lightweight equipment made outdoor activities more comfortable and feasible and therefore more desirable. But new companies, as they garnered often cult-like followings among consumers, were responding to a changing culture that fed their businesses' success.

✻

Expert outdoorspeople had access to high-end equipment in the 1950s and early 1960s, but ordinary outdoor enthusiasts struggled to find affordable and effective goods for leisure-time activities. While friends of outdoor company founders and climbers such as the Holubars in Boulder (Holubar Mountaineering) and the Andersons in Seattle (REI) could turn to the resources at hand, those who didn't live in outdoor hubs or have personal connections to company owners had a more challenging path to acquiring their own kits. In the second half of the 1960s, as more outdoor stores opened across the country, the supermarket model of outdoor stores provided access to a far wider range of consumers.

Generally, the new stores opened in locations with populations already interested in outdoor sports. Hubs included Los Angeles, San Francisco, Portland, Seattle, and Boulder. And generally, many company founders had been young men who were avid participants in their sports and saw room for improvement in particular types of equipment. They often had military backgrounds or experience in the field of engineering, and they often got the support of their wives in the form of sewing, selling, and beyond. In the Bay Area, for instance, where young people skied, camped, backpacked, and climbed, the North Face did well, as did Sierra Designs, building on the longer history of the Ski Hut. Many people who worked in the outdoor industry in Boulder cited Roy and Alice Holubar's shop as their inspiration, including Dale Johnson of Frostline, Gary Neptune of Neptune Mountaineering, and George Lamb of Alp Sport and Camp 7.[13]

These participants and their stories, however, hide the fact that by the late 1960s the outdoors was a big business, and there were plenty of reasons to be involved beyond being an outdoor enthusiast with a good idea and a romantic, countercultural vision. The origins of three outdoor stores—Patagonia in Ventura, California; Eastern Mountain Sports in Boston, Massachusetts; and Columbia Sportswear in Portland, Oregon—show that while the notion of an anti-business hippie climber selling to his friends has some truth, the growth of the industry in the 1970s was far more complicated and varied. Together, these stores are representative of retail changes in that decade, specifically the rise of specialty clothing stores more broadly.

In Ventura, California, a decades-long business partnership and friendship began with a rebellious teenager sulking at her parent's beach home. Kristine McDivitt—known as Kris—had already decided she would not go to a posh boarding school that her oilman father wanted her to attend when she met Yvon Chouinard at the beach. Chouinard, a twenty-something climber, would have called himself a dirtbag at the time. Since 1957, he had been making his own chrome steel pitons and selling them to fellow climber friends, and the customers who followed. Chouinard was part of the Yosemite climbing crew at Camp Four. The makeshift business became a more established one as Chouinard Equipment emerged as the climbing industry standard. Kris McDivitt's life changed when she met Chouinard, who was by then beginning to sell clothing under the label Patagonia. She was not an environmentalist then, although she did love outdoor activities. McDivitt later guessed that if not for Chouinard hiring her at fifteen, and the surfing, skiing, and climbing friends he introduced her to, she would have ended up "an alcoholic old woman with pearls around her neck." Instead, McDivitt became a ski racer in college, a friend of the Chouinards, and within a few years Patagonia's first CEO at twenty-eight.[14]

In Denver, Colorado, lawyer Roger Furst liked to spend time hiking and fishing with his friend (and client) Alan McDonough, who managed a local hotel. They were like so many residents of the city at that time, eager to prolong their time in the mountains, away from work and the city. They had both camped and skied before, but it was only in Colorado that they learned backpacking as well, which allowed them to fish as soon as they woke up in the morning by a mountain lake or stream, rather than having to make an early-morning or late-night trek to or from the car. The hotel where Mc-Donough worked had a mountain climbing shop, and both men saw the potential of selling outdoor clothing and equipment. They didn't want to set up shop in a place like Denver, however. Indeed, most big cities in the West had their share of outdoor stores—but not the East. So in 1967 McDonough and Furst moved to Boston, close enough to mountains to be attractive to outdoor athletes, but in a region with far fewer dedicated mountaineer, climbing, and backpacking stores. Within seven years Eastern Mountain Sports (EMS) was manufacturing goods; making retail and catalog sales; operating mountaineering, rock, and ice climbing schools; and planning to expand by two or three new EMS stores per year.[15]

Although McDonough and Furst's motivations were clear—build an outdoor clothing and equipment company in the East to rival those in the West, others in the outdoor industry came to the business with murkier goals. In Portland, Oregon, Gert Boyle inherited Columbia Sportswear in 1970 when her husband died unexpectedly. Boyle was a generation older than Furst and McDonough. Born Gert Lammfromm in Augsburg, Germany, she moved with her parents to Portland at age thirteen, in 1937. Gert's father borrowed money to buy the Rosenfeld Hat Company, probably in part because of the well-established presence of Jews in the sportswear and textile industry in Portland. To replace the German Jewish–sounding name with an American one, just as the Hirsches had done earlier with White Stag in Portland, Lamfrom (his Americanized surname) renamed the company after the Columbia River. Gert met her husband Neal Boyle at a fraternity party at the University of Arizona, and he joined her father in the company, which became Columbia Sportswear after a merger in 1960. Neal had his finger on the pulse of the growing interest in outdoor sports, and Columbia expanded from hats into outerwear for hunters, fishermen, and skiers. Gert Boyle contributed by sewing a fishing vest with generous pockets, although she had never gone fishing. She raised her three children as her father slowly built the company. The deaths of her father and her husband within a few years of each other left Gert Boyle at the helm of Columbia Sportswear. Along with her son Tim and the help of others in the outdoor industry in Portland, especially fellow Jew and outdoor company owner Harold Hirsch, Boyle gradually elevated the struggling company to new heights.[16]

Jim Whittaker, Kris McDivitt, Roger Furst, and Gert Boyle catered to slightly different markets, but all benefited from a cultural milieu where it was cool to go to the outdoors. They also benefited from customers' enthusiasm for new technology and often, although not always, had a personal interest in outdoor activities. They all shared the belief that the outdoor industry could be a profitable place to work. But not everyone in the industry was as comfortable discussing balance sheets.

✳

Looking back on this so-called golden era, many outdoor entrepreneurs called themselves "reluctant businessmen" who got into the outdoor industry for the love of sport and only accidentally became millionaires. Whereas the retrospective disavowal of early career ambitions seems idealistic, and perhaps apocryphal, this attitude is consistent with the outdoor industry's moral qualms about selling the Great Outdoors to an ever larger market. There were two prevailing tensions in the outdoor industry in the late 1960s and early 1970s. The first was a general resistance to, or suspicion of, capitalist systems. Not all of these company owners considered themselves hippies, but many did have sympathy for the politics of the New Left, a taste for drugs shared by counterculture youth, and a general sense that the outdoors represented an alternative career and life to an office job. These factors offered new twists on the immanent tensions, from the 1800s on, between a commercial outdoor industry and an outdoors idealized as non-commercial. The second tension was specifically about reconciling new environmental politics with the business of selling the outdoors. The concern wasn't just the overpopulation of wild lands reaching their carrying capacity, but also the consumerism they promoted, the plastics they sold, and their companies' contribution to litter and pollution.

To address these concerns, many outdoor industry companies in the 1970s chose to run their businesses differently. With store classes, swap meets, and other meeting grounds for customers and owners alike, outdoor shops were interested not in toppling older economic systems but rather in reconfiguring American business to emphasize environmental values, appropriate technology, and human connection. The historian Joshua Clark Davis calls business owners like these activists. For Davis, outdoor stores were activist businesses, along with Black booksellers, women-owned credit unions, natural food stores, and head shops. Some, like REI, promoted shared ownership as a cooperative that returned profits through dividends. Others, like Patagonia, established more democratic workplaces by providing on-site childcare facilities. Many more small outdoor companies fit under the activist label, including retail stores such as Adventure 16.[17]

Mic Mead, founder of the outdoor store Adventure 16 (A16), sensed an incongruity between his work and his play. For Mead, the beginning of a resolution was to change the way he did business. A16 was a small outdoor chain in Southern California with stores from Los Angeles to San Diego. Founded in the late 1960s, the company's claim to fame was a backpack, modeled after a military pack, that transferred most of the wearers' weight from shoulders to hips. A16's role in the social fabric of outdoorspeople's lives in the 1960s and 1970s exemplifies how approaches to business had changed from the cottage industry days of the immediate postwar era. Customers still visited outdoor shops as the first stop on their road to the wilderness, but they were less likely to know workers, store owners, and founders.

On the surface the supermarket approach seemed at odds with the activist approach and the sense of community and belonging in the cottage industry years. By 1970, the more intimate communities of the previous decades had disappeared, but new forms of commercial connection were forged in their place. Customers at A16 and other outdoor stores around the country found connection through classes held in the stores and through company-run trips that ranged from weekend campouts to Himalayan treks. They shared outdoor catalogs and guidebooks and met up at informal commercial sessions such as swap meets organized by outdoor shops. The large footprint of stores and their expanding customer base allowed for a new kind of interpersonal connection that hadn't been possible when the storefront was a family basement. Managers filled their stores with folding chairs, made their stocked shelves the classroom walls, and invited customers to return on evenings and weekends to learn. Through classes and, later, trips run by companies such as REI of Seattle and Adventure 16 of Southern California, outdoor companies invited a new generation of aspiring backpackers into the outdoors.

At A16 in San Diego founder Mic Mead gave classes once a week on the skills and goods of backpacking that included weekend campouts with fellow customers and A16 employee experts. Don Deck, known to his students as Mountain Mouse, led the A16 Backpack Training program, teaching classes and leading trips for the company. For Deck, teaching in the A16 store and extending that education outdoors helped fulfill his vision of a company "dedicated to the proper use of our back-country and wilderness areas through education." Deck connected his work as a teacher and guide to a larger company ethic. The leader of the Los Angeles A16 branch's weekend campout also linked outdoor ethics and backpacking practices in his course: on a hike in the San Gabriel Mountains, he would stop to discuss how to locate campsites or practice good sanitation in the field. These courses and trips were intimate, small group affairs, yet they were also corporate. There was a set curriculum, a schedule, and no impromptu stops just to chat, as neighbors hoping for a slice of pie might have done at Alice Holubar's. These teachers were businessmen, and they carefully guarded their time. Of course, they were also bringing people together who all patronized the store.[18]

Footprints magazine, A16's publication, captured some of the relaxed community formation that could happen on these skills-building trips. One trip leader, Jim Bailey, taught the "fun of sleeping on the ground and cooking in the wilderness." Some attendees sought expert advice on outdoor photography. The informal connections often continued long after Bailey went to sleep: "The socially inclined in the group often make a late night of it around the warming glow of a campfire." Whereas REI or Holubar customers in the 1950s had known store owners or salespeople personally, even these corporate, less personal classes and trips helped connect outdoor shop customers over shared learning and gear accumulated.[19]

Outdoor stores also organized annual or semi-annual sales that drew large, enthusiastic crowds. REI's annual owners' sale and A16's Mother's

Parking lot gear swaps were both shopping events and community events. (Image courtesy of John D. Mead, Adventure 16)

Day swap meets were more than just shopping events and price reductions. They were outdoor community events where enthusiasts could geek out over gear together. A16's swap meets began in 1972. Crowds could buy old equipment at a discount from the store's rental shop and trade with fellow backpackers, bringing gear in car trunks to sell and trade. Attendees by 1978 included "anxious traders" who arrived at 6 a.m. to share coffee before the cordoned-off area opened. As news of the bounty of cheap goods spread over the years, potential customers began to arrive even earlier to ensure access to the best gear. In camping out the night before, they made the sale a kind of celebration and communal gathering.[20]

Although it might seem that swap meets contributed a part of the counterculture ethos within the outdoor industry, historians have shown that secondhand distribution networks were often profitable businesses central to the development of corporate capitalism. From Salvation Army and Goodwill to suburban garage sales, this seemingly "anti-consumption consumerism" was in fact big business, even though swap meets created a mood for participants of crafting more authentic individual identities that defied middle-class consumerism.[21]

The scene of these parking lot mobs evoked the makeshift surplus stores of the late 1940s and early 1950s, transposed to a corporate key. Customers practiced their skills of discernment. They had to pick through the lot of used goods to find treasures. Like their Khaki Gang forerunners, these customers embraced the grubbiness ethic—used gear was usually a plus rather than a concern because it meant a cheaper price and conferred a certain authenticity. Often these sales were the only things that made specialty outdoor stores affordable. Most of all, the swap meets encouraged exchanges of enthusiasm and information. For much of the year, these outdoor enthusiasts were connected only because they read the same guidebooks and catalogs. In the parking lot by the A16 store with cups of coffee, or camping on the sidewalk outside the Seattle store, customers bonded over their shared love of gear. They forged their bond not on the solitude of the trails but in the bustle of a sale made possible by urban corporate interests.

The most expansive community of outdoor enthusiasts in the 1970s formed from the connections catalog readers imagined with each other. Catalogs of the 1970s resembled hefty tomes with beautiful illustrations that aimed to provide didactic but enjoyable reading about how to shop for the outdoors. Belief in a community of like-minded outdoorspeople, one that existed both in face-to-face conversation at store sales and in reading material, paved the way for customers who demanded political action from the companies they had come to believe in. Outfitters published not just catalogs listing products for sale, but also newsletters and bulletins that kept readers informed of the latest in-store sales, environmental legislation, and the ethics of minimal impact camping.

Outdoor catalog aesthetics appealed partly because of their approach to modeling. Catalog designers selected models carefully and staged them in natural settings even more carefully to promote a particular vision. To distinguish their catalogs from more fashion-oriented brands, outdoor companies often emphasized that they did *not* use professional models, but instead recruited from family and friends, well-known athletes, or readers themselves. "You may be the person we're looking for," read an advertising insert from Early Winters, a Seattle outdoor company that encouraged outdoor catalog readers to send in a photo and body measurements so that they might be considered as a model for the next catalog. Perhaps the best example of catalogs visually embracing the freedom of the counterculture came from Jack Stephenson's Warmlite, notorious—or lauded—for using nude models lounging in front of high-tech tents and sleeping bags.[22]

※

Although Jim Whittaker presided over the garage sales as REI's general manager, he was no hippie. He climbed Mount Rainier with Robert Kennedy. He was a celebrity whose poster, featuring a photo of him standing on Everest in a puffy red down jacket, was a bestseller at $1.50 at REI. And perhaps most consequentially for REI members looking for a cause, Whittaker thought REI should not be involved in environmental politics. In the mid-1960s, companies such as REI had shied away from espousing political values directly. A storefront was hardly the place for political posters or pamphlets. When REI member Patrick Goldsworthy stopped at the Co-op before a Conservation Committee of the Mountaineers meeting with a stack of flyers advocating for the creation of a North Cascades National Park, he received a brusque reply. Whittaker told him that controversies such as the park were not something the Co-op involved itself in and added that the literature he was carrying was not welcome in the store.[23]

By the 1970s, however, Whittaker and REI could not afford *not* to get involved: heeding the demands of customers, outdoor companies reshaped themselves into leaders in the dialogue about wilderness preservation. Many outdoor catalogs of the 1970s show that employees and company owners were eager to be vocal and visible in their support of environmental causes.

Community experience through classes, swap meets, and DIY kit hotlines paved the way for engagement in political activities through outdoor companies and disseminated the new outdoor ethics. These consumers had not lost sight of the larger social questions that had animated generations of outdoorspeople before them. What place, or role, did the modern economy and consumerism play in the wilderness? Clad in used boots and brightly colored vests they sewed themselves, they argued that consumerism was precisely the point at which to engage with questions in environmental protection. Consumers argued that they could find both pleasure and politics as they shopped en route to the wilderness. Environmental historians have examined the ethics of the outdoors and noted links between outdoor companies and changing consumer decisions. The Leave No Trace campaign of the 1990s, for instance, championed the idea that contemporary high-tech, often synthetic gear might alleviate stress on the wilderness and the recreational landscape. Certainly, high-tech goods occupied, and continued to occupy, an ambivalent position relative to the wilderness, but whatever the case, the new, dominant ethic in outdoor recreation in the last quarter of the century developed from consumers as much as it did from lawmakers or outfitters.[24]

In addition to outdoor companies, leaders in outdoor conservation and education taught Americans about ethical behavior in the wilderness at outdoor clubs, new public land organizations, and wilderness skills courses. Historians have shown the critical role of political organizations like the Wilderness Society and even Outward Bound or the National Outdoor Leadership School in teaching environmental values and encouraging activism at the grassroots level. Yet, like Sierra Club mass mailings, the outdoor industry reached a broad audience not necessarily inclined toward political action.

These companies made political choices about the meaning of the outdoors. They argued that nature was a space of consumption and leisure. It was an escape, more from the humdrum of everyday work life than from consumer culture or modernity itself, since companies wanted to sell modern gadgets, after all. Accordingly, for these companies nature began where people set aside their ordinary clothes and gadgets and picked up ones made for outdoor recreation. The very boundary of nature, in other words, was delineated by stuff. As consuming became more and more central to what it meant to go outside, the language around mastering the outdoors shifted. It became less about becoming the master of nature out there and more about the battle in here—the store—to master the gearing-up process.

Outdoor company catalogs, brochures, newsletters, and other published written material reinforced one another—quite explicitly and directly in the case of REI. Harvey Manning was both the editor of a popular volume on mountaineering and an REI member. Manning wrote his guidebook, *Back-packing: One Step at a Time,* at the company's request. He developed the book's packing list and gear explanations in conjunction with REI staff. REI was the first publisher of the book as well. The CEO of REI wrote the foreword to the guidebook and REI promoted the book's release in catalogs. Guidebooks like Harvey Manning's promoted consumption as a path to mastering the outdoors. Authenticity could be purchased by carefully selecting the right products from the broad range available.[25]

The industry and customers alike recognized the paradox that selling gear made the wilderness both more comfortable and more crowded. In a letter to Harvey Manning, Gene Duenow wrote that he'd enjoyed the guidebook but regretted that the book's influence would be to aid more badly behaved beginners to head to the wilderness. He saw Manning's critique of dam builders and miners falling flat given that Manning, like so many others in the outdoor industry, made backpacking too accessible, therefore leading to more destruction. Duenow did not argue that the industry was in a hopeless bind. He thought that just like dam builders and miners, the outdoor industry needed to develop a conscience.[26]

Mic Mead, head of A16 in Southern California, mulled just this question. "When we make packs out of aluminum and nylon and make some of our best clothing out of synthetics that contribute to major problems," he said, "then as an environmentalist I have to think in terms of how I can have all that. How can I have my beautiful automobiles and use lots of oil and gasoline and do this in a responsible way?" Mead's answer reflected his constant engagement with that question: "When I take a walk and there is a tin can or bottle I pick it up. If I am backpacking in the mountains, I always make sure that I bring out more trash than I take in." Those were his suggestions for action on the trail, yet the principles ran deeper: "If you somehow contribute a little bit more than you take, if everybody understood those little bits of what Thoreau had to teach—we would have an absolutely beautiful world." Mead did not have answers for everything—he did not offer a philosophy by which it made sense as a business owner to sell high-tech synthetic clothing if one was a nature lover. And yet in his own company newsletter, he did self-consciously pose the ethical question, pushing readers to think about how their own fetishization of gear contributed to major environmental problems.[27]

These debates and conversations played out in textual communities that companies and consumers had cultivated over the previous decade. Mead's comments were published in the company's *Footprints* magazine that accompanied catalogs and shared gear news, announced swap meets, and taught outdoor ethics. The magazine's name referred to the ideal human impact on the land—leaving footprints and nothing else. The Recreational Equipment Cooperative published a similar document, *View Point*, and included it as an insert in catalogs. This recognition that problem-solving started at home and with companies and consumers in the industry inspired a new radical approach to the business of getting back to nature. Outdoor companies decided to embark on campaigns to popularize a new outdoor ethic. But this campaign emerged not only from companies but from consumers, who demanded it and helped to shape it.

In the 1960s, David Brower and Gerry Cunningham focused their guidebooks on "going light," which meant (and recommended) the purchase of new lightweight gear, but also treading lightly on the land. Although older woodcraft styles persisted in some guidebooks into the 1980s, by the mid-1970s the idea of light-impact camping dominated new guidebooks and other publications. Guidebooks had an ambitious, if at times uneasy, relationship to lightweight camping, in part because going lightweight seemed almost too easy and accessible. In other words, lightweight gear implicitly made "going light" on the land more difficult because it drew more outdoorspeople, including women. There was also a concern that talking about lightweight packs just for the sake of comfort made backpacking sound too luxurious and frivolous. A philosophy of gear developed to explain why so many women were now backpacking and also why expensive, beautiful, lightweight gear was ethically necessary for backpacking the right way.

More ambitiously, these conversations between consumers and gearmakers imagined a radical new relationship between customers and companies—one in which customers asked the shops they patronized to be explicitly political. In 1971, Chuck Bale wrote to Sierra Designs, the gearmaker based in Boulder, Colorado. Bale was an experienced outdoorsman who had hiked the

When outdoorspeople lamented the growing trash problem in their beloved wilderness, outdoor companies stepped in with solutions. (REI Newsletter, Winter 1972–1973, p. 22, University of Washington Libraries, Special Collections, Lloyd Anderson Papers, Accession 2648-001, UW41657)

southern Sierra in some of the remotest areas of the range, far from established trails and at altitudes higher than 11,500 feet. Like Gene Duenow and Mic Mead, Bale looked inward at the problems of the wilderness caused by those who purportedly loved it most. He wrote of "toilet paper and soap suds in East Lake, tin foil on the summit of Mount Brewer, and garbage everywhere." His letter to the company lamented that hikers, either "innocently or maliciously," allowed even the most sacred places to be "cluttered by garbage and crap."[28]

Bale argued that as an equipment maker Sierra Designs was "in a position to inform people that either they treat the earth with respect or soon the whole range [would] be nothing more than another polluted human disgrace." Bale's reasoning was that Sierra Designs had a wide audience. He asked the company to develop a pamphlet of outdoor ethics to sell with products, which included rules for packing out trash as small as orange peels, burying human waste deep, and not washing with soap directly in streams or lakes. Sierra Designs saw Bale's message as aligned with its own. The company published the full letter, not just the list of appropriate backcountry behavior, in the first two pages of its catalog in 1971. It was accompanied by a photo of the company's employees, associating them with Bale's ideas. In each of these requests, nature problems were construed as gear problems.[29]

Bale's recommendation that an outdoor company teach consumers about outdoor ethics is important not because it was unusual but because it was common in the 1970s. Building off the enthusiasm for Earth Day, outdoor consumers regularly asked the companies they loved to engage in environmental education and politics. In a survey from 1973, 92 percent of REI members in Seattle said they wanted the store to do more environmental activities. The three most popular forms were "1) environmental education, 2) lobbying, 3) creation of an environmental fund through optional return of all or a part of members' dividends." Ira Spring asked that the catalog, used to sell goods, allocate space for "The Voice of the Hiker" to promote "better trails." Mike Weisbach suggested that REI hand out a free booklet with purchases "to educate people about proper use of the back country." John Lindstrom agreed, though he thought the booklet on "Wilderness Manners" should come with membership rather than purchase. Dale White wanted to buy a patch that said "We Leave It Cleaner Than We Found It." For these REI members, ethics developed and promoted at the point of consumption seemed like the best way to communicate ideas, with REI using its "mass power" to improve the environment.[30]

The call from consumers for companies to change practices was emblematic of the larger consumer activist movement. In the fitness world, for example, runners complained if their running heroes picked the wrong cereal to promote, because it did not represent the values of the culture. Women catalog readers critiqued the sexualization of women's bodies in sleeping bag advertisements, noting the coquettish facial expressions and suggestive poses. "Please discontinue the use of male Chauvinist pig advertisements," wrote Parker Quammen and Sheila Boss of Chicago, enclosing a clipping of the catalog from 1972 with a young woman posed shirtless, though with only her shoulders visible, in a sleeping bag. Edwin Gragert of New York wrote that "he and his wife were highly pleased with the 1972 catalog" until they saw the same image.[31]

Sierra Designs employees wrote self-reflectively in their catalog, "Since we began designing and making equipment in 1965, backpackers have multiplied to the point of having to reserve trail space, every hardware and department store has a backpacking shop and the ever-expanding group of manufacturers belch out mounting mountains of purple and orange goosegear. We at Sierra Designs have contributed to and participated in this growth, but with occasional reservation and unease." In 1972, REI wrote in its catalog that although employees had long expressed and acted on environmental concerns as individuals, as an organization, "REI feels it must speak to you, pointing out ways in which you can help save the land, and on occasion speak for you by presenting the concerns of our members to public officials." REI hung posters that, according to company literature, urged "customers to think about their purchases in terms of environmental effects. One poster urges customers to 'Save a tree . . . Don't Take a Bag.' Statistics show that for every ton of paper saved, up to 17 trees can be spared. In the boot department another sign reads, 'May these boots be used on trails only, and not for cutting switchbacks.' " Echoing consumers' desires that REI "sell nothing that lends [sic] to destroy the wilderness such as snowmobiles," company policy limited products to human-powered activity.[32]

Patrick Goldsworthy, who had been rebuffed for trying to pass out political material in the store, was gratified to later discover that the Seattle REI had an "Environmental Center" to share information about environmental politics, with a particular focus on conservation activism. In planning for this center, REI invited customers to send literature about environmental groups they were involved in, both locally and nationally. Other campaigns highlighted in company catalogs included the Sierra Designs practice of finding nature close to home. The 1975 catalog explained that previous catalog photo shoots had taken the company to "big name" wilderness spaces like the Sierra Nevada or Vancouver Island. In 1975, the copy writers explained, rather than contribute to the "dreaded glut" of tourists at these famous locations, Sierra Designs forewent "traveling considerable distances" and instead looked "closely around [their] own home" to find "reasonable solitude and isolation." This move certainly would save on costs but was also indicative of a deeper philosophy.[33]

Catalogs and newsletters encouraged outdoor enthusiasts to write to government officials to support recreation infrastructure or the preservation of particular places. Sierra Designs asked customers to write to state and national park officials to make space for people who came on foot or by bicycle. REI also urged the preservation of beloved wild landscapes. "Write your Representative today," said one insert in a catalog, "and urge that Congress begin Alpine Lakes hearings soon." REI's *View Point* in 1976 reprinted "Letter Writing: Whys and Hows" from a Sierra Club publication.[34]

Consumers and company organizers worked together most visibly in trash cleanups in national parks. REI organized company-sponsored trash pickups in national parks that drew enthusiastic crowds. The fifth wilderness cleanup organized by REI, for instance, drew 141 volunteers who boarded buses chartered by REI and camped together at Lake Crescent for a night in early May 1976. The next morning these volunteers targeted thirty-nine miles of beach, "collecting trash and oil globules from recent oil spills." The Olympic National Park superintendent, Roger Allin, estimated that the REI cleanup crew collected four thousand pounds of litter that day. For the Snow Lake cleanup, enthusiastic volunteers "hitchhiked across town" or traveled twenty-five miles with their families to reach the store meeting point by 6 a.m. The REI "Wilderness Clean-ups" were so popular that the company had to limit group size by requiring interested members to send an application. Given their popularity, the Wilderness Clean-up coordinator Mike Collins offered suggestions about how members might organize their own cleanups, including working with national agencies, training group leaders, and arranging transportation. Anyone could, of course, organize a cleanup, but the REI-backed ones had particular clout: the REI general manager and famous Everest summiteer Whittaker led the Lake Melakwa cleanup, and got the Seattle mayor, Wes Ullman, to agree to join.[35]

These trash pickups were well-intentioned actions, yet they also placed responsibility on consumers rather than on companies or the government. The former Washington state governor and U.S. senator Daniel J. Evans, an REI member since the early days, argued that companies such as REI should invest more in preservation, environmental cleanups, and consumer education precisely because these activities would motivate people to buy equipment for outdoor adventures. Here was a senator arguing not for government involvement in environmental policies but rather for company engagement, and limited engagement at that, in political issues closest to home.[36]

Companies saw themselves as part of the problem, because their comfortable gear invited more people to enjoy the wilderness, yet their solution was to sell activism alongside gear, not to cut back or limit the materials used or types of gear sold. Indeed, these environmental actions were good for business because, as the REI Board of Directors articulated in their new guiding philosophy, "The recreational uses of the outdoors, which are the reason for R.E.I.'s existence, depend on the preservation of open space available to the public, and upon a healthy environment in which natural processes can function." They thought about their impact in the wilderness, but not out in the world. There was less concern for the health of workers or land beyond the boundaries of what had been defined and demarcated as wilderness, and they placed both the blame and the solution more on individual consumers—their customers—who could pick up a tin can rather than change their way of living.[37]

One REI member, Don Wittenberger, concerned about leadership at the Co-op and the direction the company was headed in, wrote an open letter in 1971 to REI members. He noted that some had accused REI of "selling the outdoors in order to promote their business." The t-shirt for sale in catalogs in the 1970s, with the REI Co-op logo prominently displayed, is one example of this effort of selling the outdoors, and did promote the business, but for many REI employees and customers the shirt also symbolized an earnest call to action.

The gear, along with education from stores and guidebooks and magazines, helped elaborate the outdoor ethic into one of using technical gadgetry to leave a lighter footprint in the wilderness. Even as this ethos was attuned to "going light," it nevertheless simultaneously underscored American reliance on the shopping experience as central to what it meant to hike.

In contrast, aficionados of the "woodsman school" shared the view that "wilderness was inexhaustible," despite the denuded and polluted campgrounds that were becoming increasingly common. Guidebooks began to criticize woodcrafters—descendants of the earlier woodcraft tradition—for the heavy footprints they left behind in the form of tree stumps and campfire scars. In the woodcrafter's place, guidebooks celebrated a "new outdoor ethic" that made old camp craft practices unnecessary. Modern equipment changed the backpacker's needs: buy a tent and "there's no need for sapling frame structures" to do the same work. A modern sleeping bag similarly "does away with bough beds and hip holes." Buying new gear allowed people to feel proud of their environmentally friendly shopping habits. To be sure, outdoor companies, guidebook authors, and magazine contributors all stood to benefit from an increasing focus on equipment as the path to mastering the outdoors ethically and authentically.[38]

Patrick Byrne of Malibu grew up in the woodsman era, started backpacking at eleven, and was a Boy Scout. He taught ax and survival classes at Lake Arrowhead Scout Camp. But by 1974, he said, he came full circle and had embraced the philosophy of taking nothing but pictures and leaving nothing but footprints. In Byrne's modern conception of outdoor recreation, woodsman-era and scouting talk no longer applied. The outdoors was not to be used, but preserved. Byrne's reeducation was emblematic of thousands of others', and of how environmental politics seeped into outdoor industry writings and practices.[39]

The transition from woodcraft to Leave No Trace, as one historian termed it, shifted the politics of the outdoors more broadly. Outdoorspeople learned what to buy as a way of learning what not to chop down. Consumption became a solution to the now-visible problems of woodcraft. For companies, outdoor stores became places to educate users about the new ethics along with selling their brands. Stores became the classrooms, trip organizers, and scolds when outdoorspeople didn't do things the new right way. Company owners and employees welcomed this chance for engagement, even as they realized that they could not ultimately reconcile selling industrially produced goods with their nascent environmental values. For their part, consumers saw company involvement in environmental issues as a central part of the value of the brand they bought—and were buying into. An ecological consciousness convinced millions of Americans to rethink their outdoor practices and pervaded even the stodgiest of outdoor guides: the *Boy Scout Handbook*.

✳

The outdoor industry had built itself on giving consumers something they couldn't find anywhere else: not only a tent or a fishing pole but also an authentic connection with nature. In the 1970s, stores expanded into everyday items like t-shirts and sneakers that really could be purchased anywhere. But informed by a vision of an activist business that was good for the environment, cheap t-shirts emblazoned with a Patagonia logo signaled an alignment with the new wilderness ethic of leaving no trace on the land. As companies used swap meets and in-store classes to educate newcomers about outdoor ethics and practices, the status of outdoor products in popular culture rose and became—to the concern of many—fashionable in spaces anything but wild.

Activist businesses that grew into supermarkets of the outdoors left a complicated legacy. Together, these companies succeeded in transforming American consumers' conception of outdoor ethics and guided them down the road from woodcraft to Leave No Trace. The price of growth for many of these early activist companies was that environmental politics could no longer remain central to how they did business. These self-identified hippie businessmen went corporate quickly. Their recreational interests and their sense of a growing market were a good read of the landscape, and the new brands that started in the late 1960s and early 1970s benefited from their understanding. One result of outdoor recreation's expansion was having enough of a market share, and a distinct focus, for the outdoor industry to start distinguishing itself from the sporting goods industry. The outdoor industry split along a clear line: motors and guns on one side of the line, and non-motorized backpacking and climbing on the other. For hunting and fishing companies, selling licenses offered a key way to participate in conservation conversations. For many, the sport itself constituted activism, since the Pittman-Robertson Act of 1937 had established a tax on firearms, the proceeds of which went to wildlife projects. Crucially, this meant that buying became conservation, in some ways. Corporatization of the outdoors also allowed companies to see their power and flex it for collective political action. And in conceptions of environmental politics, companies everywhere saw lightweight, low-impact gear as a solution to the problem, rather than the problem itself.

The language of environmental activism from outdoor companies now is as unremarkable as a Whole Foods ad featuring organic food. Preserving the outdoors *is* the business of outdoor companies, it now seems. As Joshua Clark Davis, a historian of activist businesses, has argued, although companies that work in earnest for social justice are rare, the legacy of activist businesses from the 1970s is substantial: they changed how consumers envisioned the responsibilities of a business to citizens and community.[40]

How big should outdoor business get? This was a constant question throughout the twentieth century, especially since many aficionados still thought that business, and purchased goods generally, had little place in the authentic outdoors. But the challenge of growth, and the enduring, inherent paradoxes of the "outdoor industry," were more urgent than ever simply because of the popularity of the outdoors in the 1970s. These were dilemmas to balance and solve—or hide.

EIGHT

Gore-Tex and Do-It-Yourself Kits

Corporatizing the Outdoors

B y the mid-1970s, the outdoor industry was both corporate and counter-cultural, depending on your perspective. On one hand, long-haired hippies were selling gear with friends in little shops in mountain towns to help young people get away from civilization with a trip into nature. On the other hand, gearmakers designed and tested new equipment according to specifications initially developed during World War II, using techniques that emerged out of the military's investment in research laboratories, and chemical corporation investments in new materials that similarly dated back to World War II. On top of that, large corporations targeted outdoor companies for buyouts, with giants as varied as General Mills, Johnson Wax, and the Gillette Corporation all pursuing outdoor outfitters as promising investments.

New companies such as Patagonia, Sierra Designs, the North Face, Cabela's, Bass Pro Shops, and Eastern Mountain Sports joined older firms like Abercrombie & Fitch, L. L. Bean, and Eddie Bauer as outdoor recreation retailers. For all the time and energy company owners spent thinking about environmental politics, it was ultimately products, not politics, that brought customers in the door. And these shopping outings were a source of joy and consternation for enthusiasts. Joy: because in the 1970s new, lighter designs and improved materials were appearing constantly on store shelves. Consumers knew they were living through an equipment revolution. Consternation: because the equipment was very expensive, and also rarely as miraculous as advertisements claimed.

The 1970s are now often called the golden age of the outdoor industry for a few reasons. First, corporate outdoor companies still squarely envisioned their target market as outdoorspeople, and with good reason. Second, participation in outdoor sports expanded in the early 1970s. The outdoor industry was especially interested in reaching the previously untapped market of outdoorswomen, who had been active outdoorspeople since the nineteenth century but for whom clothing and equipment were usually an afterthought. And the number of outdoor companies themselves was growing. These companies were founded by what historians of business have called "lead users"—expert participants at the leading edge of their sports, who helped to create new designs that matched their needs and commercialized them in companies, either as consultants or by starting their own companies. Yvon Chouinard and his companies Great Pacific Iron Works and Patagonia fit this model. So too did JanSport and Sierra Designs. The 1970s are often evoked as a golden age because people think of the decade as less corporate than it actually was.

Outdoorspeople, for their part, sought better equipment that solved immediate, pressing problems such as staying dry, and warm, on the trail. Synthetic materials, new creations from chemical companies, promised better protection from the weather. Readers flipping through the pages of popular magazines such as *Backpacker* or *Field and Stream* would have seen page after page about a "revolution" in materials. There were numerous technological changes, including internal-frame packs, dome tents with telescoping aluminum tent poles, freeze-dried food, and more that changed the practice of outdoor recreation.[1]

These new materials came at a high cost. Chemical companies, with a sense that the outdoors could be one among many end markets for their products, helped to commercialize synthetic waterproofing material and insulation in the 1970s. Lead users at Patagonia and its kin benefited from the R&D departments at chemical companies but did not craft or design this gear. Hence the equipment revolution proved less romantic and more corporate than golden age proponents would like to believe.

Outdoorspeople also began to make their own gear. Indeed, one of the biggest trends in the 1970s was sewing tents, jackets, and bags at home—but this trend was not like the craft era that preceded it. Do-it-yourself (DIY) kits, as they were called, were products of the corporate outdoors. Outdoor companies mass-produced these kits to sell to customers who were eager to have high-end performance gear at a lower cost. And the kits clearly spoke to the moment because they recognized women as outdoor consumers. Frostline—the most popular brand—and other companies provided budget-conscious outdoorspeople pre-cut fabrics and materials along with directions for how to assemble them. DIY kits have faded in popular memory, but they loom large for baby boomers who came of age with Frostline and similar kits in the 1970s. Do-it-yourself was not an anomaly in the progress of equipment: rather, it was a popular trend precisely because it combined older values that celebrated craft skill with the excitement surrounding new equipment.

Together, these trends constitute the maturation of the corporate outdoors. Although they were not the only important changes in design and technology, DIY kits and synthetic technical fibers like Gore-Tex together exemplify how the outdoor industry sold these new technologies and the ideas that accompanied them. Making use of phrases like "high-tech" and "space-age" to talk about everyday items, not just rockets, had begun decades earlier. In the outdoor realm, clothing that was scientifically designed and technologically sophisticated and that had its origins in World War II–era research laboratories peaked in the late 1970s.

In popular memory, the equipment revolution of the decade was centered around synthetics. Gore-Tex is still well known today. In fact, Frostline and the DIY kit imitators it inspired were a far bigger phenomenon than Gore-Tex. Consumers know Gore-Tex now, but Frostline's rise was central to the story of the corporate outdoors of the 1970s, as it captures both companies' approaches to growth and customers' relationship to new equipment and clothing during the revolutionary era. Remarkably, Gore-Tex initially proved a failure, whereas DIY was popular.

The braiding together of one of the biggest trends of the equipment revolution of the 1970s, which ultimately failed, and another trend that ultimately surpassed it shows the surprising evolution of the corporate outdoors. Do-it-yourself kits and technical synthetics like Gore-Tex juggled differently

the competing demands of effective and exclusive yet accessible and affordable outdoor gear. Consumers tended to either love or hate these new
trends, which speaks to how the outdoors as corporate big business played
out in Americans' lives and perceptions.

*

Colorado native Dale Johnson went on his first backpacking trip in the
summer of 1949 before he attended the University of Colorado. Johnson
and a buddy went to the Needle Mountains in the southwestern part of
the state and the equipment, he later recalled, was "terrible." Johnson carried a heavy surplus backpack, a cheap sleeping bag stuffed with a vegetable
fiber called kapok, and jars and cans full of trail food. His memory of
cold nights and uncomfortable days served him well as he began to work
in the outdoor industry after a few years as an engineer in midwestern oil-
fields. From his eight years of work with Gerry Cunningham at the Boulder-
based Gerry Mountain Sports, Johnson learned both the principles of
design and the outdoor customers' interest in making gear, and these
things inspired him to create the first DIY kits for outdoor clothing and
equipment.[2]

The earlier Gerry method entailed drawing out of graph paper the individual shapes that formed a parka, for example. Dimensions for curves and
deconstructed torsos were included on the graph paper so that consumers
could scale up as necessary. This was a prohibitively complicated process:
Adventurous home-sewers needed to buy individual pieces of material of
the correct weave and tear-strength—a simple process, but only if they knew
where to find the material. They needed to buy small sacks of goose down—
easy enough, as long as they knew how much down to buy and how to
keep it from wafting away in their living room. Of course, the method didn't
include nylon thread, buckles, D rings, rivets, and zippers, all available sep-
arately for purchase in the Gerry catalog. It was an ambitious plan for all but
the most expert sewers. Cunningham found that few customers wanted to
scale up tiny sketches onto butcher paper, cut them out, estimate how much
of each material was needed, find various shops to purchase the components and material, and then follow the directions, especially if using down
feathers that led to a "terrible mess." It was so difficult that Johnson, who

worked for Cunningham at the time, estimated that they sold only "seven or eight kits the whole time" they appeared in Gerry catalogs.[3]

But Cunningham was on to something. Making gear oneself had been a celebrated part of masculine outdoor culture for more than half a century. According to the woodcraft ethic, a *real* buckskin suit was one handmade by the wearer. Anything else was a costume. As the DIY culture became more widespread, making gear at home continued, although inspired by economic necessity as much as or more than the woodcraft ethic. Do-it-yourself remained especially important for those living distant from outdoor hubs with specialty stores. Bob Gore himself grew up going to Boy Scout camp with a homemade pack and sleeping bag, designed by his dad and sewn by his mom. Gerry Cunningham's business partner Margaret Hansson sewed sleeping bags for her kids' trip to the Grand Tetons. For aspiring outdoorspeople who couldn't afford the specialty goods at Holubar Mountaineering or REI, surplus was one option, and DIY the other.[4]

Dale Johnson found the answer to Cunningham's puzzle of how to scale up and commercialize DIY with kits that allowed consumers to skip many of the harder steps in the sewing process. While he commuted back and forth from his home in Boulder to an uninspiring bank job in Denver, Johnson sketched designs on his clipboard in the bus. His efforts to break down the individual elements of design and the steps necessary to make a jacket both simplified the process and made it accessible to a wide range of consumers who might have been intimidated by the labor required by the Gerry outdoor kits.[5]

The outdoor industry's DIY kits were part of a much larger trend in the 1970s that combined know-how with a new brand of consumer ethics: from food to housing to energy, DIY was a buzzword that represented frugality, American-made consumer goods, and individuality. The historian Andrew Case describes the Rodale Press's success marketing do-it-yourself books to gardeners and natural health enthusiasts. The success of Rodale magazines, books, and pamphlets, Case argues, was directly related to larger concerns about energy and the American economy. Publishers like Rodale "found they could recast organic living and homesteading as an energy-saving and frugal means of being self-sufficient in uncertain times."[6] Similarly, outdoor equipment and clothing companies capitalized on their customers' anxieties by offering hands-on interaction with the production process that mimicked self-sufficiency.

Frostline kits belonged to a broader DIY movement that dated to the early twentieth century, when homeowners—again with more time than money—embraced fix-it tasks around the house. With the dawn of companionate marriage and as daily office work required less physical exertion or skill, men were especially eager to perform masculine competence in domestic spaces. Do-it-yourself was a nostalgic performance of that male competence, as well as a contrast to sedentary office labor. In the postwar era, DIY culture was still largely associated with men. Magazines like *Popular Mechanics* published how-to guides for building things like toy boats or even pianos that taught craft skills as a part of recreation. For all their promise of ease and frugality, however, Frostline kits contained the same "jumble of contradictions" that historian Steven Gelber has described with other DIY projects: Kits seemed, at first, to be cheaper than ready-made goods, but hours invested in building skills and then sewing the kit often belied that assumption. It was hard work—not just leisure—especially for inexperienced sewers, though the manual dexterity it required often was a welcome contrast to their day jobs. Like piano kits, Frostline kits were not fully DIY, but hybrid objects that required both purchase and assembly. Like other postwar kits, Frostline kits were eventually mass-produced in factories with standardized fabric pieces and zipper pulls and down sleeves. But like other kits, Frostline nonetheless evoked feelings of self-satisfied independence.[7]

Within the realm of outdoor leisure, DIY kits seemed to imply a contrast to mass-produced goods. The label hearkened back to late nineteenth-century woodcraft—crafting what was necessary for survival from nature's storehouse. But as one historian has argued, DIY relied on industry—and on women's labor: fifty million women sewed at home in 1972.[8]

Johnson set up his business in his basement at 1965 Dartmouth Avenue in Boulder, a town with a number of thriving mail-order and local outdoor companies, in addition to Gerry. He called the company Frostline because "it sounded kind of outdoors and cold weatherish." He ordered in bulk—

one hundred yards of cloth, a twenty-five-pound bag of down. On evenings and weekends, Johnson would cut patterns from the cloth, stuff little bags of down feathers, and box up and mail customer orders. Frostline reduced work for the home sewer because the package included the required notions: "All they needed to supply was the sewing machine and the labor."[9]

Down vests, down-filled sleeping bags, and a rain parka were among Johnson's first products in 1966, and the ads Johnson ran in the *Sierra Club Bulletin* and *Backpacker* magazine emphasized cost savings—the Big Horn sleeping bag, which cost $49.95 for a complete kit, was "equal of most $75 to $95 down bags on the market." Of course, such a claim depended heavily on a competent kit user to sew it together and whether the labor of assembly exceeded the savings.[10]

Frostline grew quickly. As soon as Johnson thought the business could support him, he quit his bank job, although it meant a six-month period of daily work in the basement. Eventually, he sped up production by changing the scale of design: he learned to cut one hundred layers of fabric at once and hired someone to compile package orders into kits. By 1967, he had eight employees and had outgrown his home basement. Within a few years, Frostline catalogs offered down jackets, down pants, ponchos, rain gear, children's clothing, backpacks of all sizes, and tents. Ten years after starting the business, Frostline mailed 2.2 million catalogs annually.

Do-it-yourself kit producers like Dale Johnson hoped to attract the millions of men and women who participated in outdoor recreation after the late 1960s and early 1970s. The draw for these customers was high-quality yet affordable equipment and clothing, along with the benefit of clear directions and the possibility of customization. The ease of making a kit depended in part on the support a company offered. Frostline had a reputation for writing clear direction booklets, and as Frostline stores began to pop up nationwide, the company also offered in-store sewing assistance and a toll-free support line.

Recollections from DIY sewers and company ads suggest that more women than men sewed DIY kits and that the experience differed according to gender. Men, mostly young and single, sewed for themselves, while women sewed for themselves and their families. Women who made Frostline

When Kristi DuBois moved to Bozeman, Montana, she needed
an affordable mountain parka. DuBois sewed this Frostline parka
in 1976. (Photo courtesy of Kristi DuBois)

kits emphasized cost savings, while men focused on customization and craft.
Many of the women were seamstresses and hobbyists and delighted in giving
economical equipment to family members. Moms got assistance from their
children, who would help finish the garments by singeing the edge of the
nylon thread.[11]

Frostline inspired many competitors, and at its peak in the 1970s the DIY
trend yielded more than fifteen other companies, including Altra, Holubar,
Plain Brown Wrapper, Mountain Adventure, Eastern Mountain Sports,
Country Ways and Sun Down, Adventure 16, and REI. These companies,

which like Frostline often offered the kits at a major discount to similar products in ready-to-wear form, advertised them in a wide range of venues, including *Boys' Life, Backpacker* magazine, and the *Whole Earth Catalog*, as well as *Mademoiselle*, the *Country Gentleman, Popular Mechanics*, and *Pennsylvania Game News*. Frostline was the biggest, however, and by its own estimate it controlled 75 to 85 percent of the outerwear kit market. But they all belonged to the larger trend of home sewing, which was a $3 billion industry by 1973.[12]

The trajectory of one company, Altra, illustrates that DIY was, perhaps counterintuitively, part of the corporatization of the outdoor industry. Frostline's expansion throughout the West convinced a young Jon Hinebauch to pursue selling DIY kits. Hinebauch's MBA got him hired by General Recreation, a conglomerate of outdoor companies. After its first choice didn't work out, General Recreation sent Hinebauch from Ithaca to Boulder to run Alpine Designs, originally Alp Sport. When General Recreation wanted to send him to another company away from Boulder in 1975, Hinebauch—inspired by Frostline as well as Holubar Mountaineering's expansion into the kit business—instead decided to build a company, which he called Altra, to market to retail stores. Building off Hinebauch's and Alp Sport founder George Lamb's personal networks of outdoor stores in "every college town in the country," Altra quickly entered into competition with Frostline, Holubar, and other kit companies. The vision was to sell at-home craft, the art of doing things for yourself, at a mass scale.[13]

While General Recreation's $30 million in sales in 1974 seemed like a wild success, another soon-to-be-launched company was taking a much longer and more ambitious approach.

✳

The path from the establishment of the chemical company W. L. Gore to the creation of Gore-Tex, a well-known waterproof, breathable material used in outdoor clothing and equipment, was long and winding. The Gore family's goal was not primarily to get into the business of outdoor gear but to find commercial applications for the unique qualities of polytetrafluoroethylene (PTFE), a plastic polymer on which Gore was founded. Like Dale Johnson's early years at Frostline, father and son Bill and Bob Gore tinkered with their product at home and on vacations to find better end uses. The difference was that they were professionally trained chemical engineers, and had the financial backing of a chemical company that had already succeeded in the industrial and medical fields, so they didn't have the financial imperative to make an immediate success of their technology, as Johnson did.[14]

The invention and marketing of Gore-Tex and its synthetic fiber cousins reveal the consequence of so-called miracle materials both for American closets and conceptions of nature. Chemical companies and consumers together built a new outdoor tradition. Experts gradually began to recommend synthetic fibers—polymers of petrochemicals, created by scientists in laboratories to mimic or improve upon natural fibers—as the best (albeit ironic) choice for getting back to nature. Between 1970 and the mid-1980s, man-made films, filaments, and fibers replaced plant-based fibers as the most desirable raw material for fabrics in everything from socks to sleeping bags. From polypropylene long underwear to polyester fleece jackets to Gore-Tex rain protection, synthetic clothing and equipment received rave reviews and a mass following in outdoor sports.[15]

The seemingly separate—even antithetical—worlds of chemical engineering and outdoor recreation converged in this era with one man, Wilbert L. Gore. Long before Bill, as he was known, became the CEO of the chemical company that invented Gore-Tex, he was an outdoor gear enthusiast. Bill was a mountain climber and skier in the early 1930s. Along with his future wife, Vieve, he got a job as a "demonstrator skier" at Jackson Hole, Wyoming. Demonstrator skiers climbed up mountains and skied down "just to show it could be done," he remembered. Skiing was hardly a profession, though, so Gore's study of physical chemistry and chemical engineering at the University of Utah determined his next steps. In 1945, after a stint as a chemical engineer for the American Smelting and Refining Company, Gore became a chemical engineer at the chemical giant DuPont. DuPont's major postwar product was synthetic chemicals. First nylon and then a long list of other new chemicals promised "better living through chemistry." Gore later transferred to the plastics division at DuPont, where he experimented with PTFE. This material would first be known popularly as Teflon cookware and later as the chemical base for Gore-Tex. Gore enjoyed his chemical engineering work at DuPont but was not content to leave his outdoor interests behind.[16]

On the weekends, Gore liked to experiment with building better camping equipment using the materials from his workweek and sharing those inventions with his family of five children. Much like Gerry Cunningham and backpack designer Richard Kelty, Gore was a basement tinkerer, and his professional training helped him access special materials for his experiments. In 1945, for example, Gore ordered coated nylon from the Cordo Chemical Company so he could experiment on inflatable sleeping mats for camping. To seal seams, he also ordered a special solution.[17]

Over the next decade, Bill, Vieve, and their five children experienced this camping test equipment firsthand as they took it to camp or on family trips. Bill Gore and his son Bob experimented with ventilation challenges in one of Bill's ventures in the late 1940s. Bill made a transparent plastic tent so that he and his son could see the stars at night together while camping in the Utah mountains. As it turned out, the tent created a bonding experience of a different kind: the tent walls were impermeable to water vapor. Bob later remembered that "[i]t was as hot as a greenhouse in the sun during the day, and at night the moisture from our breath condensed on the impervious walls of the tent, making them less than transparent. As the moisture collected into droplets, it would run down onto our sleeping bags[,] making things pretty soggy." As a kid, Bob might not have had the language to call this process "condensation," but he certainly registered the imperfect sleeping arrangements. Bob Gore had learned what generations of people who lived and played outdoors knew through experience: bodies exude moisture and need materials that allow moisture to escape.[18]

Ventilation offered the solution. Any item of clothing that was meant to thermally protect the body from cold should ideally transport humidity from the inside to the outside, from the body to the surroundings. Popular outdoors materials like wool and cotton/nylon blends let sweat vapor escape when a person was active and moving. These materials could be water-resistant, but never fully waterproof. The rain from outside eventually soaked in. Conversely, a wholly impermeable rain jacket made of rubber- or polyurethane-coated nylon kept the rain completely off the body, but sealed in the body so that a teakettle's worth of sweat built up underneath.[19]

Like many outdoorspeople, the Gores knew that the consequences of non-ventilating insulation could be far worse than an uncomfortable night's sleep. Headlines reporting on deaths from hypothermia indicated that the problem was not bad weather but bad clothing. Outdoor columnist Nelson Bryant explained that how a trip "turns out depends almost entirely on whether you are knowledgeable enough to dress properly for the weather." Narratives of deaths and near misses on the trail often began with ominous references to inadequate clothing and seemingly good conditions: "It was a sunny, 40-degree day. She was dressed in jeans and a T-shirt." In this case, all it took was a heavy wind and a sudden bout of rain: "She began to shiver violently and stumble. Her speech slurred." This woman was out for a jog in a New England city, so friends and shelter were nearby and she survived her hypothermic symptoms. But newspapers often ran stories about the "Outdoor Killer" in the wilderness: "4 Dead Hikers Were Lightly Dressed," read one headline. "Carelessness Keeps Rescue Teams Busy," read another. Insulation and protection from rain was the "key defense" against this "No. 1 killer of outdoor recreationists."[20]

Bill Gore and his son were part of a professional and recreational milieu that understood the need for a fiber that would simultaneously insulate and ventilate. The elder Gore saw the possibility of solving some problems of the outdoor body with the singular product PTFE. When DuPont declined to pursue a new application of PTFE, Gore left to start his own company. He started W. L. Gore & Associates in 1958 in his Delaware basement to pursue new PTFE applications.[21]

When Bob Gore joined his father's company in 1963, the firm had already successfully used PTFE in a range of applications. With the exception of Teflon, PTFE remained an industrial plastic, rather than something consumers would find on a shelf. It was hydrophobic, so it repelled water, and nonreactive, which made it useful for pipes, wiring, industrial seals, and other places with the potential for contact with reactive materials. NASA used PTFE fibers on the outermost layer of the Apollo space suit. Bob Gore's task was to find new applications of the same material.[22]

It would be simplistic to draw a direct line from the impermeable plastic tent in the Utah mountains that failed to keep Bill and Bob Gore dry to the invention of Gore-Tex. Years of education and experience at DuPont happened between the first moment and the second. Nonetheless, memories of his father's failed experiments remained prominent in Bob's mind as he imagined what a miracle material might accomplish. His experience outdoors shaped part of his lab agenda.[23]

In 1969, Bob Gore wanted to make PTFE cheaper, and use it in textiles. The best way to do that, he found, was stretching it. Day after day in the lab, he heated an oven full of thin white cords of PTFE, hoping to stretch them about 10 percent. Wearing thick oven mitts, he carefully pulled the cords apart. The PTFE kept breaking. One evening, as Gore retold the story over the following years, he got so fed up that he yanked a cord out of frustration. When he pulled quickly, he was surprised to find the PTFE cord "stretched the full length of [his] two outstretched arms"—an amazingly expanded PTFE. The next morning, Bob called his father in to see how the extruded material expanded when stretched, and they both recognized it was the future path of the company.[24]

Plastics World, the trade magazine of the plastics industry, announced the next year that expanded polytetrafluoroethylene (ePTFE) was "a whole new ball game." It could be made in yarn or fabric, films and sheeting, core insulators for cables, and tubes of all sizes. The new structure of ePTFE—it was 70 percent air—allowed great control over the porosity of the material. Under a microscope, ePTFE looked like a maze of webbing. The semipermeability of the pores, along with the hydrophobicity (it repulsed water) that had characterized PTFE all along, made the development of new products promising. With Bob's discovery of ePTFE, a rain jacket or tent that ventilated and shed water finally seemed possible.[25]

As early as 1970, Gore announced its ventures into textile fibers and rainwear fabrics using the lattice-structured ePTFE. Ever the experimenters, Bill and Vieve took a prototype tent on their annual Wyoming camping trip the same year. Vieve Gore had sewn patches of ePTFE on the outside of the tent. Recalling Bill Gore's tent experiment decades earlier, this trip did not go as planned. A storm brought hail and then rain. As Vieve remembered, hail tore through the patches of ePTFE, leaving their sleeping bags "sopping" from rain that entered the tent through the holes. Nonetheless, Bill Gore saw the

THE FORCE BEHIND THE DREAM

Bill & Vieve Gore

Bill Gore is an entrepreneur.

In 1958, with two of their five children in college, he left a challenging job at the Du Pont Company to pursue a dream. Working in the basement of his home with the aid of his wife Vieve and son Bob, Bill developed materials that would one day pioneer new frontiers of modern technology.

For outdoor people like Bill and Vieve — who've spent years backpacking from the Tetons to the Himalayas—his work meant a truly waterproof and breathable fabric, fulfilling a need felt by serious outdoorsmen for decades.

For the medical profession it meant artificial arteries and other devices that could save a limb—or a life. Their work also created air cleansing filters to eliminate pollution and electronic components widely used in computers, satellites and other phases of telecommunication.

In 1971, Bill received an honorary Ph.D. in the humanities for his progressive personnel programs. As a prominent physical chemist, with 13 U.S. patents to his name, Bill has remained intensely involved in all facets of the business, from the testing of new shoe constructions to the development of a progressive new heart valve. Through it all, Vieve, as an officer and director, has worked side by side with Bill, guiding the business.

Brilliant, unorthodox, innovative, compassionate... Bill and Vieve Gore. An Inspiration to Us All.

GORE-TEX®
fabrics

Bill and Vieve Gore took Gore-Tex prototype equipment with them on family backpacking trips. (Copyright 1982, W. L. Gore & Associates, Inc. Reprinted with permission. All rights reserved. GORE, GORE-TEX, and designs are trademarks of W. L. Gore & Associates) promise of an ePTFE textile in that initial field test: the tent held water "like a bathtub," which made it clear that the Gore company textile—coined Gore-Tex—was waterproof. Gore-Tex films were quite thin, but laminating them to the inside of fabrics, rather than the outside, increased the strength of the material and gave it a wide range of outdoor applications.[26]

The first direction the company pursued was not recreational but military. Gore sent an early prototype of the fabric, a nylon-ePTFE-nylon sandwich, to the U.S. military's testing facilities at Natick in 1973, where it was evaluated alongside current and potential wet-weather parka materials. Bill Gore had long thought that "the ideal target [for Gore-Tex] was the soldier" because the fabric could offer comfort as "an integral part of an efficient military operation." The laminate, which allowed moisture vapor to permeate, was evaluated as one of the "best candidates for wet weather suits" by Ralph Goldman, the director of the Military Ergonomics Laboratory in Natick, Massachusetts. Despite this enthusiastic endorsement from a merchant of comfort, the military never moved the material past copper manikin evaluations into the next set of physiologic chamber trials. With the military sector uninterested, Gore decided to pursue the consumer industry.[27]

When Gore made the pivot to consumers, the company structure had supported more than a decade of research and development on what eventually became Gore-Tex. The material came of age around the same time as other synthetics with outdoor applications from chemical companies such as 3M and DuPont.[28]

The first commercial product made with Gore-Tex came out in 1976, seven years after Bob Gore learned to stretch cords of PTFE. Early Winters, an outdoor company in Seattle, introduced the Gore-Tex tent in May 1976. The Light Dimension was "an instant hit," according to Early Winters. The company followed up within a year with rainwear and sleeping bags also made with Gore-Tex laminate. By 1977, many other outdoor companies, including Marmot, from Grand Junction, Colorado; and Banana Equipment, from Estes Park, Colorado, produced tents, sleeping bags, and jackets made with nylon and a layer of Gore-Tex laminated to it.[29]

Soon after its introduction, equipment reviewers and consumers alike "duly proclaimed [Gore-Tex] the Holy Grail." Ads in 1976 extolled

Gore-Tex as a "revolutionary new fabric" that kept rain out but allowed sweat to escape.[30]

Why choose a Gore-Tex jacket over a similar-looking one at half the cost? Shiny gold hangtags attached to the garments educated consumers with diagrams and technical images that used infrared heat or micrograph photography to zoom in on how a fiber worked. Logos, diagrams, and trademarks were seductive—at least until a potential customer flipped another tag over and saw the price. How could this be worth it? As Gore-Tex strategized, however, the premium price itself boosted the product's status. Bill Gore espoused a philosophy of "value pricing," by which he meant pricing products based on their worth in the marketplace rather than on how much they cost to manufacture. Yes, Gore-Tex laminate required decades of experimentation and investment, but the high price was more about creating a sense of status, exclusivity, and performance.[31]

Remarkably, the ingredient branding programs worked. Outdoor enthusiasts really did sit down and read technical ads. Gore's strategy was to educate both in specific outdoor markets—advertising in *Backpacker, Outside, Skiing,* and *Bicycling* magazines, for example—and in publications that reached a broader audience, such as *Vogue, Esquire,* and the *New Yorker.* These technical ads challenged common-sense ideas, such as the bulk-equals-warmth myth targeted by Thinsulate ads, for instance. With a new vocabulary and a new method for perceiving comfort as a function of performance, American consumers were well armed for the outdoors not just with stiff, even squeaky new jackets but also with the understanding that these new jacket technologies were necessary components of the "right way" to do the outdoor experience.[32]

Gore-Tex is just one example of the many new fibers chemical companies promoted as miracle materials in the 1970s. Although each fiber followed its own thread from discovery to market, many followed the same timeline. Embedded in scientific journals such as *Textile Organon* were stories of fibers invented in the 1950s and modified in the 1970s, as fiber producers with high capital investment costs sought markets. A few became specialty high-performance fibers well known to consumers—in addition to Gore-Tex, for example, was the aromatic polyamide Kevlar. Two other mir-

Outdoor consumers learned about the technical performance of otherwise-invisible synthetics like Gore-Tex by reading advertisements and hangtags. (Copyright 1984, W. L. Gore & Associates, Inc. Reprinted with permission. All rights reserved. GORE, GORE-TEX, and designs are trademarks of W. L. Gore & Associates)

181

acle materials from the same time that also challenged scientists to sell in new ways to a consuming public were polypropylene, from the olefin family of fibers, and fiberfill, from polyester. The revolution in outdoor fabrics promised new luxuries: sleeping bags that would still work when wet; long underwear that would not absorb water; and rain jackets that would prevent condensation from forming underneath. By the mid-1980s, an alphabet soup of trademarked goods dominated outdoorspeople's packing lists, such as DuPont's Hollofil, Quallofil, and Sontique polyester fiberfill insulation and 3M's Thinsulate insulation. Like DuPont and 3M, Gore had no stores and, indeed, no consumer products. It was just a material, and its contracts with manufacturers such as Frostline, the North Face, or Early Winters relied on its reputation with and appeal to consumers. This new world of gear was so complicated that guidebooks recommended that readers make a "schedule of purchases" to prioritize when to buy the necessary, but expensive, new goods.[33]

Despite the celebration of the "Holy Grail" at Gore-Tex's arrival, the first-generation laminate was a failure. The company had promised more than this experimental material could deliver. The reviews for Gore-Tex trickled in, and—as they explained—so too did water through this supposedly waterproof material. Reviews conceded that Gore-Tex was nearly perfect in a laboratory setting, and showed promise in the field, but, among other examples, the founder of Early Winters, the first company to use the Gore-Tex laminate in its products, reported that in the first few years, jackets "were being returned . . . like crazy." Richard Kelty, the founder of Kelty packs, said that the company had "horrible luck with the original Gore-Tex." One equipment columnist reported that members of a sailing team, fed up with their free and supposedly waterproof Gore-Tex rainsuits, actually threw their garments into the ocean after a race. Part of the issue was that the original Gore-Tex laminate didn't deal well with salt water. Other contaminants, such as body oils and insect repellents, also seemed to cause leaks. The first-generation rainsuits required lots of care and washing.

The seams were another major issue. Like any other rain jacket, Gore-Tex garments had seams, and the needle would leave tiny holes as the thread stitched the pieces together. This was a standard problem in the industry. To address the problem, when Frostline began selling Gore-Tex rain jackets in 1978 or 1979—a steal at $51.95 for a kit compared with $90 to $100 for a ready-made jacket—it came with seam sealant. The sealant, called Seam-Stuff, was produced and sold by Gore. Users would trail a line of the clear goo along the seams, smear it with their fingers and wait for it to dry and plug up the holes. The expectation that users would need to do some waterproofing at home was not unique to Gore-Tex jackets but true for most outdoor gear.[34]

Steve Shuster, who began working for Gore as a research chemist in the early 1980s, called this approach "aesthetically horrific." The seam holes might not have mattered in city clothes, since few urban people planned to stay out in the rain for extended periods of time. However, when a garment's whole raison d'être was microscopic holes that keep water out while letting sweat escape, the comparatively huge holes caused by needles were a glaring problem.[35]

For people hoping for a miracle fabric, leaky seams were serious, especially when outfitting companies started blaming consumers for imperfections in the expensive garments. Orvis, an outdoor outfitter that sold Gore-Tex products, blamed careless do-it-yourselfers when the sealant they would apply along each seam at the start of every season didn't work. Orvis sales manager Donald Owens claimed that "most returns either weren't sealed by the owner or weren't sealed properly." Even the guidebook author Colin Fletcher remembered that hikers "botched" the seam-sealing when they tried to do it at home. With seams still leaking, Gore-Tex was not enough of a miracle to end the wet bodies problem. *Backpacker* equipment evaluator David Sumner wrote that a July thunderstorm in the Rockies put his rainsuit to the test, and it performed only adequately. "There was some leakage through the seams, which I'd sealed only once. I was rock scrambling and did perspire a bit, but," he conceded, "I would have sweated like a pig wearing the coated rain gear I'm used to."[36]

Despite the leaking, Gore-Tex found an enthusiastic group of boosters who applauded not just its function but its style. Even two years after its introduction to the commercial market, people beyond the "mountain-club fraternity" were talking Gore-Tex. Wealthy customers were often equated with extreme users, and this connection gave them more status by suggesting that they were true athletes and adventurers. Gore-Tex was for the "BMW set," a competitor explained, with high prices to go with it. According to Peter Gilson, the manager of Gore's fabric division, Gore-Tex sought the tip of the triangle of users: not casual joggers who run because it is a fad, but the serious ones—all seven million of them—who put in more than twenty miles a week, no matter the weather.[37]

That Gore-Tex weathered this initial storm had everything to do with its commitment to the corporate outdoors.

✳

While Gore struggled, the DIY kit industry thrived. Frostline founder Dale Johnson had worked for Gerry Cunningham and was part of the Boulder outdoor community, whereas Gore was outside all of that—geographically but also professionally removed. It seemed the future of the outdoors pointed more toward DIY than Gore-Tex.

DIY kits were so popular and profitable that multiple companies wanted to buy Frostline. Dale Johnson fielded inquiries from the Greyhound Bus Company and Southland Life Insurance, and ultimately went with the Gillette Corporation. Gillette bought Frostline in 1978 for just under $6.5 million. Gillette's goal was diversification, especially by having access to Frostline's mail-order sales. For similar reasons, Johnson Wax bought Holubar (and it already owned Camp Trails and Eureka).[38]

These buyouts were part of a larger trend, and seemed to cement DIY kits as a central part of the outdoor industry. Maurice Pomeranz explained in a *Backpacker* article in 1974 that companies securing a piece of industry success included General Mills (Eddie Bauer), the Olin Corporation (Comfy, Trail Blazer, and Seattle Quilt), Fuqua (Mountain Products Corporation), Cummins engine (JanSport), and Warnaco (White Stag). In all, Pomeranz tallied $400 million in backpacking equipment and clothing sales, a small percentage of these corporations whose business totaled nearly $6 billion.[39]

Despite the initial failures of Gore-Tex, Gore's corporate strength was building, and Gore leaned on that slow build and the laboratory research made possible only by his decades of experience in chemical engineering.

The company could invest time into research and development and potential commercial applications with no guarantee of success because it already had markets in industrial and medical applications. Gore-Tex first turned a profit in 1979, a full decade after Bob Gore made ePTFE. This was due to the expense of raw polymers and the slow production of the Gore-Tex laminate, as well as problems with the initial Gore-Tex run. Gore was a $100 million dollar company, even without Gore-Tex's profit, so its slow path to profitability had little impact on the company.[40]

Gore-Tex gained momentum in the years that followed thanks to technical improvements, the spread of technical knowledge through the advertising the company had initiated, and the cultural resonance of technical performance wear as a popular style. Second-generation Gore-Tex was less squeaky and stiff and could be laminated to a wider range of fabrics. Gore also allowed returns of first-generation Gore-Tex, worth nearly $4 million, which was possible only because the company could weather the hit financially. Finally, by the early 1980s, lessons about comfort as something that fabrics and fibers should actively provide had settled into popular consciousness. Consumers believed that synthetics offered a marked improvement in "adjustment for weather changes and exertion level." Compared with older surplus-style parkas, for example, Gore-Tex jackets were "easy to put on and take off, with plenty of flaps and zippers for ventilation." This was important because it could extend the temperature range and length of time spent outdoors. In boating, for example, outdoor reporters recalled the leaky wet-weather gear that "retained perspiration and wetness." New synthetics were an "unparalleled success" for the sport, allowing moisture to be wicked away.[41]

Another technical change in the manufacturing of products with Gore-Tex signaled the slow demise of the DIY era. This shift began in 1979 when outdoor manufacturers started to seal the seams in-factory with a seven-eighths-inch-wide tape welded "onto sewn seams with hot air and pressure." This small change in production marked a larger shift: outfitting companies no longer assumed that customers had the skill or the equipment to modify their clothes at home. The shift away from consumer participation had begun. Home-sealed garments started to look "as if snails have crawled all over it," both unprofessional and unfashionable. Colin Fletcher assured his readers that "no hand-sealing seems as effective as the factory job with tape."[42]

Many large outdoor outfitters, including Early Winters, L. L. Bean, REI, Patagonia, and the North Face, contracted with Gore-Tex in the early years. Gore sold the laminate to select manufacturers that rented the seam-sealing machines from a chemical company. Gore wanted to maintain its fiber's reputation, so the firm likely stopped selling Gore-Tex to kit companies within a few years of the introduction of the seam-sealing machines. Companies like Frostline started to seem "dated and behind the times." A Frostline Gore-Tex Parka kit in 1981 was $69.95, still a significant discount compared with the $114.95 for a sewn parka, but the kit included seamsealer, by 1981 a clear indication that a home-sewn parka would not live up to the standard Gore had set with its factory-sealed seams.[43]

The seam-sealing shift connoted a larger shift in attitude: homemade goods were not just inferior, but also a problem. As one former gear company owner asked, "Do you really want to climb Denali with a tent you sewed yourself?" Popular features on outdoor equipment echoed this attitude. One article offering tips on dressing for cold argued that "store-bought outfits are far better than home fashions" because of performance features. Gore-Tex and the suite of synthetics that accompanied it in the mid- to late 1970s replaced at-home sewing kits as emblems of how to get back to nature "the right way"—the corporate outdoors way. Lower-cost, long-lasting craft projects could not compete with expensive, branded, off-the-rack technologies. DIY kits could not be high-tech, which meant their performance characteristics were suspect, too.[44]

The decline of DIY kits by the 1980s reflects not only technical changes but also broad social and economic transformations in the industry, to say nothing of the demise of the earlier woodsman ethic of crafting as a measure of authenticity and expertise. These kits straddled the earlier woodcraft approach and the corporate outdoors. Frostline kits did not seem as cost effective, and customers were less willing to spend leisure time sewing the kits. New materials made outdoorspeople less interested in sewing for themselves what they could purchase new. And many of the customers who at twenty or twenty-five could not afford a ready-to-wear item were willing and able to pay more for a down sleeping bag by the time they reached their thirties.

At Frostline, still the biggest of the outdoor DIY kit companies, Johnson witnessed the industry's quick decline. Johnson's sale in 1976 to Gillette was good timing: American companies moved production to Southeast Asia at the end of the 1970s and started selling finished products for prices that equaled or beat the DIY kit prices. After three unprofitable years, Gillette liquidated Frostline. At the same time, sales of Gore-Tex reached an estimated $250 million, far outpacing the struggling DIY kit companies and even matching the sales of the biggest outdoor company in the business, L. L. Bean. The 1970s might have begun as the decade of DIY kits, but ended as the decade of the corporate outdoors, and Gore-Tex.[45]

By the mid-1980s, even marketers whose job it was to promote the DIY kit had to face reality: it had failed commercially. Lou Barnes, a former marketing manager for the kit company Holubar, suggested that by the 1980s, any male who expected his wife to sew a kit for him was "road kill." Owing to the wild success of women's liberation movements, Barnes suggested, piles of "unsewn kits still sit in attics." Other Frostline customers explained that they simply got distracted. As a cyclist and proud owner of an unsewn dark green Frostline kit explained in 1994, more than a decade after Frostline was liquidated, "I just never got around to it."[46]

The broader shift away from DIY culture cannot be attributed solely to liberated women who refused to sew for their husbands, the competitive pricing of vests made in China, or the rise of synthetics like Gore-Tex. The DIY movement in outdoor recreation was also upended by new ideas about American consumer culture. That fifty million women who sewed in 1973 decided within a decade that they didn't want to coincided with the rise of a status culture focused on brands and bodily performance. A product made with Gore-Tex signaled not only wealth and status, but something equally important: an active body. Fitness, activity, performance—these were values to be achieved, and a brand-name piece of clothing helped get people there. This brand popularity is evident on the bottom line: after a decade of tepid earnings, sales of Gore-Tex totaled $50 million in 1985.[47]

For the outdoor writer Nelson Bryant, the equipment revolution proved a revelation. In 1982, in his column on the outdoors for the *New York Times*, Bryant wrote that "it is much easier to keep warm outdoors in cold weather than it was a decade or more ago." In his writing on hunting, fishing, and camping over the course of four decades, Bryant often recalled his days in the army during World War II, shivering through the Battle of the Bulge in trousers, wool shirts, and a "monstrous heavy" wool army overcoat. After the war he could afford no better than army surplus and scarcely knew of more specialized clothing. Bryant, like so many outdoor athletes of the 1970s and 1980s who could remember the years before Gore-Tex, was especially pleased that "neophytes" could have access to comfort, safety, and performance as readily as experts—as long as they could afford the new products. For him, the "continuing improvement" of the equipment revolution had made "what was often an ordeal into pleasure."[48]

The technology trickled down from sportswear into everyday wear. Gore-Tex's entrance in the public lexicon could be dated to 1994. That year, the hit television series *Seinfeld* made a Gore-Tex jacket part of a punch line. The character George wears a large Gore-Tex coat because of the cold weather and is eager to talk about it. He shows it off to his friends indoors, looking a little silly because the shiny green jacket is so puffy he can hardly put his arms down. "What is *that?*" Elaine asks him. "It's Gore-Tex," he says with a smarmy look on his face. "You know about Gore-Tex?" On the surface, the joke is that he is ridiculously over-equipped, looking like a Michelin man when he is simply heading out to dinner in New York City. But there is a different joke at play for viewers who grasp exactly what the Gore-Tex laminate was and is. The jacket cannot be made of Gore-Tex because Gore-Tex is an ingredient, only ever used when bonded to another fabric out of which the clothing is made. And the jacket looks silly not because it's waterproof and breathable but because it's puffy and filled with down. The joke, then, is about consumers who bandy about technical terms without fully knowing what they mean. George loves to say, "It's Gore-Tex," but doesn't actually understand what Gore-Tex does.[49]

Critics of Gore-Tex and other high-tech materials still existed, and still warned about the safety of less experienced backpackers. Mountaineer Lou Whittaker warned novices against "taking too literally the abundant claims that Gore-Tex will keep them dry" and told of being "called on to carry people off the mountain who thought their raingear could perform miracles."

Gore-Tex may have been breathable, said Early Winters founder Bill Nicolai, but it was "not an antiperspirant." Whittaker warned that "no raingear will keep you dry in the mountains unless you know how to function." They were not saying that Gore-Tex was ineffective, but that consumers needed to know principles of body heat transfer and layering to use the material properly. However, these expert voices of the previous generation were often drowned out by the overwhelming marketing campaigns meant to convince potential customers that the newest stuff could help them perform, or create an aura of high performance.[50]

To other critics, Gore-Tex worked well enough but was still an environmental issue. In the 1970s, living with chemistry could sound more like a threat than a celebration. After all, audiences watching *The Graduate* in 1967 sensed the distaste in the recommendation to Benjamin Braddock that his future was in "plastics." Popular environmental consciousness since Rachel Carson's *Silent Spring* made Americans question more and more the health impacts of what they ate, breathed, and put near their bodies. The guidebook author Harvey Manning privately shared concerns about the equipment revolution: "I'm appalled at the industry and ingenuity of Science. Since the last edition it has produced such a bundle of miracles that no wonder we're running out of oil and money. Gore-Tex. Pile. Thinsulate, for Chrissake." Publicly, though, Manning's hefty guide to backpacking equipment dedicated scores of pages to these technologies.[51]

A final type of critique had little to do with the material function or composition of Gore-Tex and more to do with the changes it brought to outdoor culture. One effect of the synthetic revolution was that men who had adhered to the practices and beliefs of the Khaki Gang era felt they had lost part of the exclusivity of their identity. Ward Irwin, a longtime REI member, and other self-labeled outdoor purists like Earl Shaffer of the first Appalachian Trail thru-hike were skeptical about the abandonment of army surplus gear for the latest in technology. Irwin complained in a letter about REI in the 1980s: "new and stylish colors; synthetics; pile and high tech insulation; GorTex (Bah!)." Irwin and the Khaki Gang looked back and saw earlier traditions that seemed more authentically tough, less based on gadgets and more based on pure performance. In the pre-synthetic days, a

World War II veteran and his sons "made do with layers of cotton and wool," and despite suffering "occasionally," "there was never any frostbite or hypothermia." Each generation constructed its own boundaries on gear improvements and dangers. Gore-Tex, with its high-ticket price and conspicuous logos, was certainly not about "making do."[52]

Hierarchies of outdoor recreation meant packing a bag heavy with morals, admonitions, and warnings about the right way to go back to nature. Using the cultural reference points of his era—guidebooks, peer advice, and his own experience—Irwin had mastered his generation's craft of hiking: where to go, what to wear, what to bring, and how his body should enjoy the delights of nature and suffer through its less hospitable impositions. But chemical companies' technical advertisements, guidebooks, and equipment catalogs spoke for the values of the next generation. The badges, hallmarks, and material manifestations of the niche culture's "insider" vocabulary were evolving rapidly. Irwin may have dismissed Gore-Tex, but the material was still available in REI catalogs—and, judging from the trail traffic, widely popular.

✳

The Adirondack Museum and Library, nestled in the side of a mountain in the village of Blue Mountain Lake, New York, upgraded its exhibit about Americans and their outdoor recreation practices at the end of the millennium. The mannequin Apple Annie, so named for the apple she held in her hand, had worn a typical outfit of the 1970s outdoors: an L. L. Bean plaid shirt and jeans, both made of cotton, which had come to appear obsolete to recent visitors who had grown up in an age of synthetic wilderness apparel. To anyone who read a how-to guide to the outdoors published after 1975, natural fibers were increasingly suspect. These guides argued that new innovations from chemical companies like DuPont, 3M, and Gore offered the best chance at comfort, safety, and high performance.[53]

Not even a plastic mannequin could escape criticism. Visitors to the exhibit believed so deeply in synthetic fibers as the right way to dress for the wild that they asked the museum to change the exhibit. Sue Whitcomb, writing in 1998, asked if the mannequin's clothes could be updated to non-cotton. Whitcomb suggested that the way Apple Annie was dressed made

The original Apple Annie from the Woods and Waters exhibit at Adirondack Experience donned heavy boots, blue jeans, and a plaid cotton shirt from L. L. Bean. (Courtesy of Adirondack Experience)

the exhibit "less authentic" because her clothes represented the outdoors of the past rather than of today. A group of students from a nearby college had similar suggestions a couple of years later. Cotton "can be a lethal material in a wilderness setting," they wrote. The students proposed to update the exhibit and accompanying sign on display as a part of a school project. They sought equipment donations from nearby specialty stores, including Eastern Mountain Sports.[54]

The updated Apple Annie wore high-tech synthetics. As the new sign accompanying the display explained, "Advancements in fiber technology created new fabrics such as nylon, Dacron polyester, Gore-Tex, synthetic fleece, and polypropylene, which are light and strong, repel water, retain body heat, and allow for increased safety and comfort outdoors." It was almost as if the technical advertisements were speaking through them in the

Adirondack Experience visitors asked that Apple Annie change her outfit to include more "authentic" synthetic materials that characterized late twentieth-century outdoor wear. (Photo by author, 2013)

students' praise for high-tech synthetics. Synthetic chemical manufacturers had clearly influenced Americans' conceptions of the "authentic" outdoor experience, goading it, paradoxically, toward synthetics, polymers, and the corporate outdoors that produced and sold these high-tech "authentic" garments.[55]

"Cotton kills" was repeated as if it were ancient wisdom in outdoor guidebooks for fishing, Boy Scout handbooks, *Backpacker* magazine, and even *Travel and Leisure* magazine. Yet the notion had saturated popular consciousness with widespread education (advertisements, mostly) about synthetics during the 1970s and 1980s. Before that, jeans were deemed perfectly acceptable, if slightly uncomfortable, attire.

"Cotton kills" suggested another change in outdoor recreation: old or homemade clothes would no longer do and, the catchphrase implied, could be deadly. With the equipment and synthetics revolution, the cutting edge replaced the home-crafted as the epitome of outdoor culture "the right way." Successions of new technology replaced old ones, and even participation in the conversation and reviews of the new technology—how waterproof is it, does it work, is it lighter—moved outdoor culture toward the idea that newer, rather than traditional and crafted, is better.

By the 1980s, the outdoor industry had reached previously unimaginable heights. It was more corporate, more scientifically oriented, and more stylish than company founders of the late 1960s would have ever thought possible. Conglomerates focused more specifically on portfolios of outdoor clothing and equipment brands, like American Recreation Products, and the practices of testing materials and clothing as a science spread to other outdoor companies. Finally, as newspaper reports suggested, corporate-run manufacturers of technology were riding a fashion wave. Gore-Tex, and its many siblings, were not just functional outdoor gear by the 1980s but also stylish indoor, urban fashion. For the company founders who started their work in family basements selling to friends, the industry structure and its products, and their popularity, would have been confounding—and that profitability and popularity had only begun to take off.[56]

NINE

Bean Boots and Puffy Jackets

Lifestyle and America's Outdoor Heritage

Abercrombie & Fitch, the storied outdoor outfitter of the first half of the twentieth century, remained financially successful through the heyday of outdoor recreation. The company boasted retail branches in big cities around the country as well as a robust catalog. In 1968, sales peaked at $28 million. The headquarters, still in Manhattan at 45th and Madison Avenue, was a "mecca of affluent sportsmen" with its log cabin on the roof and floors of novelty items like mini Ferraris and dogsleds. Yet in the early 1970s, the store's sales declined as sportsmen increasingly turned to more affordable and newer brands for sportswear. In New York City, wealthy customers left for the suburbs, while in the city Abercrombie & Fitch increasingly had to compete with local stores like Paragon Sports and army surplus stores in addition to mail-order outfits. By the mid-1970s Abercrombie's paradoxical outdoor consumer opulence—selling gold-and-onyx chess sets for $18,000 or custom-made rifles for $6,000—no longer made sense. The company was $1 million in the red in 1975, and it declared bankruptcy in 1976.[1]

What was once a model for retailing success now became a warning to other outdoor companies such as L. L. Bean and Eddie Bauer. The lesson for these companies was that Abercrombie & Fitch had strayed too far from its rugged frontier image—after all, they had sold to Theodore Roosevelt and outfitted Antarctic expeditions—when it tried to broaden its appeal. Executives looking to learn from the bankruptcy saw a company that sacrificed its history for fashion. The surest sign of this brand dilution, according to outdoor industry observers, was openly marketing Abercrombie & Fitch attire to women. Aspiring mass-market outdoor companies struggled after the 1970s to expand sales while maintaining control of the brand's history and reputation.[2]

To resolve this dilemma outdoor companies established themselves as lifestyle brands. In the 1970s, outdoor companies began to slowly reposition both their product lines and marketing toward more casual and less sport-specific lifestyle attire. In the 1980s, participation in outdoor sports leveled off as Baby Boomers' enthusiasm for high-impact outdoor sports waned with age. Yet as outdoor sports participation decreased, the business in outdoor equipment and clothing increased. According to a federal study in 1989, yuppies of the 1980s supported the concept of the wilderness, but were less likely to actually go to it. Many were perfectly happy to enjoy wilderness from the comfort of home, by looking at books, films, and outdoor company catalogs and mall locales. The concept of an outdoor lifestyle was ubiquitous in the 1980s—in how advertisers talked about cars, houses, neighborhoods, and, especially, clothing. Responding to its ambitious but busy customer base, the outdoor industry began to sell the notion of a vicarious outdoor lifestyle: their customer might not hike, fish, or hunt, but construed leisure-time activity self-consciously as part of their identity, way of life, and consumer choices. Of course, those who had been backpacking or climbing for decades typically associated their pursuits with the counterculture and saw it as a lifestyle, too, but by the 1980s this lifestyle was more about what Americans consumed than what Americans did, and the concept was now going mainstream. An outdoor lifestyle connoted health, wealth, and the sporting aspirations, if not activities, of tens of millions of people in white suburbia.[3]

The question for company executives, remembering the demise of Abercrombie & Fitch, was how to appeal to these new customers without conceding too much of what the company had once been, or, at least, what these executives imagined the companies to represent. To appease their older customer clientele, companies established what they called heritage, almost as a marketing complement to lifestyle. Commercial narratives and images appealed to an authentic past that was almost exclusively white and male. Heritage marketing offered a way to appease existing customers while attracting new ones who were more interested in embroidered tree logos than finding that tree in the wild. Heritage, in catalogs, advertisements, and other company material, was not simply history, but a selective and carefully curated set of vignettes—often conveyed in catalog copy—that communicated a company's nostalgia for a past self. Heritage was the answer for how to maintain an idealized customer base even as outdoor clothing became more popular with a far broader, even antithetical, customer base. Industry discussions about ideal target markets reveal the latent misogyny and racial anxiety of the post–Civil Rights years. As women, the industry's historical foil as it promoted authentic masculinity, and nonwhite people bought outdoor products, companies reiterated and established their company brand identity and heritage, firmly grounded in a white, male, and thus authentic past, using stories and claims about the frontier, rugged West, and American military to reinforce this narrative.[4]

Historians at this time were revising the history of the American West, revealing a diverse and complicated western conquest, and examining how the myths of the frontier and the cowboy erased so many from the American past. But marketers had little use for these new interpretations of histories, and so the outdoor industry reiterated conservative tropes of earlier stale and often exclusionary histories. Through heritage, the brand story remained constant over time even as the customer base changed.[5]

Neither lifestyle nor heritage, as the two concepts developed together and complemented each other, appeared in outdoor company materials until the late 1980s, when companies courted the lifestyle market in different ways. Some, like L. L. Bean, used expanded catalog mailings; Eddie Bauer built up its mall retail spaces; Cabela's combined big box stores with museum-like displays; and the North Face and Timberland reached for a broad base of nonwhite consumers. Despite their different approaches, all these companies simultaneously evoked heritage to reaffirm their idealized customer base, history, and values.

✻

In 1981, executives with L. L. Bean revisited an ongoing debate—where should women's clothes appear in an outdoor catalog? Did a woman's cotton-polyester blend corduroy shirtdress belong in a catalog that strove for a "hard-core outdoor jock image," and, if it did, then in what category? Was the dress outerwear or underwear—the only options in Bean's rigid production orientation? And would such a dress go out of style too quickly for a retailer known for classic design? The proponents of the shirtdress won out—the $29 garment was listed as outerwear, and was quickly on back order.[6] But the larger debate and tension did not go away.

As the mail-order giant L. L. Bean transitioned from hardcore outdoors to lifestyle, the shirtdress epitomized for company executives the larger conundrum of how to expand to meet consumer tastes while maintaining the company image. The company had an uneasy relationship with popular fashion, especially with women's wear, because it seemed to dilute the brand. Ultimately, despite the careful public disavowal by company president Leon Gorman that L. L. Bean was focusing on women's wear, the company was doing just that: it was now selling primarily to suburban women, and men, who were not hardcore outdoorspeople. This was a gradual and not a radical transition, since Bean had long made a business of selling to urban easterners who preferred a "taste" of the outdoor life rather than "a full meal." So the company's concern was less about losing a hardcore market and more about integrating women as a larger component of it. The company resolved this tension by continuing to sell hardware, and by focusing especially on legacy items such as the very popular Bean Boot, to emphasize the longevity of the company, its consistent design as a retort to fashion, and the legacy and character of its founder. L. L. Bean successfully cultivated a customer feeling of communing with nature in Maine's north woods, even if that interaction happened only vicariously, through catalogs.[7]

In 1979 the Bean Boot, offered since 1912, became a surprise hit. A few years earlier these tall, laced hunting boots with leather uppers began to wander from the woods to city streets. Gorman remembered being "inundated with orders" for women's sizes of the traditional hunters' boots in the early 1970s as urban and suburban women embraced the rustic chic look. By 1979, designers like Calvin Klein were sending the boots "stomp[ing] down fashion show runaways." The boot was so popular it was back-ordered for months at a time, and other companies produced knockoffs that sold nearly as quickly.[8]

Bean Boots were part of the preppy fashion trend of the late 1970s and early 1980s that launched L. L. Bean to national and even international fame. "Preppy" referred to and imitated the world of elites, usually WASPs from private preparatory schools and Ivy League colleges. The prep costume, also called "East Coast cool," included items such as khaki pants, Fair Isle sweaters, and Sperry Top-Siders. It had deep roots in American elites' use of sportswear to connote a life of conspicuous leisure, but took off on a broad scale with the rise of designers such as Ralph Lauren, Calvin Klein, and Donna Karan. L. L. Bean was one place to find preppy clothes for people like Kent Yalowitz, a Yale freshman looking for pants to start out the school year. One Yale student estimated that 75 percent of her classmates in 1981 owned the same navy and white sweater from L. L. Bean. As a student from a Connecticut liberal arts college exclaimed: "Thank God for L. L. Bean. Without that, half the campus would be naked."[9]

The Official Preppy Handbook, a wildly successful work by Lisa Birnbach, was the bible of the preppy trend. The book, with its plaid cover, dissected the aesthetic, lifestyle, and predilections of elite, white Northeasterners and the fashion choices that signified their membership in the group. Birnbach intended to satirize this population, but she captured their style so succinctly: practical and expensive sporting attire, particularly clothes appropriate for a duck blind but also at home in sophisticated suburbs. Bean Boots were comfortably matched with salmon-pink Lacoste polos and khaki pants. The style suggested an everyday casual look that complemented everyday access to leisure. The implication of the style was that wealthy, tasteful prepsters were immune to frivolous fashion, and instead invested in expensive but high-quality brands like L. L. Bean that were acceptable for everyday wear because they signaled that leisure time was always at their fingertips. The book itself sold more than a million copies, enough to amplify this group's squash and yacht pretensions to a broader audience, and even to affect L. L. Bean's bottom line. It saw more catalog requests than ever and became one of the most robust and coveted mailing lists in the country.[10]

Gorman didn't like the preppy trend. He thought it betrayed the essence of the company image. And when Gorman compared a "core market" to the "fashion" market, he was implicitly making a gendered claim about the ideal customer. The problem with preppy was a gender problem. He acknowledged that the preppy trend had helped the company's bottom line, but emphasized that the company had not pursued the fashion cycle. Furthermore, Gorman thought these new customers were buying Bean "for the wrong reasons." Fashion was temporary, its benefits to a company's bottom line fleeting, and Gorman was worried about ending up like Abercrombie & Fitch, selling flared pants rather than focusing on the core and authentic market of "the average guy who likes to enjoy the outdoors."[11]

As Gorman predicted, the preppy craze waned after a few years, but the discussion within the company of how to grow persisted. Leon Gorman wanted to maintain the company's reputation for ruggedness and its core focus on the male outdoorsman customer. Bill End, L. L. Bean's vice president, thought differently. End saw casual wear, and especially products for women, as L. L. Bean's future. Both executives believed that mail order was the best direction for growth, at least at first. The debate, then, came down to two choices: active versus casual, and male versus female products. By these binary formulations, active products were for men, and casual products were for women, even though the boundaries were never clearly defined. Notwithstanding their differences, Gorman and End shared a deeply gendered sense of what the "real" outdoor market was, as well as a limited conception of women as outdoorswomen. Company executives persisted in seeing women as primarily drawn to L. L. Bean fashion rather than function. Even Charlie Kessler, a proponent of expanded womenswear, poked fun at women as outdoorspeople: "Well, you just can't predict what a woman will wear outdoors. I mean, look at what some of them wear to go fishing!" The ladies' department had been around for decades, but executives still struggled to conceive of women collectively as sports-oriented buyers who sought functionality.[12]

From Gorman's perspective, L. L. Bean's "unique core values" became more important, counterintuitively, as the company moved toward a less differentiated market. Abercrombie & Fitch, as ever, was his cautionary tale of an outdoor company trying to do it all and losing its core in the process. Without guarding the core of "rugged individualism," the branching out into women's apparel was a "guaranteed disaster." Nonetheless, End did concede that the women's market had the biggest growth potential, but beyond adding a few more pages of women' apparel, "I don't know how much more we can modify our merchandise mix before we jeopardize our image."[13]

As this debate transpired, the company developed new ways to find and advertise to casual outdoorspeople. The company was well positioned to use mail order to navigate its way toward new customers. Mail order accounted for 2.5 percent of retail sales nationally and benefited from social and economic shifts in the 1970s and early 1980s. More women were working, the U.S. population was older, and there was more discretionary income around. These were all reasons to buy from a catalog rather than shop at a store. The expansion of toll-free 800 phone numbers, credit cards, the development of scientifically managed mailing lists, and the high cost of gasoline as well as the inconvenience of finding parking also contributed to the popularity of shopping by mail catalog. Companies mailed 5.8 billion catalogs in 1980, with that number increasing to 13.4 billion by 1989. For an individual household, that amounted to nearly five pieces of third-class mail per week.[14]

L. L. Bean mailed twenty-six million catalogs in 1980, sometimes sending as many as nine catalogs a year to its best customers. The company developed themed catalogs—one focused on womenswear, for instance, and another on fishing equipment—as an outdoor lifestyle merchandising strategy. The company learned about consumer habits by organizing them into different segments by zip code. L. L. Bean surveyed non-customers and learned that people leafing through the catalog in Houston or Washington, D.C., in 1980 saw L. L. Bean as "oriented toward fisherman, campers or serious outdoor sportspeople"—as opposed to competitors who made products for people "casually enjoying the outdoors." This distinction was important; it gave Bean the edge of authenticity because of its link to outdoor sports, even if the customers' actual outdoors practices were distinctly more casual than the "authentic" image suggested.[15]

In 1982, despite Gorman's concerns, the outdoors was "in" fashion-wise, and L. L. Bean even earned a Coty Award, a kind of Oscar for fashion designers. The company won this award, usually given to the likes of Dior or Saint-Laurent, because of the gum-soled hunting boots that were pounding pavement in midtown Manhattan. One reporter enjoyed the irony, noting that the award "flies in the face of everything L. L. stood for. Quality, dependability, durability. Not fashion." Predictably, Gorman was unhappy. "It's something we try to downplay," explained one employee. The public affairs representative agreed, saying it was "no big deal" that L. L. Bean had won fashion industry awards.[16] As L. L. Bean moved more toward the mainstream of everyday wear in classrooms and at backyard barbecues, the company remained secure in the belief that these fashion accolades did not matter—precisely because of its strategy of emphasizing company heritage.

The company worked hard to cultivate an outdoor feeling through the catalogs themselves, even as most customers flocked toward casual dress. The most important strategy was continuing to sell equipment, or hardware, in the catalog, even if it didn't make money, since the casual consumer knew of L. L. Bean because of the gear. For example, the company reintroduced guns and duck decoys, to clarify and reassure that they were in the outdoor business, and sold guidebooks on things like fishing or outdoor photography. Even the slightly altered company logo conveyed a broader interpretation of what counted as outdoor sports: for years, L. L. Bean had used the logo "Hunting, Fishing, and Camping" but now subtly tweaked the logo to "Outdoor Sporting Specialties."[17]

The two most important products for showcasing the company heritage even as lifestyle consumers swarmed were the warden jacket and the Bean Boot. The Bean Boot ads showed how the design was consistent through the decades, and often invoked the story of the company's founding. The Maine Warden jacket was rarely purchased but effectively conjured the authentic, rugged outdoors. As a longtime customer put it, "I didn't want one. I didn't need one. But I got used to seeing it and thinking, well, maybe someday I'll need a heavy wool jacket with lots of pockets." The hardware and the stories behind them in the catalogs allowed nearly everything else to change in the product offerings without changing the company feel. In the 1980s, the worst-performing department was fishing and hunting gear, which generated less than one-third as much as the women's clothing department sales.

Yet the gear department did important work in another way: it maintained the L. L. Bean image, because those things were linked to company founder Leon Leonwood Bean. The approach worked. Business writers interpreted the success of L. L. Bean in the 1980s as a story of not succumbing to trends. The authors of *Corporate Cultures* (1982), for instance, wrote that "[u]nlike his unfortunate competitor, Abercrombie & Fitch, Gorman never moves far from the Maine Hunting Shoe, or the Warden Jacket. Employees and customers can depend on the culture of L. L. Bean." But this was not the case. L. L. Bean had indeed "moved," but successfully hid the transition to a new market behind old window dressing. In the 1980s, L. L. Bean attracted new female customers and sold mostly casual attire but used the story of heritage and its gear to keep the same store and catalog feel, even as the catalog content itself changed dramatically.[18]

L. L. Bean found that the literary readership of the *New York Review of Books* responded more favorably than even the outdoor-sports-oriented subscribers to *Sports Afield* or *Backpacker*. An apparel products manager at L. L. Bean explained the lifestyle customer this way: "I suspect that many of the products we sell, particularly clothing, never make it into the woods," he said. "Our customers are probably buying them as much for their looks as for their function. However, we do design and manufacture the items as if they really are going to be used in the wilderness."[19]

In the "wilds of suburban New Jersey," Maryanne Garbowsky's husband anxiously awaited the arrival of the L. L. Bean catalog in the mail. The goods in the catalogs had a special allure, she wrote in the 1980s in a profile of his experiences. Her husband—unnamed in the article—imagined himself "transformed into a bold outdoorsman" simply by reading and ordering from the L. L. Bean catalog. Ordering products such as a Moose River hat and thermal boot socks from the comfort of home, he was not simply dressed but rather outfitted by L. L. Bean. Garbowsky's experience was shared by millions of Americans in the 1980s, transforming L. L. Bean into the nation's biggest outdoor retailer selling specifically to weary city men living the "perilous life of a sportsman," from their armchairs.[20]

In this transition L. L. Bean effectively honed an idea of the outdoors that catered to suburbia. Being an "L. L. Bean type" in an L. L. Bean zip code meant something different from how many nights someone spent camping in a year. Richard Smith, an author based in New York, described his affinity for L. L. Bean attire: "People who work all day inside an office, crunching numbers and shoving stocks around, want to have an escape. So they go home, change into their rugged, outdoor clothes, look in the mirror and say, 'Hey, I'm free.'" This feeling of freedom had less to do with the specific clothes, to say nothing of outdoor recreation, than with L. L. Bean's reputation around outdoor heritage.[21]

L. L. Bean's approach inspired a number of imitators such as Lands' End and J. Crew. In part because of these competitors' success selling womenswear, the role of casual clothing and clothing for women remained a sticking point within the company. Leon Gorman remained with his family's company until his retirement. But Bill End eventually took a job at competitor Lands' End, which was more aggressively pursuing casual wear.

In 1980, nearly 40 percent of New Englanders were familiar with L. L. Bean. Eddie Bauer, the next closest competitor, had limited awareness in that region, only 5 percent, but was stronger than L. L. Bean in its home region of the Pacific Northwest. Eddie Bauer was also moving toward lifestyle, and weighing the same tension between brand history to maintain authenticity and new markets. But Eddie Bauer came up with a very different answer than Bean: the company decided that retail stores in suburban malls were the next hot spot for selling the casual, or entirely vicarious, nature experience.[22]

✳

Perhaps no company in the industry veered more from specially designed equipment for extreme athletes to workday and weekend apparel for white suburbanites than Eddie Bauer. From the 1950s to the 1970s Eddie Bauer was resolutely an equipment manufacturer and retailer. The company sponsored expeditions led by American mountaineers in far-flung locations. By the 1990s, Eddie Bauer had shunned this hardcore image and sought out a nation of dog walkers who liked the look of outdoor clothing but didn't need the functionality of an Everest climber. Unlike L. L. Bean and its catalog empire, Eddie Bauer found these alluring customers at the mall. Its story is one of corporate takeovers, transformed retailer landscapes, and an unusual partnership that ensured that even when stuck in freeway traffic, Americans imagined themselves as adventurers in the Great Outdoors. To make this transition Eddie Bauer changed the very history it invoked in its own company materials and stores. Through the 1970s and 1980s, the legacy of expedition sponsorship had fueled company advertisements. By the 1990s, Eddie Bauer marketers had invented a very different heritage, one more focused on conquest of an imagined western frontier than on mountain climbing, to suit its new customer base. The company created a new historical identity, paradoxical as that is, focused less on a particular adventure sport and more on general myths of the American West. This new history invited fad-followers to imagine themselves as both athletes and adventurers, regardless of their sedentary ways.

In 1971, General Mills acquired Eddie Bauer as a catalog company with $9 million in sales and advertisements that emphasized the company's links to international expeditions. Owing both to its high prices and its high quality, Eddie Bauer equipment had a reputation as the "Cadillac" of outdoor wear. Catalogs emphasized that gear had been tested on mountaintops and given good reviews by these elite athletes, even if the expeditions had happened years earlier. In addition to food products, General Mills owned other brands in apparel, chemicals, and games and toys. It had more than $1 billion in total sales. Eddie Bauer was attractive specifically because of the strength of its catalogs and computer system for processing orders and managing consumer information. Its retail store in Seattle had only been open one year at this point, but General Mills saw potential. Eddie Bauer executives retained control of many things—day-to-day decisions like what to sponsor—but the ultimate strategy came from General Mills, which would send newly minted MBAs to Seattle as a kind of seasoning, regardless of their interest in the outdoors. In the years that followed, General Mills guided Eddie Bauer away from its reputation as an outfitter of expeditions and toward a bigger, broader market.[23]

Turning attention to a broad market made sense in part because the allure of the outdoors as a lifestyle continued to grow. In 1978, Eddie Bauer sent out 1.3 million catalogs and the rugged-clothes trend was still in vogue. After the acquisition by General Mills, Eddie Bauer opened new retail stores regularly. It added San Francisco and Minneapolis in 1972, Chicago and Denver in 1973, and throughout the mid- to late 1970s expanded to Canada and the East Coast. By 1984 it had eight new stores, from Santa Monica, California, to Minnetonka, Minnesota, to Stamford, Connecticut. The expansions paid off. In 1980, with seventeen stores in the United States and Canada, Eddie Bauer had increased sales from $9 million (at the time of General Mills' acquisition) to $80 million. The retail stores represented a big part of that growth—they made up 50 percent of sales, up from 10 percent nine years earlier. Eddie Bauer was only 2.3 percent of giant GM's total net profit, but it remained an important part of GM's apparel division, which also included Talbots. By 1981, it was the second-largest outdoor company in the country, after L. L. Bean.[24]

Along with the new retail stores came new inventory. Clothing accounted for two-thirds of sales, but the company also offered sheets and bathrobes alongside sleeping bags and winter boots. Jacket offerings, specifically, help illustrate the strategy. A heavyweight jacket called the Karakoram, designed for an expedition to the mountain range of the same name, was among Eddie Bauer's top-selling jackets for decades. In 1971, Eddie Bauer introduced the Suburban Sports Parka. It had design nods to earlier products, but the nylon taffeta shell and fashion photography—not to mention the name itself—suggested it had a very different purpose. Not fit for the Karakoram or the Rocky Mountains, the Suburban Sports Parka served quite different (suburban) buyers. Eddie Bauer still designed and sold for the sports market but had begun its tack toward the casual consumer.[25]

The search for this casual consumer was organized around shopping malls. Eddie Bauer executives looked for anchor stores—the department stores that drive traffic to malls, such as Nordstrom's and Macy's, and that reached a middle- and upper-middle-class customer. The demographics of these customers matched the profile of their targeted "casual outdoorsman." Under General Mills' guidance, Eddie Bauer customers had gone from "hardcore" to nature-adjacent. They weren't climbing or backpacking. Instead they were taking their dogs on walks or lounging in backyard hammocks. The outdoor athlete was a niche market, but the outdoor enthusiast—the type who had gone out to nature as a college student but who now nostalgically recalled those times while focusing on raising a family—was the new Eddie Bauer ideal. Outdoor lifestyle meant loving the outdoors in theory, and vicariously, but not in practice, as shown by the fact that less than a quarter of Eddie Bauer customers regularly participated in outdoor activities.[26]

These stores, the malls and the goods, were crucial in defining what outdoor lifestyle, as opposed to outdoor activities, looked like. One product that contributed to this new definition was not sold in Eddie Bauer stores at all, but nonetheless in the 1980s came to represent Eddie Bauer's rugged outdoor style, heavy on conspicuous consumption, over-equipping, and suburban life: the Eddie Bauer–branded Ford SUV.

In 1984, Ford approached Eddie Bauer with a proposal for a partnership that radically expanded the look and feel of marketing to the general outdoorsperson. Ford proposed that it use the Eddie Bauer name on the Ford Bronco. Essentially, this would be a designer truck, meant to appeal to outdoorsmen who loved Eddie Bauer. It would teach yuppies about American trucks, and it would teach Ford fans about Eddie Bauer. SUVs were getting more popular in the 1980s. Following the oil crisis of the early 1970s, American consumers decided they wanted to go bigger and sportier. Ford designed SUVs for suburbanites who liked the idea of a rugged truck but never planned to test the truck on so much as a dirt road. For Ford, the deal promised to attract Eddie Bauer fans who saw the company's rugged outdoor reputation embodied in truck colors like dark canyon red and dark spruce green.[27]

The agreement included no cash, but rather a series of agreements around advertising and co-branding partnerships. Eddie Bauer arranged to have Ford give free Eddie Bauer luggage—not called suitcases but gear bags—to those who purchased trucks. Special products for the co-branding arrangement included ten thousand visor organizers and ten thousand travel blankets, all with the Ford and Eddie Bauer logos. Ford also paid $1 million for a mailing insert in a catalog to sell these goods. Ford anticipated selling 1,500 to 2,000 trucks that bore the Eddie Bauer name, all with special trim and custom interior details such as little evergreen trees on the seat backs. Instead, it sold more than 7,000 in 1984.[28]

Ultimately, the truck branding shows the development nationally of a particular marketing category: the general outdoors*man*, who, like the SUV incarnate, was equipped for the outdoors but rarely headed there. The demand for SUVs and outdoor clothing for everyday use reinforced and mirrored each other as elements of the same phenomenon. Between 1982 and 1985, SUV sales went from 132,000 to 800,000 nationwide, with no more than 10 percent of those vehicles ever leaving the road. And by 1994, nearly half a million Americans had purchased Eddie Bauer–branded trucks. Functionality was a big discussion point, especially for men—these vehicles could tow, were big enough for the family, and were safer in extreme conditions. Like heavy sports equipment and clothing, all of this might have been true, but, ultimately, the usage conditions suggest that these functions were aspirational qualities and also "accessories to Boomer conceptions of masculinity." Their ruggedness was conditionally valued. The SUVs *could* leave the road, but for the doctor and lawyer crowd, rarely did.[29]

During the early years of the Ford partnership, at least half of Eddie Bauer's business was focused on fishing, and most of the people walking into its retail stores were men. But Michael Rayden, the new company president in 1984, wore pinstripes and polka dots rather than a fishing vest and was intent on changing the consumer demographics. Rayden explained that those "caught up in the mania of outdoor sports," a declining breed, were no longer as desirable as consumers. Instead, Rayden embraced fashion. He wanted to aim at the "function-emphasized outdoor lifestyle," which to him meant the consumers "who want a barbecue in the backyard as much as a backpacking stove."[30]

Eddie Bauer's store layout tracks these marketing changes. By the 1980s, Eddie Bauer had stopped sponsoring expeditions, but equipment was still an important part of store displays. Gear and menswear had prominent positions in the front, while womenswear was in the back. As womenswear got more important, it moved forward toward the shop entrance. Dedicating floor space to equipment seemed increasingly less useful, dropping to 25 percent of floor space by the end of the 1980s. The migration to malls factored prominently in this shift. Corporate offices often gendered floor space: gadgets were about the male shopper and clothing about the female

Eddie Bauer, like its competitor L. L. Bean, sold the outdoor lifestyle to American consumers, and the shift in stores away from equipment and toward soft goods reflected that trend. (Eddie Bauer, Madison, Wisconsin, 1991; photo courtesy of the Eddie Bauer Archives)

shopper. Mainstream clothes would appeal to these desirable "women mall shoppers." As "hard-core items" further declined, Rayden moved into selling not just clothes but also frisbees, kites, and sunglasses. Customers, he confirmed, liked the "outdoor ambience" that these items created—even if they never ventured into nature. Being outdoors could now connote a backyard patio as much as the wilderness.[31]

The more pronounced the pivot toward a lifestyle market, the more Eddie Bauer doubled down on the exclusionary ideals of the outdoor identity's history. Heritage was not simply Eddie Bauer history, but rather carefully structured stories designed to suggest that contemporary customers were the inheritors of particular values. Eddie Bauer's heritage was malleable and manipulable, as the retouching of an iconic early company photograph suggests. In the 1980s, Eddie Bauer executives quietly altered a photograph of the company's original store that adorned the company's marketing materials. The original photograph of the Seattle store included trophy heads—a symbol of the founder's hunting acumen—arrayed on the sidewalk. The

Eddie Bauer executives wanted to use this historical image of the founder posing in front of the old store but found the animal trophies out of sync with the company's contemporary branding. (Photo courtesy of the Eddie Bauer Archives)

deer also indicated who the customers were: hunters and fishermen, mostly, in the Seattle area who would come to the retail store for conversation as well as equipment. But as the CEO at the time explained, "We're taking down the animal heads and guns . . . having that hard-core outdoor stuff makes women feel uncomfortable." Likewise the gun cabinets. Women and younger customers were "turned off" by guns, so those too had to go.[32]

The retouched photograph was sparse and clean in comparison to the animal head original. In the 1980s, the very history of Eddie Bauer, Inc., was too gory for the General Mills subsidiary making headway with lifestyle clothing and home goods in suburban shopping malls. The history of hunting expertise mattered mostly because of the nebulous aura of authenticity in the thick, colorful catalogs. Changing its company origin story in a photograph was one of Eddie Bauer's small answers to the industry's ubiquitous

The retouched historic photograph created a new heritage the company could claim in selling to lifestyle consumers. (Photo courtesy of the Eddie Bauer Archives)

riddle of the 1980s: how to expand into lifestyle wear while maintaining an aura of authenticity. With the photograph and other moves, heritage was revised and customized to fit the new marketing model.

When Spiegel purchased Eddie Bauer from General Mills in 1988, equipment in the Eddie Bauer stores became an homage to the company's past rather than an indication of its future direction. Spiegel helped facilitate the introduction of All Week Long, a women's workwear brand within Eddie Bauer. The company also brought the outdoor lifestyle to the indoors directly, with a home goods division. Eddie Bauer Home sold tables, chairs, upholstery, and floor coverings as well as compost bins and mailboxes. The catalogs conveyed a "traditional lifestyle" purveyor of flannel sheets. Around the same time, the company also launched a fragrance, bottling the "lifestyle" as defined by Eddie Bauer. The scent was called Adventurer, and according to Eddie Bauer's president, it conveyed "the individual sense of discovery that lies at the heart of Eddie Bauer's heritage." The "masculine scent," available in deep-forest-green bottles and packaged in rawhide, "embodies the spirit of the outdoors." Together, these products sold the fantasy of mountain climbing in a way that a mountaineering jacket might have in earlier decades.[33]

In the best example of Eddie Bauer's paradox of "new" heritage, a catalog in fall 1989 used black-and-white photographs of bush pilots, World War II pilots, and ranchers alongside the more well-known images of mountaineers to create a new history. Some of these stories were consistent with the older version of company history—Eddie Bauer had indeed designed equipment for the Air Force. But the catalog also introduced new heroes to honor the masculine ideal at the heart of the outdoor identity. Although it was 1950s-era ranch workers who bought Eddie Bauer–branded products, the catalog celebrated—bizarrely—"the last hurrah of open-range grazing" in the 1870s when, the catalog explained, the market for cattle was governed by neighborly trust. The catalog celebrated "the old ways," when chivalrous cowpunchers slept outdoors from spring to fall and wouldn't dare insult a woman. What did this have to do with Eddie Bauer, Inc., a twentieth-century enterprise focused since its founding on leisure wear? Very little: no cowboys wore Eddie Bauer clothing during the big freeze of 1888. But this celebrated cowpuncher past was a part of the company's "heritage," if not its history, because the Eddie Bauer of 1990 wanted to associate with the values of pioneer authenticity. Company marketers reached back a full century—past their legacy of outfitting expeditions in the twentieth century—for the right kind of history for Eddie Bauer to sell down vests and work socks at the mall.[34]

J. Samuel Lowham, a fourth-generation rancher from southwest Wyoming who appeared in Eddie Bauer's 1991/1992 winter catalog, is another example of invented heritage. In the cover photo, he is feeding cows and wearing an Eddie Bauer parka. Lowham had been recruited by a company employee who was friends with his daughter. He was "the real thing," they both thought, someone who works outdoors in negative fifty-four degree temperatures, living a "traditional ranch lifestyle." It was, in essence, a message that suburban men could use this "wanna-be attire" to imagine themselves as "urban cowboys and big-game hunters."[35]

This new kind of heritage, which other outdoor companies mirrored (though not always with the same success), reveals the associational power of outdoor clothing as part of a deeply held mythology of white American manhood. Eddie Bauer was part of the growth in the men's functional-wear market, which imparted a heady romance to customers about the clothes they wore to the local bistro. Tom Julian, of the Men's Fashion Association, explained in 1989 that while "a man may not be able to flee to the country every weekend, . . . he can wear clothes to create that mood." Clark Bromfield, who managed the Eddie Bauer and L. L. Bean competitor Orvis hunting and fishing store in Philadelphia's Center City, guessed that more than half of the clothes bought there were for streetwear use. The Philadelphia publisher Larry Teacher was one of these customers. He used a fly-fishing bag for his work briefcase and enjoyed heading to his office in a fly-fishing vest. Teacher did enjoy fly-fishing, but the outfit was part of his city look, not his outdoor one.[36]

Like L. L. Bean, Eddie Bauer's new reputation was "upscale" and "outdoorsy" rather than just outdoorsy. The columnist Anna Quindlen described Eddie Bauer clothes as part of the "affect" urbanites don when they head to the country "to be at one with nature." The catalogs, according to one description in 1994, showed "uniformly upscale models still along beaches, sail and cast fly lines in a seductive assembly designed to take the urban fantasist out to the country." Projected sales for 1994 for Eddie Bauer were $850 million, eclipsing L. L. Bean's $775 million and second only to Foot Locker on the list of Specialty Sporting Goods Retailers.[37]

The message traveled far and wide. In 1992, 230 stores in the United States and Canada sent catalogs to 65 million potential customers. By then, the store was selling the outfitter's "casual, outdoor lifestyle heritage," using the industry's new buzzwords. Dismantled, this phrase highlights the new approach to selling the outdoors: "casual" as opposed to technical; "outdoor lifestyle" as an identity rather than an active life; and "heritage," to highlight the ranchers, pilots, and mountain climbers the company once outfitted (or wishes it did) but does no longer.[38]

"Outdoor lifestyle," a term that had not appeared in any corporate materials in the 1970s, was commonplace by 1990. It accommodated and embraced a seemingly boundless merchandise expansion, from the selling of candles and comforters as well as camping equipment, so long as companies were willing to consider women.

Sporting industry insiders predicted the trend of the 1990s would be "consumers wanting to look like Eddie Bauer models." To that end, Eddie Bauer, like L. L. Bean, inspired a number of imitators, including Nike, Nautica, J. C. Penney, and even Victoria's Secret, all of which created outdoor clothing lines in the early 1990s. Despite this expansion, the emergence of a new set of consumers in the 1990s provoked the industry's decision that outdoor lifestyle was not for everybody, and neither was the heritage that these companies invoked.[39]

✻

In the 1990s, outdoor clothing once again left the trail for the city street. But this time, it was not the white wine brunch crowd or even over-geared dog walkers, but rather young Black and brown men who celebrated what they called Timbs, Eddie, and the Face. Outdoor gear became urban chic. Hip-hop fashion, as the broader trend was called, was directly inspired by the preppy looks that preceded. Hip-hoppers made use of the ski jackets and hiking boots that white, middle-class Americans embraced, though they remixed those styles in new ways. The outdoor industry was ambivalent about—or even hostile to—this newfound market. As with the preppy trend of the early 1980s, outdoor companies had to decide how to respond to this new consumer base. Other firms had seen the potential of female and Black markets in previous decades, but by the time outdoor companies participated, there was a marked retreat from these expansive visions of the market.[40]

The hip-hop fashion trend of incorporating outdoor clothing brands and workwear brands into urban chic began with musicians and spread to young people around the nation. Hip-hop culture, dominated by musical artists in New York, Chicago, and Detroit, helped to shape national trends in fashion. Some of the best-known elements of the style of groups like the Wu-Tang Clan included bright colors, oversized logos, and attire associated with white Americana such as Polo Ralph Lauren and Tommy Hilfiger. The styles appealed to celebrities and their followers alike because of how they played with both elite white culture and Black, lower-class masculinity. Hip-hop styles that made use of Americana and outdoor brands allowed customers to subvert the notion that white masculinity was an unmarked and unremarkable category. Brands such as Timberland, a work and hiking boot company, and the North Face, a climbing and backpacking brand, as well as Eddie Bauer were all part of the "fresh" look and featured in the lyrics of Black hip-hop artists.[41]

Individual artists' attire for their music videos beamed old brands into living rooms—and new potential markets—around the country. Although no single artist or group can be credited with bringing Timberland boots from the trail to the sidewalk, such artists as Jay-Z, the Notorious B.I.G., and Timbaland—whose moniker came directly from the boots—all wore the shoes. For instance, music videos that aired on MTV, the music television channel, often featured Timberland boots. While the company had been selling the yellow leather boots to outdoor enthusiasts and trade workers since 1973, music videos from Wu-Tang Clan gave the boots exposure. As RZA, a Wu-Tang Clan member, explained, he saw the boots as both "cool and rugged." For performances, RZA preferred "fresh" black boots, which meant they were both polished and spotless. He also preferred to tuck his pants in to show off the boots. Eventually, RZA expanded his collection from "construction color ways" to nearly every color the company offered, including baby pink and baby blue. In addition to MTV and magazines of hip-hop culture like *Vibe* and *The Source*, mainstream reporting picked up on hip-hop style, calling outdoor clothing "dope" and "phat."[42]

Artists didn't just wear these styles. They sang about them too: RZA's line "I rock the boots with the trees," shared his love for Timberlands. "Timbs for my hooligans in Brooklyn," rapped the Notorious B.I.G., aka Biggie Smalls, in "Hypnotize." In "The World Is Yours," Nas said, "Suede Timbs on my feet makes my cipher complete." Other lyrics from Raekwon, Lauryn Hill, and Diddy similarly referenced Timberland boots.[43]

The North Face was another outdoor-turned-lifestyle brand popularized by hip-hop artists in the 1990s. Musicians such as Notorious B.I.G., Missy Elliott, Method Man, LL Cool J, Heather B, Erykah Badu, and Big L wore yellow and red boldly branded North Face jackets in music videos. The Bay

Area company had first outfitted mountaineers in the 1960s, and by the 1980s expanded its line to include skiwear and equipment. Urban brand enthusiasts of the 1990s had a particular way of wearing the Nuptse puffy down jacket from the North Face: usually three sizes too big and paired with baggy pants and Timberlands. Though less common than lyrics about Timberland, songs referencing the brand's puffy jackets—the Notorious B.I.G.'s "Dead Wrong" being one example—continued in rap and hip-hop, including Ratking's 700 *Fill* album from 2015, which comments on the quality of the down in a North Face jacket, and YL and Roper Williams's "Fly Out" from 2018: "We keep half a zip / Still poppin' in that North Face / You known what I'm sayin', for them cold nights / 700, know what I'm sayin', goose feathers / Strong shit." Lyrics like these celebrated Timberland boots and Nuptse jackets as functional as well as markers of identity.[44]

Hip-hop's affinity for outdoor lifestyle brands spread from artists to their fans. One fashion consultant observed that 90 percent of the young people she encountered in Harlem were wearing high-tech down jackets during the winter of 1997. Ramon Herrera's experience working at Tent & Trails on Park Place in Tribeca supported that observation. For Herrera, the 1990s was the "golden age" of the North Face, when Tent & Trails stocked seven or eight colors of the brightly colored Nuptse jackets. Peter Yeh recalled that though it wasn't cold at his childhood home in Southern California, he "knew all about puffy Nuptse jackets thanks to Bad Boy [Records]." Brooklyn rapper Masta Ace said he knew teenagers who owned five or six pairs of Timberland boots—each costing a hefty $100.[45]

Corporations guarded the association of outdoor clothing with whiteness, but nonwhite Americans created new "brand stories" nonetheless. A fan of Timberlands wrote in *Vibe* magazine, "The tree-stamped shitkickers" worked well on broken glass, concrete, or barbed wire. Like white suburbanites who were unlikely to climb a mountain or go yachting, Black customers sought upscale Americana in the form of branded sportswear. It was specifically a "lifestyle aspiration." As Just Blaze, a hip-hop producer and collector of Polo Ralph Lauren attire, explained: "I'm not a cattle wrangler, I'm not a skier, and I don't race yachts for a living, but as a young kid in the hood I wished I could be that, and that's why we wear the clothes we do." In 1993, Joey Ones got a North Face–branded bag as a gift. His favorite branded product soon became a Ski Patrol jacket from 1990, in red, black, and white. As a North Face superfan and "goretex hoarder," as he called himself, he was part of a much larger trend of urban sportswear in the cities. For Ones, the city-based fans had just as much of a claim on the brand: "we live in NYC bro, we're surrounded by fucking concrete. One minute it's raining, one minute it's hot, one minute it's cold." Though the language is different, the sentiment—a focus on the necessity of functional equipment for everyday usage—was nearly identical to that of L. L. Bean lovers.[46]

Outdoor corporations were ambivalent about the popularity of their products among this market even as they welcomed the boost in sales. Timberland saw a 52 percent increase in sales in one quarter of 1992. Timberland CEO Jeffrey Swartz reflected on this growth in two ways. He explained of the young Black and Hispanic fans of Timberland that "their money spends good," while at the same time insisting that "we are not going to build a business 'on smoke.' " In other words, the trend might be good for business temporarily—as preppy style had been—but over the long term Swartz didn't envision these new fans as core customers.[47]

Another concern, which few executives said directly, was that the hip-hop generation "cheapen[ed] their brand names." A fashion editor for a magazine on hip-hop culture suggested that outdoor companies were purposefully hiding their popularity in the "hood." Echoing Leon Gorman's feeling about preppies, Timberland advisers suggested that buying these clothes for fashion was emphatically the "wrong reason." Fashions change, while timelessness was the essence of these brands. L. L. Bean and Eddie Bauer executives had made the same argument about preppies or women undermining brand heritage in the 1980s, but the argument in the 1990s was tinged with racist ideas about brand identity. When Swartz said the company's primary desirable market was "honest working people," the description struck many in the hip-hop world as an underhanded suggestion that they were neither honest nor working. Regardless of the intention, customers interpreted these white-owned brand statements as an attempt to "distance themselves from the customers who were making them street chic." Along those lines, Timberland made the choice to direct all company advertising to its "primary consumers" rather than building the business to include young Black and Hispanic customers.[48]

When outdoor industry executives and reporters described the trend of outdoor clothing among Black youth, they used the language of co-optation or appropriation. By painting Black customers as "outdoor-wear-for-style devotees," they suggested that the white customers were wearing the same clothes and boots for function, out of necessity. It reified the "outdoor life-style" as one about function rather than fashion—even at a time when a vast majority of customers and devotees were buying for fashion. The primary white customers donned their "rural chic" look for their professional jobs in the city or leisurely weekends in suburbia. This middle-class market was that of an "urban fantasist." In that sense, few customers bought the attire for the function for which it was originally designed—they were aspirational consumers and valued the outdoors hypothetically more than anything else. But only one set of customers drew the suspicion and accusations of "corrupting" the outdoor lifestyle.[49]

The suggestion that a Black teenager was not a primary customer had broad ramifications. In 1995, sixteen-year-old Alonzo Jackson entered an Eddie Bauer store near Washington, D.C., wearing a green and white plaid shirt he had purchased there the day before at a half-off sale. The store was in a primarily Black neighborhood, likely sited there as a result of Eddie Bauer's diversity outreach—their term for marketing to nonwhite populations. Back to shop with friends, Jackson was part of the much larger trend of what newspapers were calling the "lumberjack-with-a-trust-fund look" popular with urban teens and young adults. Jackson's friend Marco Cunningham was with him, looking for an Eddie Bauer parka that was "all the rage" in his neighborhood of Oxon Hill. So was Rasheed Plummer, a fellow Oxon Hill High School student.[50]

It was common enough to see a Black teenager in outdoor lifestyle cloth-ing, but being young and Black in an Eddie Bauer store was reason enough for the store security guard to be suspicious. He stopped Jackson and told him to prove the shirt was his. Even when a shopkeeper remembered the customer from the day before, the security guard—an off-duty police officer wearing a gun—insisted the young man leave shirtless and bring a receipt to get the shirt back. Jackson returned with evidence of his purchases the next day and retrieved his shirt. Upon hearing of the incident, the company headquarters said that, even though Jackson had a receipt, it wasn't itemized and they "gave him the benefit of the doubt."[51]

Eddie Bauer's corporate office initially viewed the incident as trivial and declined to return concerned phone calls from Plummer's mother. Then, after negative national press coverage, Eddie Bauer publicly apologized, created a "diversity initiative" for the corporate office, and donated some jackets to a homeless shelter. Jackson brought a lawsuit against Eddie Bauer, charging false imprisonment, defamation, negligent supervision, and violation of the Civil Rights Act. The case included Eddie Bauer employees testifying about the company's culture. They described being told to follow nonwhite customers around the store because of the presumption that they would shoplift. Nearly two years after the initial encounter, Jackson and his friends were awarded $1 million in damages. Jackson never wore the plaid Eddie Bauer shirt again. Jackson's friend decided to boycott Eddie Bauer and also most other white-owned stores.[52]

The lumberjack look didn't fade from popularity among Jackson's peers as quickly, however. A couple of months after the incident, Jackson witnessed a botched robbery that left a fellow student dead right next to him. The robber, a Black teenager, still got away with his intended prize—an Eddie Bauer coat.

The case exposed the race-based definition of outdoor lifestyle. It revealed the broader network of institutional racism within Eddie Bauer. Like Timberland, Eddie Bauer had begun posting uniformed security guards at many store exits to combat shoplifting, as if this was a problem specific to "the ghetto." Another outdoor store, Tent & Trails in Manhattan, also hired three undercover cops to work as security guards in the stores because of shoplifting. The scrutiny of nonwhite customers in the stores along with the language and imagery in advertisements made Black people think that they were perceived as a problem.[53]

The disconnect between catalog imagery and customer use of clothing and equipment illustrates how ideas about appropriation and "co-optation" unfolded in outdoor companies. Companies featured photographs of

sponsored expeditions in their catalogs, yet there was little suggestion that customers who did not do those things had co-opted the brand. The sponsored
athletes were white, however, and that was sometimes enough for customers
to imagine themselves as free adventurers when they donned the apparel.
Black models, on the other hand, rarely appeared in outdoor catalogs and
magazines. In 1994, only twelve photographs in 174 pages of an Eddie Bauer
catalog featured Black models. In outdoor as well as national magazines, advertisements usually portrayed Black models in much smaller numbers, and
when they did appear, they were depicted in urban spaces—running or playing basketball, for instance—rather than in the Great Outdoors.[54]

Outdoor lifestyle in the 1990s yielded a language of clothing that had remarkable flexibility. One journalist's take on the outdoor scene captures this
phenomenon: On a cold, sunny day outside the Museum of Natural History in New York, one could see a cross section of America all dressed in
Gore-Tex, the North Face, and hiking boots. The group included tourists
with kids, homeboys, and private school kids. Their strikingly similar attire
offered soccer mom functionality for out-of-towners; a wink at mainstream
prep, with a healthy dose of yearning for the American dream for the young
Black kids; and a hip rebelliousness for angsty white adolescents.[55]

✻

By the 1990s, the consensus in the outdoor industry was that the casual
outdoorsman—white, suburban, a lover of tree decals as much as if not
more than trees—was here to stay. The outdoors as a lifestyle, reconciled
with older, function-based notions of authenticity through careful inventions and reinventions of heritage, now dominated the industry. Tom
Mendl, a product manager at Patagonia, called the phenomenon of selling
high-tech goods both to an "inner circle of outdoor athletes" and "to the
mass of consumers" the "80–20 rule": "Eighty percent of the people who
purchase premium outdoor clothing don't buy it for the use it was intended.
They're out there walking the dog in cold weather, and that's it." But though
white suburbanites' and Black city residents' use of outdoor clothes was similar, few suggested white dog walkers were parodying or wrongly appropriating outdoor culture. Companies worked to create a specific heritage, and
policed those who didn't fit their vision of an outdoor lifestyle consumer.[56]

By using the concept of heritage to solidify the roots of their brands while simultaneously embracing the new casual market of the outdoor-adjacent or vicarious consumer, companies promoted archetypes of the outdoorsperson that remained largely unchanged even as the demographics of customers and participants shifted. How the industry constructed its own history is key to understanding how businesses saw the future of outdoor recreation as part of American culture. Despite some nods to diversity and marketing adjustments to reflect new customers, their uses of heritage allowed them to continue to privilege the authentic white outdoorsman, thereby reinforcing conservative values. By the 2000s, when outdoor stores conjured the outdoor lifestyle as an American heritage, they were referencing a concept of their own invention, created earlier as a response to female and nonwhite consumers—people often criticized as lifestyle consumers who bought for the "wrong reasons."

After L. L. Bean, outdoor companies continued to grapple with the balance between selling the company's past and reaching a new lifestyle consumer. Abercrombie & Fitch, the storied outdoor outfitter of the first half of the twentieth century and cautionary tale of the 1970s, was reborn as a teenage clothier in the 1990s. No longer an outdoor company, A&F nonetheless made use of its successors' legacies by embracing both a preppy legacy and the cultivation of lifestyle. In the 1990s, catalog giants Eddie Bauer and L. L. Bean remained close to the top of sales lists for sporting goods retailers, beating out more traditional sporting goods stores (those that also sold baseball mitts and football cleats) such as the Sports Authority, Champs Sports, and Sportmart. For the first time, in 1994 Eddie Bauer sales surpassed L. L. Bean's, at $850 million to Bean's $775 million. Smaller, regionally based outdoor companies such as REI ($400 million in sales) continued to grow and eventually adopted the big-box retail format. REI, like its industry competitors, continued to sell equipment but also welcomed lifestyle consumers.[57]

The broader market that industry now reaches is visible across the country. In a gateway town to a national park, such as Estes Park, Colorado, or Gardiner, Montana, it is unsurprising that so many people passing through don trail-ready attire. But so too do Americans at sites far from the trail, including farmers' markets and office buildings from midtown Manhattan to

"I hate camping, but I love shopping at L. L. Bean."

CartoonStock.com

Outdoor lifestyle consumers were well aware that their shopping habits were at odds with the origins of the stores they frequented. (Amy Hwang, *New Yorker*, October 21, 2013, www. CartoonStock.com)

Silicon Valley. There is even a term for this wardrobe: "Gorpcore" is a popular term for outdoor wear for decidedly indoor folks who may or may not be familiar with the trail mix after which the style was named. The spread of outdoor style can have an elite bent: a collaboration between Gucci and the North Face in 2021 brought the spirit of exploration to a $3,300 down jacket in a dizzying kaleidoscope pattern. More common, though, is the pedestrian use of outdoor products. College students wear long down jackets because it is cold; urban dwellers wear waterproofed and insulated boots because the roads have winter slush; and even toddlers wear fleece vests because they (OK, their parents) recognize the usefulness of layering.[58]

By the mid-1990s, with the stylistic influence of outdoor companies evident in everyday dress across geographical, class, and race lines, the outdoor lifestyle consumer appeared to have been willed into existence. They were punchlines in *New Yorker* cartoons. There were usually two kinds of jokes about the American outdoor consumer. The first poked fun at the under-achiever who liked gear—the phenomenon of the outdoor-adjacent fan who buys but doesn't camp (or camps but doesn't backpack, or backpacks but doesn't climb mountains). The second kind of joke centered around the tendency to over-equip for the outdoors. Americans would buy out a whole catalog if they had the chance. The implication was that these people were unlikely to need or use most of what they acquired. Companies continued to debate whether they were about the casual or the adventurous consumers, a debate that played out internally and on store shelves and layouts. This debate over function or fashion remained both gendered and raced.

The function or fashion question has recurred in the industry for the past fifty years. When L. L. Bean Boots made an appearance on fashion runways in 2020—not for the first time, as an article erroneously suggested—Lisa Birnbach, whose *Official Preppy Handbook* had contributed to the national popularity of Bean Boots as part of the preppy trend of the early 1980s, asked, "Are they fashion or are they gear?" Of course, Birnbach likely knows better than most that this question cuts to the heart of how outdoor style has worked in this country for many decades: products that toe the line between fashion and gear can claim the more authentic status of equipment.[59]

Epilogue

The outdoor industry in the twenty-first century remains a complicated web of relations that tie manufacturers, retailers, and consumers together. Americans maintain a deep interest in outdoor recreation and in gear, as both shopping trends and data collectors show. In 2020, Americans purchased in record numbers tents, bicycles, and other outdoor equipment, items that promised escape from the lockdown and contagion through the relative safety of outdoor recreation. The national lobbying arm of the industry and national and state governments have worked to quantify the impact and influence of outdoor recreation on the national economy. The Bureau of Economic Analysis measures the activity and sales generated by recreational activities with the Outdoor Recreation Satellite Account. These aggregations of information can hardly capture the broader changes in the industry that consumers and industry professionals alike are most interested in discussing. There are many contemporary trends in the industry that could warrant chapters or whole books in their own right, including the shift toward big-box retail and the political activism espoused by some companies. This epilogue will outline just two of these trends that point to what comes next for the outdoor industry, one coming from the bottom up and another prompted by industry voices.

For activist and business owner Rue Mapp, it is high time to tell a new story about the outdoor identity. Mapp felt a "Black joy in nature" participating in outdoor activities but didn't see people who looked like her represented in outdoor media. Her nonprofit, Outdoor Afro, founded in 2015, sought to reconnect Black people with nature through guided activities and outdoor leadership trainings and has successfully done so, with sixty thousand people participating in events in 2022. But it is her for-profit company, Outdoor Afro, Inc., that has directly addressed the narrowness of the historical outdoor identity. When Mapp's nonprofit surveyed event participants, they expressed that finding the right gear and equipment was one of the top five barriers to participation in outdoor activities. Mapp saw an opportunity. She wanted to highlight a "whole new reality that Black people could see themselves in, in nature." How she did that was with a clothing collaboration between Outdoor Afro, Inc., and REI, the national outdoor retailer.[1]

The collaboration yielded what REI called a hiking collection, which includes trail pants, a fleece pullover, and a couple of different t-shirts, among other products—nothing remarkable at first glance. There are two elements that make the products stand out, however. First, the design and colors are meant to resonate with Black customers. As Mapp put it, it is clothing that will fit her body and she can also feel good in. Second, the graphic on the collection water bottle, bandana, and shirt pays homage to Black oases in the American past. Rectangular blocks in mustard, plum, and a fiery orange offset the all-caps black text with the names of recreational hubs for Black Americans such as Sag Harbor and Idlewild Beach. Drawing on the argument the historian Carolyn Finney made in *Black Faces, White Spaces*, the graphic lists outdoor spaces around the United States "that have long been safer havens for Black people to find joy in nature." Since most REI customers will likely not recognize that Lincoln Hills, Colorado, or Lake Ivanhoe, Wisconsin, were where Black Americans gathered to fish, hike, swim, and enjoy the woods, the design offers an education in outdoor recreation history. For Mapp, her nonprofit participants, as well as representatives of REI who worked on this project, this gear is a way to express a new kind of history, where a more diverse set of Americans are explicitly named as a part of the back-to-nature experience.[2]

The REI and Outdoor Afro, Inc., collaboration is just one example of the way many advocacy groups in the twenty-first century are claiming space in the outdoors by participating in the outdoor clothing and equipment industry. Another example is NativesOutdoors, which has a distinctive origin story but a similarly broad goal. Len Nece, Diné, founded NativesOutdoors as a social media project to broaden the outdoor identity. The goal was to "highlight the stories and photos of Native people in outdoor recreation to address the lack of representation of Indigenous people in the outdoor industry." As it did for Mapp, the industry gave activists a way in to a critique of narrow representation. NativesOutdoors is now both a media company and an outdoor products company. The company has partnered with Eddie Bauer to consult on current designs that Eddie Bauer uses on gear and apparel and to help Eddie Bauer "make reparations to Native communities and artists." In 2023, Eddie Bauer offered a notable acknowledgment of its history, writing on its website: "We acknowledge that some Eddie Bauer product designs and names have been appropriated from Indigenous artists, peoples and cultures." Given how recently Eddie Bauer catalogs celebrated a romanticized cowboys' American West while continuing to erase Indigenous pasts and presence, this is a surprising but welcome admission.[3]

Other examples of advocacy groups working hard to define an alternative set of access points and relationships to nature show imagination about what the outdoor identity can be. Together, these projects suggest that there might be a new way to define the Americanness at the core of the outdoor identity. The Venture Out Project leads backpacking and other wilderness trips for the queer and transgender community. Blackpackers addresses the gap in representation and provides gear and lessons for how to pack for a backpacking trip for Black Americans. Fat Girls Hiking creates a community for safer spaces and more access with online advice on gear that fits, while Alpine Curves sells that kind of equipment, from base layers to ice fishing gear, all in true plus sizes. Unlikely Hikers, a nationwide hiking group with a podcast and Instagram account, articulates the activists' critiques most coherently: "The outdoor industry and media has for too long displayed a very narrow definition of who is 'outdoorsy' that isn't representative of most of us." Rather than accept the "normative, one-dimensional" representation that is common in the outdoor industry, Unlikely Hikers works to increase access and build community for "adventurers who are plus size, Black, Indigenous, People of Color, queer, trans and non-binary, disabled, neurodivergent" and beyond. With such a list, the organization both recognizes the existing outdoor archetype and invites a new population to claim their identity as authentic recreationists.[4]

A second trend of note in the outdoor industry is visible to any attendee of recent Outdoor Retailer trade shows: new ways of addressing climate change. The trade shows gather brands, retailers, designers, manufacturers, and other industry representatives for three days to meet, make deals, and generally fawn over new products. At the Snow Show in Salt Lake City in 2023, the products on display during the Innovation Awards demonstrated the industry's commitment to considering its impact on the climate from both production and consumption ends. The awards honored ski makers looking to replace plastics with natural alternatives, running shoe and sandal designers planning for a circular economy by allowing for recurring subscriptions with returns to address shoe waste, and creative thinkers who hope to keep products out of the waste stream to begin with by making sure users find the gear they've lost and resell the gear they're done with. Educational sessions at the Snow Show mirrored the innovative products: topics for the week included "Rethinking Materials, Processes, and Product Design for Sustainable Experience" and "Supply Chains and Climate."

The lessons of these recent outdoor industry conversations vary based on the hopefulness or cynicism readers bring. For some the cumulative lesson of these efforts might be that the industry has shifted from selling an image of the "green" outdoor lifestyle to its consumers based on surface-level gestures at sustainability to an earnest and sustained effort at changing how manufacturing and selling itself work. It is also possible to be critical of the notion that making skis with fungi rather than carbon will adequately address the climate crisis. Can the solution really be more consumption? Similarly, the activist organizations working outside industry structures to create more access to outdoor recreation for a wider range of people seems like work to be celebrated, but will the industry's current positive response continue? Is the embrace of a broader American outdoor identity a calculated recognition of a new, potentially lucrative market?

Although these questions about the future cannot be answered here, there are lessons to be had from this foray through the outdoor industry's past. As we have seen over the course of this book, the outdoor industry has changed substantially in 150 years because it has responded to broader trends such as war, innovation, and cultural movements. The new gear meant to address climate change and the collaborations with outdoor brands that diversify both workforces and designs show this responsiveness. Much like their counterparts in the 1880s or the 1950s, outdoorspeople cannot escape to nature without carrying packs heavy with expectations of expertise, belonging, and the notion that there is a right way to be outdoors. Recognizing these histories, embracing the tensions and joys alike that they bring, has the possibility of making each step a little lighter. May our future journeys welcome that curiosity.

Archival Collections

Adirondack Experience (formally Adirondack Museum and Library) (ADK)
Adventure 16 Corporate Archive (A16)
American Alpine Club (AAC)
American Recreation Archive (Sierra Designs and Kelty)
Autry National Center Library and Archives (Autry)
Bancroft Library
Boulder Public Library (BPL)
California Historical Society
Denver Public Library (DPL)
Eddie Bauer Corporate Archives (EB)
Hagley Museum and Library
Honnold/Mudd Library
Library of Congress (LOC)
National Archives and Records Administration (NARA)
Oregon Historical Society (OHS)
Science History Institute (formerly Chemical Heritage Foundation) (SHI)
Smithsonian Archives Center (AC)
Smithsonian National Museum of American History (NMAH)
Smithsonian National Museum of American History Library (NMAH Library)
University of Washington Special Collections (UWSC)
U.S. Army Military History Institute
Utah State University Outdoor Recreation Archive
W. L. Gore & Associates Corporate Archive (Gore)
Washington State History Research Center
Wichita State University Special Collections and University Archives
Winterthur Museum and Library (Winterthur)

Introduction

1. Weaver and Merrill, *Camping Can Be Fun*.
2. Orvell, *The Real Thing*; Banet-Weiser, *Authentic™*; Lears, *Fables of Abundance*. For authenticity via cheap and secondhand goods, see Le Zotte, *From Goodwill to Grunge*, and Woloson, *Crap*.
3. On gender and consumption, see Roberts, "Gender, Consumption, and Commodity Culture"; Swiencicki, "Consuming Brotherhood"; Jacobson, "Manly Boys and Enterprising Dreamers"; and Lubar, "Men/Women/Production/Consumption."
4. On consumption and national identity, see Hoganson, *Consumers' Imperium*, and Domosh, *American Commodities in an Age of Empire*. On clothing and national identity, see Schorman, *Selling Style*.
5. For the debates around consumer versus industry control, see Packard, *Hidden Persuaders*; Ewen, *Captains of Consciousness*; Lears, *Fables of Abundance*; Marchand, *Advertising the American Dream*; Ohmann, *Selling Culture*; Strasser, *Satisfaction Guaranteed*; Tedlow, *New and Improved*; and Leach, *Land of Desire*. On consumers as active agents in consumption, see Anishanslin, *Portrait of a Woman in Silk*, and Alexander, *Treasures Afoot*. On white people linking authenticity to Native pasts, see Deloria, *Playing Indian*, and Paige Raibmon, *Authentic Indians*.
6. This book draws on the tradition in the field of environmental history of taking seriously American leisure practices in nature that dates back to Nash, *Wilderness and the American Mind*, and Schmitt, *Back to Nature*. Cronon's essay "The Trouble with Wilderness" (1992) suggested that Americans' attachment to the wild was based on culture. For environmental histories of outdoor recreation, see Cronon, "The Trouble with Wilderness"; Price, *Flight Maps*; Coleman, *Ski Style*; Philpott, *Vacationland*; Schrepfer, *Nature's Altars*; Taylor, *Pilgrims of the Vertical*; Young, *Camping Grounds*; Young, *Heading Out*; and Childers, *Colorado Powder Keg*. On nature tourism, see Shaffer, *See America First*; Rothman, *Devil's Bargains*; Shapiro, *The Lure of the North Woods*; Sears, *Sacred Places*; Price, *Flight Maps*; Kirk, *Counterculture Green*; and Sutter, *Driven Wild*. On environment and business history, see Elmore, *Citizen Coke*; Berghoff and Rome, *Green Capitalism?*
7. For cultural histories of fashion, see Clemente, *Dress Casual*; Rabinovitch-Fox, *Dressed for Freedom*; Le Zotte, *From Goodwill to Grunge*; and Ford, *Liberated Threads*. For material culture studies on consumption and identity, see Bushman, *Refinement of America*; Anishanslin, *Portrait of a Woman in Silk*; Cohen, *Luxurious Citizens*; Alexander, *Treasures Afoot*; and Blaszczyk, *American Consumer Society*.
8. For industry histories, see Elmore, *Citizen Coke*; Chatelain, *Franchise*; Davis, *From Head Shops to Whole Foods*. Founder memoirs include Cabela, *Cabela's*; Yowell, *The Hippie Guide to Climbing the Corporate Ladder and Other Mountains*; and Chouinard, *Let My People Go Surfing*.

Chapter 1. Buckskin

1. Hough, *Out of Doors*, 90–91.
2. Young, *Heading Out*, 43.
3. Aron, *Working at Play*, 168.
4. Sears, *Woodcraft*, 2, 3, 13.
5. Kephart, *Camping and Woodcraft*, 2.
6. "Smoothing it" does not roll off the tongue easily in the twenty-first century, but it was a common invocation of early twentieth-century guidebook authors who wanted to assure readers they did not have to rough it to enjoy the woods. See, for instance, Sears's third chapter in *Woodcraft*, which includes a section on "Roughing It or Smoothing It."
7. Kephart, *Camping and Woodcraft*, 2.
8. Kephart, *Camping and Woodcraft*, 2–3.
9. Kephart, *Camping and Woodcraft*, 5.
10. For "Ideal Indian," see Seton, *The Book of Woodcraft*, 8. For more on Seton's views on Indians and woodcraft, see Anderson, *The Chief*. On visions of Indians in a mythic frontier past, see Deloria, *Playing Indian*, 103. For "light but right," see Kephart, *Camping and Woodcraft*, 218. For "less a man carries," see Kephart, *Camp Cookery*, vii.
11. James C. Allan, "Snowshoeing in Canuckia," *Outing* 13 (1888/89); Hough, *Out of Doors*, 93.
12. Hough, *Out of Doors*, 95–100. See also Stewart Edward White, "The Silent Places or The Trail of Jingoss," *Outing: Sport, Adventure, Travel, Fiction* 43 (October 1903–March 1904).
13. "From Caribou to Clothing in Quick Time," *Forest and Stream*, March 11, 1899; J. W. Schultz, "The Sportsman Tourist: Some Old Time Plainsmen," *Forest and Stream*, July 4, 1903, 2.
14. "When Everybody Called Me *Gabe-bines*: 'Forever-Flying-Bird': Teachings from Paul Buffalo," Timothy G. Roufs, ed., www.d.umn.edu/cla/faculty/troufs/Buffalo/PB10.html. See also Hough, *Out of Doors*, 101.
15. For "ideal woodsman," see Breck, *The Way of the Woods*, 26. For "no white man," see Hough, *Out of Doors*, 39,
16. Sears, *Woodcraft*, 22–23; Henderson, *Practical Hints on Camping*, 22; White, *The Forest*, 106.
17. On buckskin's qualities, see Roosevelt, *Hunting Trips of a Ranchman*, 40; White, *Camp and Trail*, 38–39; and Kephart, *Camping and Woodcraft*, 280.
18. On the strenuous life and straddling the divide, see Brinkley, *The Wilderness Warrior*, 39, 182. On Roosevelt and buckskin, see Canfield, *Theodore Roosevelt*, 5, 157.
19. On "playing at frontier hunter," see "Urban Woodsman: Theodore Roosevelt and His Buckskin Suit," MCNY Blog: New York Stories, November 4, 2014, blog.mcny.org/2014/11/04/urban-woodsman-theodore-roosevelt-and-his-buckskin-suit/.

On "picturesque" and "first-class," see Roosevelt, *Ranch Life and the Hunting-Trail*, 81 and 99. On "terrible vigor," see Hagedorn, *Roosevelt in the Bad Lands*, 150.

20. Beard, *Camp-Lore and Woodcraft*, iv–v, 24, 171.

21. Beard, *Camp-Lore and Woodcraft*, 81.

22. For "rudely fashioned," see "The New England Exposition," *Forest and Stream*, November 20, 1897, 409. For "frontierish," see "Tirador," "The Sportsman Tourist," *Forest and Stream* 15 (August 1880–February 1881): 384.

23. For photograph, see "Spotlight On . . . Ute Cradleboards," History Colorado, December 10, 2018, www.historycolorado.org/story/articles-print/2018/12/10/spotlight-ute-cradleboards. For poor mothering, see Jacobs, *White Mother to a Dark Race*, 120–121. For contrasts to scientific mothering, see Theobald, *Reproduction on the Reservation*, 51–53.

24. White, *The Forest*, 6.

25. White, *The Mountains*, 6–7, 131, 140–141.

26. Kephart, *Camping and Woodcraft*, 280.

27. "Floating on the Missouri River," *Forest and Stream*, April 5, 1902, 264.

28. ["That Bible Man"?], *Forest and Stream*, November 2, 1876, 199.

29. Gould, *How to Camp Out*, 38, 266.

30. For "sufficiently in fashion," see Gould, *How to Camp Out*, 35. For gentleman and "two-dollar a day laborer," see White, *The Mountains*, 265, 267.

31. For "clad" and "real Indian," see White, *The Mountains*, 267. For additional examples of white men whose identities were uncovered later because of their dress, see Young, *Heading Out*, 89, and Shrepfer, *Nature's Altars*, 73.

32. Nordhoff, *California for Health*, 69; Pinkerton, *Woodcraft for Women*, 164.

33. "Deer Hide Jacket," historical essay on Wisconsin Historical Museum object #2005.147.1, November 17, 2005, www.wisconsinhistory.org/Records/Article/CS2768.

34. *Pfluegers' Tips on Tackle*, no. 139 (Akron, Ohio: Enterprise Manufacturing Co., 1919), Autry; Kephart, *Camping and Woodcraft*, 110.

Chapter 2. A Green Respite

1. White, *The Forest*, 23–31.

2. White, *The Forest*, 24–26.

3. White, *The Forest*, 26–27.

4. Abercrombie & Fitch, catalog, 1922, NMAH Library; Leach, *Land of Desire*, 7, 9, 20.

5. Leach, *Land of Desire*, 66 and plates 6 and 8 (between pages 206 and 207). Store descriptions drawn from Abercrombie & Fitch, catalog, 1922.

6. Abercrombie & Fitch, catalog, 1923, AC. See also Abercrombie & Fitch, catalog, 1913, NMAH Library. On the visual tactics of display that shaped consumer experience, see Iarocci, *Visual Merchandising*, and Lasc, *Architectures of Display*.

7. Abercrombie & Fitch, catalog, 1913; Abercrombie & Fitch, catalog, 1923.

8. *Country Life in America*, May 1920, 139, Winterthur.

9. On display windows, see Iarocci, *Visual Merchandising*; Lasc, *Architectures of Display*; Leach, *Land of Desire*; and Whitaker, *Service and Style*. VL&A, catalog, n.d., NMAH Library. "Eddie Bauer has gone hunting: anecdotes from the fields and streams," pamphlet, EB.

10. Hirsch-Weis Manufacturing Co. Catalog No. 64, 1925, Hirsch-Weis (White Stag) Catalogs—1925–1942, Harold Hirsch Papers, Mss 1819, OHS. For Bissell, see Strasser, *Satisfaction Guaranteed*, 189–190.

11. Model Clothing Company to Hirsch-Weis Mfg. Co., October 3, 1929, Correspondence, 1929 and 1947, Hirsch-Weis Company Records, Mss 1436, OHS.

12. Sears, *Woodcraft*, 112. For "useless," "promiscuous," and "risky," see A. Radclyffe Dunmore, "Camping from Newfoundland to California," *Country Life in America* 12, no. 2 (June 1907): 176, Winterthur.

13. "Some Hints for the Amateur Camper," *Country Life in America*, July 1902, lx, Winterthur.

14. Dunmore, "Camping from Newfoundland to California," 176.

15. *Country Life in America*, July 1902, Winterthur.

16. On the reach of the outdoor press, see Neuzil, *The Environment and the Press*.

17. "Footing It Through the Mountains," 159, in "The Fullness of Summer: An August Calendar," *Country Life in America*, August 1902, Winterthur.

18. Sumner, *The Magazine Century*, 366.

19. Kephart, *Camp Cookery*, back pages.

20. Kephart, *Camp Cookery*.

21. Nathaniel Nitkin, "City Hiker Hits Trail," *New York Times*, May 19, 1940.

22. *Forest and Stream*, September 1919, 7–9; Henry F. Coons to Hirsch-Weis Mfg. Co., December 18, 1929, Correspondence, 1929 and 1947, Hirsch-Weis Records, OHS.

23. Abercrombie & Fitch, catalog, 1930, Winterthur; Kephart, *Camping and Woodcraft*, 146; *Outing Magazine*, Advertiser, 16, Winterthur.

24. R. Schrenkeisen to Gentlemen, December 11, 1923, Warshaw Collection of Business Americana, AC.

25. Abercrombie's Camp, Baker, Murray, and Imbrue, catalog, n.d., inside front cover, Autry.

26. White, *Camp and Trail*, vii–viii, 81.

27. White, *Camp and Trail*, viii, 104–105.

28. Abercrombie & Fitch catalog, 1908–1909 supplement, 1–3, AC.

29. Erwin Strohmaier, "Early Vacations," Erwin Strohmaier Family Papers, BANC MSS 98/159 c v.2, Bancroft Library, Berkeley, Calif.

30. Breck, *The Way of the Woods*, 59–60.

31. Gordon, "Any Desired Length," 24.

32. Miller, *Camp Craft: Modern Practice and Equipment*, 190–191.

33. Kephart, *Camping and Woodcraft*, 163; Pinkerton, *Woodcraft for Women*, 12.
34. Miller, *Camp Craft*, 191; Kephart, *Camping and Woodcraft*, 163.
35. "Grace Leach Hudowalski, #9," in Peggy Lynn and Sandra Weber, *Breaking Trail: Remarkable Women of the Adirondacks* (New York: Purple Mountain Press, 2004), 123–129, ADK; Craig Gilborn to William Crowley, July 30, 1982, ADK; "ADK and the 46ers," 82.49.1, ADK.
36. For Rondeau and "brushy," see "ADK and the 46ers," ADK. For "resignation," see Ed Hale, "Princess of the Peaks," *Adirondack Peeks* 22, no. 2 (Fall/Winter 1985–1986): 8–10, ADK. For "signature coffee," see Brian Mann, "Soul of the Summits," *Adirondack Life* (2001): 98–104, ADK.
37. Mann, "Soul of the Summits"; Breea Willingham, "Climbers Mourn 'Amazing Grace,'" *Times Union*, March 15, 2004, ADK.

Chapter 3. Buck Skein™

1. Hill, *American Menswear*, 54, 90.
2. On the Hirsches at Meier and Frank, see Whitaker, *Service and Style*. On the Hirsch family businesses, see Zeb Larson, "Max Hirsch," in *Immigrant Entrepreneurship: German-American Business Biographies, 1720 to the Present*, vol. 4, ed. Jeffrey Fear, German Historical Institute; White Stag Manufacturing Company Prospectus, March 17, 1959, Historical Reviews and Financial Report, Hirsch Papers, OHS; and Harold Hirsch, interview by Helene Hirsch Oppenheimer, 1988 and 1989, transcript, 49, SR 2831, OHS. For "through the back door," see Hirsch, interview, 47.
3. For "special Hirsch-Weis process," see Hirsch-Weis, catalog no. 64, 1925, 5, OHS. For "paraffin" and "purely for work," see Hirsch, interview, 47–50. For "taking advantage," see White Stag Prospectus.
4. "Proof: Unsolicited Letters of Approval Taken from the Many in Our Files Prove the Quality of Our OUTDOOR GARMENTS," Hirsch-Weis: Outdoor Garments Ads ca. 1930s–1940s, Hirsch Papers, OHS.
5. "The Biggest Idea Ever Developed in Outdoor Garments," n.d., Hirsch-Weis (White Stag) Catalogs—1925–1942, 3, Hirsch Papers, OHS.
6. For letters, see "Proof: Unsolicited Letters," Harold S. Bomberger to Hirsch-Weis Mfg. Co., July 26, 1929, Correspondence, 1929 and 1947, Hirsch-Weis Records, OHS.
7. For "fifteen seasons" and "shabby," see Edward T. Tandy, "Building a National Business Out of a Local Need," *Printers' Ink* 116, no. 1 (July 7, 1921): 62. For "oldtimers," see Filson, catalog, n.d., AC.
8. Tandy, "Building a National Business," 64.
9. *Von Lengerke & Antoine*, catalog, 1932, 1, Winterthur.
10. On the disagreements between Abercrombie and Fitch, see Witherell, *L.L. Bean*.
11. Chamberlin, *On the Trail*.

12. For "clannish," see Larson, "Max Hirsch." For "dormitories" and "competing," see Hirsch, interview, 5.

13. Hirsch, interview, 49–56.

14. For "foreign-sounding," see Hirsch, interview, 57. On functional regional style, see William Toll, "Acclimatizing Fashion: Jewish Inventiveness on the Other (Pacific) Coast, 1850–1940," in *A Perfect Fit*, ed. Goldstein and Greenberg, 144. On the White Stag sign in the twenty-first century, see Edwin Battistella, "White Stag Manufacturing," Oregon Encyclopedia, www.oregonencyclopedia.org/articles/white_stag_manufacturing/#.Y_07u-zML8c.

15. Tandy, "Building a National Business," 61.

16. Tandy, "Building a National Business," 61–62.

17. For "valuable business assets," see Strasser, *Satisfaction Guaranteed*, 43–47. On trademarks, see also Leach, *Land of Desire*, 45–46.

18. Charlotte D. Widrig, "He Made Back-Packing Easier," *Seattle Daily Times*, July 16, 1961.

19. Widrig, "He Made Back-Packing Easier."

20. Widrig, "He Made Back-Packing Easier"; Don Duncan, "Seattleite's Pack Holds Sentiment Load," *Seattle Times*, August 21, 1972; Peter Blecha, "Trager Manufacturing Company / Trager USA," October 22, 2013, Historylink.org, www.historylink.org/File/10625.

21. For "true grit," see Tom Swint, " 'I Dig Ozette's Diggings,' " *Seattle Daily Times*, June 13, 1971. For imitation pack, see 1661 Trapper Nelson Indian Pack Board, Accession # 013.03.01, Pemberton Museum, www.pembertonmuseum.org/collections/objects/henry-george/pack-board/; and Petzoldt, *The New Wilderness Handbook*, 97. On the notion that the authentic origin of equipment indicated its effectiveness to users, see Heggie, *Higher and Colder*, 93.

22. White, *Camp and Trail*, 38–39.

23. White, *Camp and Trail*, vii.

24. White, *Camp and Trail*, 38. All other recommendations also from White.

25. *Federal Trade Commission Decisions: Findings, Orders, and Stipulations, July 1, 1942, to December 31, 1942*, vol. 35 (Washington: U.S. Government Printing Office, 1943), 137.

26. On "links," see Lears, *Fables of Abundance*, 5. On truth in advertising, see Leach, *Land of Desire*, 179.

27. *FTC Decisions*, 132, 134. On advertising and the 1930s consumer movement, see Stole, *Advertising on Trial*. On the FTC and the unwary purchaser, see Pettit, *The Science of Deception*.

28. *FTC Decisions*, 138–139.

29. Ohmann, *Selling Culture*, 79; Harold Hirsch, "What's Ahead in Ski Fashions?" October 15, 1964, #34, Box 2, Harold Hirsch Papers, OHS.

30. For "ideal," see Cross, *An All-Consuming Century*, 2. For "new visions," see Ohmann, *Selling Culture*, 79–80. Harold Hirsch, "What's Ahead in Ski Fashions?" 4, October 15, 1964, #34, Box 2, Hirsch Papers, OHS.

Chapter 4. Feather Foam and Pocket Stoves

1. Eddie Bauer memoirs, 637, EB.
2. For "war industry," see Hirsch. On lack of updates, see Richard M. Leonard, "Mountain Equipment," November 1, 1945, 2–4, Cold-Weather Clothing and Equipment Correspondence—1945–1946, Historians Background Material Files 1941–1961, Box 7, RG 544, Records of the United States Army Materiel Command, NARA. For "utility and purpose," see "Special Report Prepared for General Gregory by Technical Information Branch," November 11, 1945, War Department Files; Reports, Box 15, Papers of Georges F. Doriot, LOC. On conferences, see Quartermaster Research and Development in World War II, 954, Historical Staff, University of Pittsburgh, Armed Forces History Collection, NMAH. Thank you to Johns Hopkins University Press for permission to use selections from Rachel S. Gross, "Layering for a Cold War: The M-1943 Combat System, Military Testing, and Clothing as Technology," in this chapter. Copyright © 2019, The Society for the History of Technology. This article first appeared in *Technology and Culture* 60, no. 2 (April 2019). Published with permission by Johns Hopkins University Press.
3. Leonard, "Mountain Equipment."
4. Spector, *The Legend of Eddie Bauer*, 20.
5. Herman, *Freedom's Forge*.
6. Bestor Robinson to Georges F. Doriot, Special Forces Section Report, March 13, 1943, War Department Files Correspondence, Box 6, Papers of Georges F. Doriot, LOC.
7. Witherell, *L.L. Bean*, 129, 133. At the time, mail order was 90 percent of the business with the other 10 percent generated through customers wandering through the factory and trying on pants in the aisles (until the showroom got built in 1942). See also Gorman, *Guaranteed to Last*, 54, 68, 86.
8. Hirsch, interview, 157. Precisely because they served as special consultants, Bauer, Bean, and Hirsch were able to secure large and often profitable contracts with the military. Bean advised the special committee on the height of footwear—he advised that the ten-inch-high leather-top boots would be preferable to suggestions of boots as tall as eighteen inches because they would be lighter and cheaper to make. The U.S. Navy ordered the Bean boot. Similarly, the Research and Development Branch of the Quartermaster Corps hired Bean as a "Departmental Expert" to design a briefcase; after he did so, L.L. Bean, Inc., "received an order for 40,000 of them." See Witherell, *L.L. Bean*, 140, 142. Eddie Bauer accepted government contracts to produce down-insulated clothing and sleeping bags, producing by his count 220,000 bags in the first year of production. Eddie Bauer memoirs, 624 and 628; Gorman, *Guaranteed to Last*, 86.
9. On testing, see Leonard, "Mountain Equipment" and "Alaskan Test Expedition," vol. 1, 1942, Mountain and Winter Warfare Board/Alaska Test Expedition-Report

Volume 1, FF53, 10th Mountain Division Collection, DPL. On product comparisons, see Report on Winter Warfare Equipment by Infantry Test Officer of the War Department, 1941, 10th Mountain Division; Mountain and Winter Warfare Board/ Winter Warfare Equip. Report/Equip Pic Captions, 10th Mountain Division Collection, DPL. On civilian experts, see American Alpine Club, Meeting Minutes, April 11, 1942, 10th Mountain Division, American Alpine Club-equipment for Mountain Troops: 1941–1942, 10th Mountain Division Collection, DPL; Vilhjalmur Stefansson, Cold Weather Clothing Report, September 22, 1949, Cold-Weather Clothing, Papers by Vilhjalmur Stefansson, Box 7, RG 544, NARA.

10. "Maine's Bean Outfits Sportsmen Everywhere," *Life*, October 13, 1941, 122–123.

11. Report on Winter Warfare Equipment by Infantry Test Officer of the War Department, 1941, plate 124, 10th Mountain Division. For the full list of participants on the Alaskan Test Expedition, see "Alaskan Test Expedition," vol. 1, 1942, FF53, 10th Mountain Division Collection, DPL.

12. Washburn quoted in Roberts, *The Last of His Kind*, 206. On Washburn's earlier work, see also Sfraga, *Bradford Washburn*.

13. There were many other military test expeditions as well, including the Wood Yukon Expedition in 1941 and the Mount Rainier Test Expedition in 1942. See Report of Wood Yukon Expedition, 10th Mountain Division Collection, DPL; Mountain and Winter Warfare Board/Wood Yukon Expedition Report, sections 1–7, ca. 1941, 10th Mountain Division Collection, DPL; and Report of The Mount Rainier Test Expedition, May 8 to 20, 1942, 10th Mountain Division; 87th Mtn. Inf. Batt. (Reinf)/ Mount Rainier Test Expedition Report, 1942, 10th Mountain Division Collection, DPL. On actual scientific data, see William House, "Mountain Equipment for the U.S. Army," *American Alpine Journal* (1946): 227.

14. For "art," see Paul A. Siple, "General Principles Governing Selection of Clothing for Cold Climates," June 1942, Expeditions/USAS, 1939–1941, Research Notes and Report, 1939–45, Box 19, Paul A. Siple Family Papers, NARA. Beginning in 1943, the Research and Development Branch, a part of the Military Planning Division of the Office of the Quartermaster General, was the branch in control of the testing.

15. On Georges Doriot, see Ante, *Creative Capital*, and "The Growth and Operations of the Military Planning Division," 166–167, Quartermaster Research and Development in World War II, Historical Staff, University of Pittsburgh, Armed Forces History Collection, NMAH.

16. Porter, *Trust in Numbers*, ix.

17. On the Cold Chamber, see Farrington Daniels, Jr., interview with Mark Van Ells, 1995, OH 499, Wisconsin Veterans Museum Research Center. See also "The Research and Development Branch," 703, Quartermaster Research and Development in World War II, Historical Staff, University of Pittsburgh, Armed Forces History Collection, NMAH. On the broader military research program, see Leonard, "Mountain Equipment," 3, and "The Climatic Research Laboratory," 816,

Quartermaster Research and Development in World War II, Historical Staff, University of Pittsburgh, Armed Forces History Collection, NMAH.

18. Folk, "The Harvard Fatigue Laboratory." Putting "skin" and "body" in quotations is the practice of military histories of the Copper Man, though in this work it serves the purpose of drawing attention to the artificial body meant to simulate real feeling. Endrusick et al., "Manikin History"; "Copper Man," *The Quartermaster Corps Reports* 1, no. 1, February 1947, Research and Development Histories, U.S. Army Natick Laboratories, Historians Background Material Files 1941–1961, Box 21, U.S. Army Materiel Command, NARA; "General Review of the Copper Man," Environmental Protection, Copper Man, U.S. Army Natick Laboratories, Historians Background Material Files 1941–1961, Box 24, U.S. Army Materiel Command, NARA. " 'Ideal GI' Gets Cold Billet Atop Bleak New England Peak," March 27, 1948, Environmental Protection, Copper Man, U.S. Army Natick Laboratories, Historians Background Material Files 1941–1961, Box 24, U.S. Army Materiel Command, NARA.

19. Harold S. Hirsch, interview by Helene Hirsch Oppenheimer, 1988–1989, manuscript, SR 2831, OHS.

20. Risch, *The Quartermaster Corps*, 72.

21. Eddie Bauer memoir; Alphabetical Listing of Major War Supply Contracts, cumulative through February 1943, vol. 1, War Production Board Statistics Division; Risch, *The Quartermaster Corps*, 72.

22. Hirsch, interview, 162; "Nylon," I-10, histories prepared by War Records Staff of Public Relations, box 29–30, DuPont Co. Public Affairs Department Collection (accession 1410), Hagley Museum and Library; Risch and Pitkin, *Clothing the Soldier of World War II.*

23. "Nylon," III-40, I-30.

24. Hirsch, interview.

25. Charlotte M. Gibbs, "The Hygiene of Clothing Materials," *Household Textiles* (Boston: Whitcomb & Barrows, 1917).

26. "The Office of the Assistant for Product Analysis," 754, Quartermaster Research and Development in World War II, Historical Staff, University of Pittsburgh, Armed Forces History Collection, NMAH. See also W. F. Pounder to Gen. Doriot, April 15, 1945, Research and Development, Clothing Items, Captain W. F. Pounder, Pounder Collection, Armed Forces History Collection, NMAH; News report, attached to letter from Isabelle C. Pounder to Donald E. Kloster, October 12, 1989, Pounder Collection, Armed Forces History Collection, NMAH; and Wet Cold Team Pacific Area, Report, 1945, Box 17, Papers of Georges F. Doriot, LOC.

27. Hirsch, interview, 155–161, OHS; White Stag catalog, c. 1943, 95.235.28, Autry.

28. "Wear for War Work Now," ad mock-up, Harold Hirsch Papers, OHS.

29. On Coleman's wartime work, see "Advisory Board to the Research and Development Branch, Military Planning Division," Army Service Forces, Office of the

Quartermaster General, QMC 17-4, War Dept Files Reports, Box 10, Papers of Georges F. Doriot, LOC. On the design of Model 520, see Portable Stove Patent, Boyd W. Tullis (assignor to the Coleman Lamp and Stove Company), filed January 12, 1942, granted April 2, 1946, Serial No. 426,421. On military orders, see Alphabetical Listing of Major War Supply Contracts. For more on the Coleman stove during the war, see Risch, *The Quartermaster Corps*, 150; "Reader's Digest Tells '520' Story," *Coleman News*, FF18, Box 41, MS 2013-03, Coleman Company Records, Wichita State University Special Collections and University Archives; and Lewis Nordyke, "Foxhole Stove," *The American Legion Magazine* 39, no. 2 (August 1945): 28, 42.

30. "Portable Stove," Kansas Historical Society, kansaspedia, www.kshs.org/kansapedia/portable-stove/10111.
31. "Reader's Digest Tells '520' Story."
32. Eddie Bauer, "Propaganda," November 1, 1982, Eddie Bauer Folder, EB.
33. On the arguments for what became Natick, see Georges Doriot, Hearings Before the Subcommittee of the Committee on Appropriations, House of Representatives, 79th Congress, Second Session on the Military Establishment Appropriation Bill for 1947 (Washington: U.S. Government Printing Office, 1946), Box 17, Papers of Georges F. Doriot, LOC. See also Roach, *Grunt*, 20.

Chapter 5. Pup Tents and Mummy Bags

1. Surplus Property Act of 1944, Act October 3, 1944, CH 479, 58 Stat. 765. On Bryant, see Ed Mitchell, "Nelson Bryant," *Fishing in Salt Water*, July/August 2008, and Nelson Bryant, "Outdoors: Today's Equipment Is Up with the Times," *New York Times*, February 16, 1981. For a similar attitude to Bryant's, see Daniel J. Evans to Larry Ferguson, March 10, 1987, Box 19, Harvey Manning Papers, Acc 2097-003, UWSC.
2. "Tent Frames on Sale in Surplus Offerings," *New York Times*, July 15, 1946.
3. Manning, *Backpacking*, 136; Bryant, "Outdoors."
4. On American business and the war, see Robertson and Tucker, *Nature at War*; Herman, *Freedom's Forge*; Kennedy, *Engineers of Victory*; Wilson, *Destructive Creation*; Baime, *The Arsenal of Democracy*; and Overy, *Why the Allies Won*. Historians of skiing and climbing have argued for the importance of the war for shaping the culture and technology of these sporting industries postwar, though they have yet to examine how surplus stores were the crucial part of that link. See Coleman, *Ski Style*, and Taylor, *Pilgrims of the Vertical*.
5. On war materiel, see "The Aftermath of War Production," Automotive Council for War Production, 1944[?], National Automotive History Collection, Detroit Public Library. On the memory of WWI, see Fredrick J. Dobney, "The Evolution of a Reconversion Policy: World War II and Surplus War Property Disposal," *The Historian*

36, no. 3 (May 1974): 499; Bernard M. Baruch and John M. Hancock, *Report on War and Post-War Adjustment Policies: February 15, 1944* (Washington, 1944). On "clogging," see "The Aftermath of War Production"; and Baruch and Hancock, *Report on War and Post-War.* On the purpose of resale, see Louis Cain and George Neumann, "Planning for Peace: The Surplus Property Act of 1944," *Journal of Economic History* 41, no. 1 (March 1981): 129–135; and Surplus Property Act of 1944.

6. Baruch and Hancock, *Report on War and Post-War*; Dobney, "The Evolution of a Reconversion Policy"; James R. Chiles, "How the Great War on War Surplus Got Won or Lost," *Smithsonian Magazine* 26, no. 9 (December 1995): 509; Joseph B. Epstein, "War Surplus Disposals," *Survey of Current Business*, October 1947, 10–11.

7. On mountains, see Dobney, "The Evolution of a Reconversion Policy," 509; "Congress Trying Now to Decide What to Do with War Leftovers," *Newsweek*, XXIV, August 28, 1944, 32, quoted in Dobney, "The Evolution of a Reconversion Policy"; "A Mile of Jeeps," *Newsweek*, quoted in Dobney, "The Evolution of a Reconversion Policy." For examples of Camp Hale coverage, see Farish, "Creating Cold War Environments," 51–84.

8. For "after the war," see Karl Truesdell to Georges F. Doriot, February 1, 1944, War Department Files Correspondence, Equipment and Supplies, Design and Development, Box 6, Doriot Papers, Library of Congress. For Carter, see H. Adams Carter, "Mountain Troop Equipment," *Harvard Mountaineering* 7 (June 1945): 26. On the influence of war on food tastes, see Collingham, *The Taste of War*, 439, 474.

9. For enthusiasts on the equipment boom, see Carter, "Mountain Troop Equipment," 26; and Recreational Equipment Cooperative News, January 22, 1943, Lloyd Anderson Papers, Accession 2648-001, UWSC. See also L.L. Bean catalog, 1945, 3, NMAH Library. On A&F, see Charles Grutzner, "Shortage in Camp Equipment; High Prices Also Limit Comfort Beside the Lake and Stream," *New York Times*, April 20, 1947. For more general deferred demand, see Horowitz, *The Anxieties of Affluence*, 46.

10. *American Alpine Journal* 6, nos. 18–20 (1946–1947).

11. Estimates for inflation here and in subsequent chapters drawn from the CPI Inflation Calculator, U.S. Bureau of Labor Statistics, www.bls.gov/data/inflation_calculator.htm. On Orkney's reselling, see Karl Klooster, "G.I. Joe's: A Surplus of Success," *This Week*, July 13, 1983, Vertical File: Portland-Business Establishments-Retail stores, Oregon Historical Society (hereafter OHS business clippings). On "warehouse," see Bob Kehoe, "From Army Surplus to Northwest Retail Giant," advertising supplement of *The Oregonian*, March 31, 2002, OHS business clippings. On waiting overnight, see "Veterans in Vigil for Old Barracks," *New York Times*, July 25, 1946.

12. On ducks and planes, see Chiles, "How the Great War on War Surplus Got Won or Lost." On Quonset huts, see Jenny Price, "Old School," *On Wisconsin*, onwisconsin.uwalumni.com/features/old-school/.

13. "Tent Frames," *New York Times*.
14. Kehoe, "From Army Surplus"; Orkney, *Growing Up with G.I. Joe's*, 8.
15. Manning, *Backpacking*, 65, 155.
16. *Cal Hirsch & Sons* 157, 1916, 21, archive.org/details/Page001_20160321; *Russell's Army, Navy, Camp Sporting Goods*, 1922, Winterthur.
17. Fink, *Backpacking Was the Only Way*, 264. For "unobtainable," see Grutzner, "Shortage in Camp Equipment." On the value of surplus, see "WAA Offers Stocks of Army Clothing," *New York Times*, April 16, 1947.
18. On "converts," see Printer's Ink Editors and Contributors, "Over $500,000 in Orders from One $1,500 Ad," *Case Histories of Successful Advertising* (Printer's Ink, 1949), 202. On "pull[ing] people" and the civilian market, see Orkney, *Growing Up with G.I. Joe's*, 24, 40.
19. Kehoe, "From Army Surplus"; "Spawned in Tent, Oregonian to Chalk up $4-Million in '73," *The Sporting Goods Dealer*, December 1973, OHS business clippings; Orkney, *Growing Up with G.I. Joe's*, xi.
20. *Fibber McGee and Molly*, radio sitcom 550104, m.youtube.com/watch?v=UFQLHYq6fn4; *The Mickey Rooney Show*, episode 11, 1955, archive.org/details/The_Mickey_Rooney_Show_Misc_ep_11.
21. Kehoe, "From Army Surplus."
22. Orkney, *Growing Up with G.I. Joe's*, 28, 6, 29.
23. Orkney, *Growing Up with G.I. Joe's*, 138, 142, 144, 149; "60 Years of Success," Worldwide, www.worldwidebuygroup.com/wps/portal/c/our-story.
24. For "vaudeville," see Manning, *REI*, 41–44. For "cheapskates," see Spring and Manning, *100 Classic Hikes*. For more on Khaki Gang members recognizing each other, see Daniel J. Evans to Larry Ferguson, March 10, 1987, Box 19, Harvey Manning Papers, UWSC.
25. A. M. Kemp, Jr., "The Prestige of the Soldier," *Quartermaster Review*, May/June 1954, www.qmfound.com/prestige_of_the_soldier_uniforms.htm.
26. Charles Williams to Larry Ferguson, February 28, 1987, Box 19, Harvey Manning Papers, UWSC.
27. On cheap goods as status symbols, see Woloson, *Crap*. For co-op prices, see Recreational Equipment Cooperative, Price List, February 1, 1950, Lloyd Anderson Papers, Accession 2648-001, UWSC; and Manning, *50 Years*, 36–46. Betty K. Nelson [to Harvey Manning?], February 23, 1987, Box 19, Harvey Manning Papers, UWSC; Alexandra Pye, interview, May 18, 1994, transcript, Mountaineers History Committee, 5038-002, UWSC. For "pup tents," see Hammett, *Your Own Book of Campcraft*, 23.
28. For Doughboy's, see "Surplus Store Grows with Time, Styles," *Los Angeles Times*, March 23, 1972. Orkney, *Growing Up with G.I. Joe's*, 26; Williams to Ferguson.
29. Printer's Ink Editors and Contributors, "Over $500,000 in Orders," 202.
30. For "rough," see Williams to Ferguson. For "terrible" and "broke [their] backs," see Johnson, interview.

31. For "peculiar," see "Hiking, Camping, Mountaineering and Trail-Clearing Equipment," Seventh Edition, 1950, Potomac Appalachian Trail Club, 3, AAC. For "muskox," see Malcolm MacKay, "The Great Equipment Dilemma," *Summit*, June 1964. See also William House, "Mountain Equipment for the U.S. Army," *American Alpine Journal* (1946).

32. Mary Lowry to Larry Ferguson, March 4, 1987, Box 19, Harvey Manning Papers, UWSC; Valerie Mendenhall Cohen, ed., *Woman on the Rocks: The Mountaineering Letters of Ruth Dyar Mendenhall* (Bishop, Calif.: Spotted Dog Press, 2006), 345.

33. On duffle bags, see Calvin M. Craig, "Basic Supplies for an Outdoor Vacation," *New York Times*, July 9, 1950. On hunters, see Oscar Godbout, "Wood, Field and Stream: New Hunter Surplus Military Arms Bargains Are Sometimes Costly," *New York Times*, August 13, 1961.

34. On the pup tent, see Craig, "Basic Supplies," and Thomas M. Pitkin, *Quartermaster Equipment for Special Forces*, Q.M.C. Historical Studies, no. 5 (February 1944): 107–108, Denver Public Library. On expressing interest, see #455 to Harvey Manning, n.d., Box 19, Harvey Manning Papers, UWSC.

35. On the imperfect tent and excessive condensation, see Conway W. Weikert, "The Development of a Two-Man Military Tent," Textile Series Report No. 115, Quartermaster Research & Engineering Center, Textile, Clothing & Footwear Division, ii, Natick, Mass., February 1961, USAMHI. See also House, "Mountain Equipment for the U.S. Army." On the latest model, see Holubar catalog, 1947, BPL. On pup tents in department stores, see Edward L. Ayers, Lewis L. Gould, David M. Oshinsky, Jean R. Soderlund, *American Passages: A History of the United States, Volume 2: Since 1865, Brief* (Boston: Wadsworth, 2010), 621. On "cheapness," see John B. Ehrhardt, "Winter Camping," *New York Times*, December 21, 1947. For "serviceable," see Nathaniel Nitkin, "With Paddle and Compass," *New York Times*, May 8, 1949.

36. On "bargain," see Raymond R. Camp, "Wood, Field and Stream: Do-It-Yourself Movement Can Be Fun, but Hunters, Anglers Should be Wary," *New York Times*, June 12, 1955, and Orkney, *Growing Up with G.I. Joe's*, 128.

37. Earl Shaffer, "Taming the Trail," draft, January 18, 1949, Earl Shaffer Papers, AC; Earl Shaffer, Appalachian Trail slides, 1999.0189, Division of Cultural History, NMAH; Earl Shaffer, "The Long Cruise," n.d., Earl Shaffer Papers, AC. For "nervous," see Dorothy M. Martin, "Do You Want to Take a Walk," *American Forests*, May 1952, 18, Box 32, Collection 828, Earl Shaffer Papers, AC. See also Middlefeldt, *Tangled Roots*. For "out of [his] system," see Douglas Martin, "Earl Shaffer, First to Hike Length of Appalachian Trail in Both Directions, Dies at 83," May 12, 2002, *New York Times*.

38. Shaffer, "The Long Cruise."

39. Shaffer, "The Long Cruise."

40. Shaffer, "The Long Cruise." For weight recommendations, see Martin, *Modern Camping Guide*, 30.

41. On the use of surplus after the war, see Oscar Godbout, "Wood, Field and Stream: Kay Starr, Just a Rabbit Hunter from Oklahoma, Sets Her Sights on Africa," *New York Times*, March 22, 1966; Oscar Godbout, "Wood, Field and Stream: In Deer-Hunting Country of Vermont, Life Sometimes Begins at 8 1/2," *New York Times*, November 15, 1961; Karl Gustafson, "The Summit Club: Boulder's Teenage Climbers, 1949–1953," *Trail and Timberline* 1020 (Fall 2013); and "Hiking, Camping, Mountaineering, and Trail-Clearing Equipment."

42. Jim Beebe to Larry Ferguson, March 11, 1987, Box 19, Harvey Manning Papers, UWSC; Margaret Dyar Ashworth to Larry Ferguson, March 12, 1987, Box 19, Harvey Manning Papers, UWSC.

43. For "amply warm," see Martin, *Modern Camping Guide*, 35. For "princes," see Manning, *Backpacking*, 155.

44. On the impact of military equipment on recreation, see John B. Ehrhardt, "Winter Camping," *New York Times*, December 21, 1947. On "shaped to fit the body" and "fine design," see Pitkin, *Quartermaster Equipment for Special Forces*, 3, 104–105. On "poked," see Brower, *Going Light*, 52. On phenomenal and prices, see "Hiking, Camping, Mountaineering and Trail-Clearing Equipment."

45. "Hiking, Camping, Mountaineering and Trail-Clearing Equipment."

46. On army-type and navy-style, see "Hiking, Camping, Mountaineering and Trail-Clearing Equipment," 15; Recreational Equipment Cooperative, Supplement to Price List, July 15, 1955; and Russell's Army, Navy, Camp Sporting Goods catalog, 1922, back cover, Winterthur.

47. *Federal Trade Commission Decisions, July 1, 1954 to June 30, 1955*, vol. 51 (Washington: U.S. Government Printing Office, 1958), 447–451.

48. For "into the fields," see Oscar Godbout, "Wood, Field and Stream: 40,000,000 Pursue Outdoor Recreation in Mass Migration to Fresh Air," *New York Times*, December 24, 1961. On Worldwide Distributors and G.I. Joe's products, see Orkney, *Growing Up with G.I. Joe's*, 67–68, 79.

49. "Our History," Bill Jackson, accessed July 27, 2017, www.billjacksons.com/our-history/; "Our History," ruggedoutdoors.com/pages/our-story.

50. For Big Business, see Arthur Carhart, "Hunting and Fishing Is Big Business," referenced in Philpott, *Vacationland*, 196. For total sales, see Alexander R. Hammer, "No Glut in Surplus Goods Business," *New York Times*, February 25, 1958. For "mass migration," see Oscar Godbout, "Wood, Field and Stream: 40,000,000 Pursue Outdoor Recreation."

51. For "droves," see Steve Finegan, "The Insider," *Daily Journal of Commerce*, 1982, OHS business clippings. For "aroma," see Kehoe, "From Army Surplus." For sales and "invading," see "Spawned in Tent, Oregonian to Chalk up $4-Million in '73," *Sporting Goods Dealer*, December 1973, OHS business clippings. For interior

descriptions, see "A Big Volume Specialty Retailer," *Camping Industry*, March 20, 1973, OHS business clippings.

52. Paul Weingarten, "Bargains: Khaki's Not Tacky—A Surplus Store Guide," *Chicago Tribune*, June 17, 1977.

53. Epstein, "War Surplus Disposals."

54. For "realize the dream," see House, "Mountain Equipment for the U.S. Army." For "interpretation," see "Hiking, Camping, Mountaineering and Trail-Clearing Equipment."

55. "A Motivational Research Study of the Advertising, Editorial, and Promotional Opportunities and Problems of Outdoor Life Magazine," conducted for Popular Science Publishing Co., Inc., New York, Conducted by Institute for Motivational Research, Inc., February 1959, 14, 22, Folder 1032C, Box 47, Ernest Dichter Research Reports, 2407 (Subgroup A), Hagley Museum and Library.

Chapter 6. Lederhosen and Tyrolean Hats

1. On postwar consumer communities, see Manko, *Ding Dong! Avon Calling!*, and Clarke, *Tupperware*.

2. LeRoy Holubar, interview by David McComb, April 18, 1974, transcript, Oral History of Colorado Project, 13.

3. Holubar, interview; Jan E. Robertson, "End of the Trail: Alice Holubar," *Trail and Timberline* 605, The Colorado Mountain Club, May 1969, 99–100, Holubar Mountaineering, BPL. On custom jobs, see also Alice Holubar[?] to Gil Roberts, April 26, 1958, Holubar Mountaineering, BPL.

4. On German, see "Boulder Profiles," *Town & Country*, December 1, 1967, 19, Holubar Mountaineering, BPL. On "female member," see Lillian Hanson White, "A Woman and Her Work: Alice Holubar: Her Heart's in the Highlands, Or Sew It Seams," *Boulder Daily Camera*, March 3, 1958, Holubar Mountaineering, BPL. On "spark plug," see Mountaineering Industry Reunion, July 18, 2008, transcript of OH 1526V A-B, transcribed by Susan Becker, Carnegie Library for Local History, Boulder, Colo.

5. On Suchteln, see Mary H. DeLapp, "Women Today: Campers' Equipment Made to Measure," *Christian Science Monitor*, March 6, 1958, Holubar Mountaineering, BPL. On "fondness," see White, "A Woman and Her Work." On Holubar's early years in Boulder, see Robertson, "End of the Trail."

6. Carol Taylor, "Holubars Were Boulder Outdoor Gear Pioneers," *Boulder Daily Camera*, June 4, 2011.

7. On the war years, see "Roy Holubar," *Trail and Timberline* 648 (December 1972); "Outdoor Pioneers: 1900–1970," *Outdoor Retailer*, 1992, Holubar Mountaineering; Alice Holubar to [?], May 24, 1943, Holubar Mountaineering, BPL.

8. Rothman, *Devil's Bargains*.

9. Philpott, *Vacationland*, 44.

10. "Outdoor Pioneers"; Holubar, interview, 8. See also Mountaineering Industry Reunion, transcript.

11. Holubar, interview, 8.

12. Holubar, interview, 9.

13. Holubar, interview, 10.

14. Denning, *Skiing into Modernity*, 10, 29–30.

15. Isserman, *Continental Divide*, 274,

16. Holubar catalog, 1950, Holubar Mountaineering, BPL; Pam Montgomery, "The Times They Are a-Changin'," *Outdoor Retailer*, 1987.

17. Gerry catalog, Winter 1966–67, Holubar Mountaineering, BPL.

18. For "Bavarian style," see Holubar catalog, 1960, BPL. For "genuine," see Gerry catalog, 1966, Holubar Mountaineering, BPL. For "traditional," see REI catalogs, 1963 and 1968, Lloyd Anderson Papers, Accession 2648-001, UWSC.

19. William Lee Adams, "Lederhosen Chic: From the Alps to the Catwalk," *Time*, May 5, 2010.

20. 2000.011.0002, hat, Germond folder ADK; 2000.011.0003, backpack, Germond folder, ADK; 2000.011.0005, Parka, Germond folder, ADK: Hank Germond to Jane Mackintosh, April 6, 2000, Germond folder, ADK.

21. Germond folder, ADK.

22. United menu card/travel schedule, 1961, Holubar Mountaineering, BPL.

23. Harvey Manning, "The Decline and Fall of Backpacking," *The Mountaineer*, 1977.

24. Holubar catalog, 1952, Holubar Mountaineering, BPL.

25. On outdoor community where hikers consumed mass-produced hiking culture, see Chamberlin, *On the Trail*, 166. For "climbers met," see "Roy Holubar," *Trail and Timberline* 648 (December 1972).

26. Jean and Tom Tokareff to Harvey Manning, n.d., Box 19, Harvey Manning Papers, UWSC.

27. On pins, see Parka, Mountaineers, 1998.39.186, Washington State History Resource Center. On Hudowalski's patch, see Grace Hudowalski's shorts, Accession 82.49.1, Adirondack Museum and Library. On the "in thing," see Mary Lowry to Larry Ferguson, March 4, 1987, Box 19, Harvey Manning Papers, UWSC. Mary Lowry was married to future Washington state governor Mike Lowry. On friendships, see Elvin Robert Johnson to Larry Ferguson, March 25, 1987, Box 19, Harvey Manning Papers, UWSC.

28. Charles Williams to Larry Ferguson, February 28, 1987, Box 19, Harvey Manning Papers, UWSC.

29. For "pitons," see Karl Gustafson, "The Summit Club: Boulder's Teenage Climbers, 1949–1953," *Trail and Timberline* 1020 (Fall 2013): 30. On the Robertsons, see Mountaineering Industry Reunion, transcript.

30. On customers, see Holubar, interview, 15; Michael and Marjorie Vickers to LeRoy and Alice Holubar, December 1, 1960, Holubar Mountaineering, BPL.; and Lee

Tidball to Alice Holubar, July 19, 1958, Holubar Mountaineering, BPL. On Redford, see Howie Movshovitz, "Robert Redford's West," *Denver Post*, 1E, Holubar
Mountaineering, BPL. On Roberts, see Alice Holubar[?] to Gil Roberts, April 26,
1958, Holubar Mountaineering, BPL.

31. On Washburn, see "Pictures of Climb of Mount McKinley to Be Shown in Boulder Feb. 19," *Boulder Daily Camera*, February 13, 1950, Holubar Mountaineering,
BPL.; and Bradford Washburn to Alice and LeRoy Holubar, February 28, 1950, Holubar Mountaineering, BPL. On Roy Holubar's leadership, see "Roy Holubar,"
Trail and Timberline 648 (December 1972), and Scott-Nash, *Playing for Real.*

32. Alice Holubar to Albert Nixon, October 26, 1955, Holubar Mountaineering; De-
Lapp, "Women Today"; Montgomery, "The Times They Are a-Changin'."

33. *Holubar*, catalog, 1962, Holubar Mountaineering, BPL.

34. Weaver and Merrill, *Camping Can Be Fun*, 160.

35. For "bright red," see "Holubars Have Products at Moscow Exhibit," *Boulder Camera*, August 1, 1959. For technological performance and consumerism, see Oldenziel and Zachmann, *Cold War Kitchen*, 4. For organization and placement in the
exhibit hall, see Tuttle, *Official Training Book*, 10, 63, 120–121. It is possible that the
Holubar equipment was part of the Outside Area display in the "Camping Equipment" section of Outdoor Living. A Boulder newspaper suggested the equipment
was part of the "outdoor sports section" of the exhibit. See "Holubars Have Products at Moscow Exhibit," *Boulder Camera*, August 1, 1959.

36. On Dinosaur, see Harvey, *A Symbol of Wilderness*. On the Wilderness Society, see
Sutter, *Driven Wild*. On the Wilderness Act, see Philpott, *Vacationland*, 224–225.
For the Holubars' official letter, see LeRoy and Alice Holubar, "Western Greet-
ings," June 1, 1959, Holubar Mountaineering, BPL.

37. May, *Homeward Bound*, 16, 18. On craftsmanship, see "Holubars Have Products."
For the Holubars' letter, see LeRoy and Alice Holubar, "Western Greetings."

38. "Holubars Have Products."

39. Casualty Loss, Holubar, 1959, Holubar Mountaineering, BPL; Daniel R. Schim-
mel to LeRoy Holubar, January 6, 1960, Holubar Mountaineering, BPL.

40. Montgomery, "The Times," 76.

41. LeRoy Holubar suggests the figure in 1968 was $357,000. Holubar, interview, 33.
On Kack, see Mountaineering Industry Reunion, transcript.

42. Mountaineering Industry Reunion, transcript.

43. Mike Brady to Roy and Alice Holubar, May 11, 1968, Holubar Mountaineering,
BPL; Robertson, "End of the Trail," 99–100; Holubar, interview, 24.

Chapter 7. Rucksack Revolution

1. For "camp stove," see Rob Carson, "The R.E.I. Card: Quintessential Northwest,"
Pacific Northwest, March 1987. For "rucksacks," see Manning, *REI*, 99. On number

of campers, see B. Drummon Ayres, "Today's Campers Bring the Comforts of Home to the Out-of-Doors," *New York Times*, August 13, 1972, and Susan Sands, "Backpacking: 'I Go to the Wilderness to Kick the Man-World Out of Me,' " *New York Times*, May 9, 1971. For $3 billion, see Joan Cook, "Jerseyans Taking to Camping in Increasing Numbers," *New York Times*, August 3, 1972. On backpackers, see John Cunniff, "Business Takes a Look at Backpacking," *Golden Transcript* 107, no. 86 (April 19, 1974).

2. J. Baldwin, quoted in Kirk, *Counterculture Green*, 70; Harvey Manning, "Where Did All These Damn Hikers Come From?" *Backpacker*, Summer 1975.

3. On the golden age, see "Outdoor Pioneers, 1900–1970," *Outdoor Retailer*, 1992, BPL.

4. For "Neiman-Marcus," see Tom Stockley, "Seattle's Supermarket of the Outdoor World," November 26, 1967, Recreation Equipment, Inc., Acc. #3129-2, Box 1, UWSC. For "help-yourself," see Klindt Vielbig to Harvey Manning, March 9, 1987, Box 19, Harvey Manning Papers, UWSC. For membership, see "The Co-op Story," REI catalog 1968, UWSC. For sales, see Record of Sales—Total Sales, Box 1, Recreation Equipment, Inc., Acc. #3129-2, and Recreational Equipment, Inc.—Net Income and Income Tax Projection for Year Ending 12/31/72, Box 1, Recreation Equipment, Inc., Acc. #3129-2, UWSC.

5. Timothy Egan, "REI: Three Initials That Changed Life in the Northwest," *Pacific, Seattle Times/Seattle Post-Intelligencer*, March 6, 1988, 4, Box 20, Harvey Manning Papers, UWSC. For "supermarket," see also Stockley, "Seattle's Supermarket of the Outdoor World."

6. For equipment making roughing it easier, see "Millions of Women Join Camping Boom," *Chicago Defender*, July 18, 1970.

7. George T. Appleton to Harvey Manning, April 3, 1974, Box 11, Harvey Manning Papers, UWSC. On guidebooks inspiring shopping, see also Burt Bartram to Harvey Manning, November 28, 1975, Box 11, Harvey Manning Papers, UWSC.

8. Kirk, "The New Alchemy."

9. Rome, *The Genius of Earth Day*.

10. Kerouac, *The Dharma Bums*.

11. McKenzie, *Getting Physical*, 2, 7–8. See also Petrzela, *Fit Nation*, and Friedman, *Let's Get Physical*.

12. Paul J. C. Friedlander, "The Traveler's World: Into the Great Outdoors, Almost," *New York Times*, June 6, 1971; Beverley Foss to Harvey Manning, February 16, 1974, Box 11, Harvey Manning Papers, UWSC; Jim Forgie to Harvey Manning, [January 1975?], Box 11, Harvey Manning Papers, UWSC. For Hoffman, see Chuck Long, ed., *Pacific Crest Trail Hike Planning Guide* (Lynnwood, Wash.: Signpost Publications, 1976).

13. Mountaineering Industry Reunion, transcript. On influence of World War II and the military on recreation, see Maher, *Nature's New Deal*, and Taylor, *Pilgrims of the Vertical*.

14. Nick Paumgarten, "Patagonia's Philosopher-King," *New Yorker*, September 12, 2016.

15. Maurice H. Pomeranz, "Four 'In' Outfitters," *Backpacker*, Spring 1974; Dennis Hevesi, "Roger Furst Dies at 78; Equipped Mountaineers in the Northeast," *New York Times*, April 8, 2012.

16. Anna Accettola, "Gertrude Boyle," *Immigrant Entrepreneurship*, October 16, 2012, www.immigrantentrepreneurship.org/entries/gertrude-boyle/.

17. Kaiser and McCray, *Groovy Science*, and Davis, *From Head Shops to Whole Foods*.

18. *Footprints* 9 (June 1975), A16 Corporate Archive; *Footprints* 1 (November 1973), A16; *Footprints* 20 (c. 1980), A16.

19. *Footprints* 20 (c. 1980), A16.

20. *Footprints* 17 (June 1978), A16; *Footprints* 11 (1976), A16.

21. Le Zotte, *From Goodwill to Grunge*, 15.

22. On the use of nonprofessional models to maintain authenticity, see Brown, "Marlboro Men"; Paul B. Brown, "The Anti-Marketers," *Inc*, March, 1988, 62–69; Sievert, *Unexpected*.

23. John Terence Turner, "REI," *Mountain Gazette* 18, February 1974, Recreation Equipment, Inc., Acc. #3129-2, Box 1, UWSC; Patrick D. Goldsworthy to Harvey Manning, n.d., Box 19, Harvey Manning Papers, UWSC.

24. On Leave No Trace and recreational landscapes, see Simon and Alagona, "Beyond Leave No Trace"; Simon and Alagona, "Contradictions at the Confluence of Commerce, Consumption, and Conservation"; and James Morton Turner, "From Woodcraft to 'Leave No Trace.'"

25. Manning, *Backpacking*.

26. Gene Duenow to Harvey Manning, August 22, 1974, Box 11, Harvey Manning Papers, UWSC.

27. James Ward, "Footprints Interview: Mic Mead," *Footprints* 40 (April 1987): 15, A16.

28. *Sierra Designs*, catalog, 1971, American Recreation Archive.

29. *Sierra Designs*, catalog, 1971, American Recreation Archive.

30. For survey, see *View Point* 2, no. 1, *Recreational Equipment, Incorporated*, catalog, 1973, Lloyd Anderson Papers, Accession 2648-001, UWSC. For responses, see Questionnaire Letters, Recreational Equipment, Inc., Acc. #3129-2, Box 1, UWSC.

31. McKenzie, *Getting Physical*; Questionnaire Letters.

32. For Sierra Designs employees, see *Sierra Designs*, catalog, Spring 1974, American Recreation Archives. For REI's organizational stance, see *View Point* 1, no. 1, *Recreational Equipment, Incorporated*, catalog, Winter 1972–73, Lloyd Anderson Papers, Accession 2648-001, UWSC. For boot department, see *View Point* 2, no. 1, *Recreational Equipment, Incorporated*, 1973, Lloyd Anderson Papers, UWSC. For consumer desires, see Lloyd Anderson to Directors of R.E.I., June 8, 1972, Box 1, Recreational Equipment, Inc., Accession 3129-2, UWSC. For a critique of motor-powered recreation, see *Recreational Equipment, Incorporated*, catalog, Winter 1976–77, Lloyd Anderson Papers, Accession 2648-001, UWSC.

33. For environmental center, see Goldsworthy to Manning, and *View Point* 5, no. 1, March 1976, *Sierra Designs*, catalog, Spring/Summer 1975, American Recreation Corporate Archives.

34. *Sierra Designs*, catalog, Spring 1974, American Recreation Archives; *View Point* 4, no. 1, *Recreational Equipment, Incorporated*, catalog, 1975, Lloyd Anderson Papers, Accession 2648-001, UWSC; *View Point* 5, no. 2, *Recreational Equipment, Incorporated*, catalog, September 1976, Lloyd Anderson Papers, Accession 2648-001, UWSC.

35. For REI cleanups, see *View Point* 5, no. 2, *Recreational Equipment, Incorporated*, catalog, September 1976, Lloyd Anderson Papers, Accession 2648-001, UWSC; *View Point* 3, no. 1, *Recreational Equipment, Incorporated*, catalog, March 1974, Lloyd Anderson Papers, Accession 2648-001, UWSC; *View Point* 3, no. 1, *Recreational Equipment, Incorporated*, catalog, March 1974, Lloyd Anderson Papers, Accession 2648-001, UWSC; and *View Point* 2, no. 1, *Recreational Equipment, Incorporated*, catalog, April 1973, Lloyd Anderson Papers, Accession 2648-001, UWSC.

36. Daniel J. Evans to Larry Ferguson, March 10, 1987, Box 19, Harvey Manning Papers, UWSC.

37. *View Point* 5, no. 1, *Recreational Equipment, Incorporated*, catalog, March 1976, Lloyd Anderson Papers, Accession 2648-001, UWSC.

38. On the "woodsman school," see Look, *Joy of Backpacking*, 1–2. On the "new outdoor ethic," see Saijo, *The Backpacker*, 6–7.

39. Patrick S. Byrne to Harvey Manning, [n.d., c. August 1974], Harvey Manning Papers, UWSC.

40. Davis, "Activist Businesses."

Chapter 8. Gore-Tex and Do-It-Yourself Kits

1. "Revolution" was a common term for referencing both changes in fabric and changes in garment and gear construction. See *Backpacker* magazine from its founding in 1973 to the mid-1980s. For revolution of fiber, see Snow Lion ad, *Backpacker*, August 1976, 2; and Gore-Tex and Marmot ad, *Backpacker*, August 1976, 67. For revolution in equipment construction (which also often included new fabrics), see "The Revolution in Three Season Tents," *Backpacker*, June 1978, 27; Seth Masia, "Design and Construction: Weekend Packs," *Backpacker*, Spring 1974, 51; and Richard Goldstein, "Adventure in an Age of Adversity," *New York Magazine*, April 1, 1964, 52.

2. Dale Johnson, interview by Gerry Caplan, 2002, OH 1113V A-B, interview transcript, Maria Rogers Oral History Program Collection, Carnegie Branch Library for Local History, Boulder, Colo. Thank you to Editions Eska for permission to use selections from a previously published article, Rachel S. Gross, "The Gender

Politics of Do-It-Yourself: Frostline Kits and the American Outdoor Equipment Boom of the 1970s," *Entreprises et Histoire*, no. 106 (April 2022): 76–91.

3. Johnson, interview.

4. Gore, *The Early Days*, 10.

5. Johnson interview.

6. Case, *The Organic Profit*.

7. For more on DIY movements, see Gelber, *Hobbies*; Steven M. Gelber, "Do-It-Yourself: Constructing, Repairing and Maintaining Domestic Masculinity," *American Quarterly* 49, no. 1 (1997): 66–112; and Reinhild Kreis, "Why Not Buy? Making Things Oneself in an Age of Consumption," *Bulletin of the GHI* (Spring 2015): 83–97. On mass market kits, see Jessica Wood, "Historical Authenticity Meets DIY: The Mass-Market Harpsichord in the Cold War United States," *American Music* 30, no. 2 (Summer 2012): 228–253.

8. Kreis, "Why Not Buy?"

9. Johnson, interview.

10. Johnson, interview.

11. Online forum, "Frostline Kit Vintage DIY Panniers," www.bikeforums.net/classic-vintage/999673-frostline-kit-vintage-diy-panniers-lets-see-them.html, accessed July 10, 2020.

12. On other kit companies, see "Kit Makers Who Made It," *Backpacker* 17, vol. 5, no. 5 (October 1976): 54–55. On Frostline's market, see Robert Williams, Letter to the Editor, *Backpacker*, August 1977. On home sewing, see "Home-Sewing: Symptom of the 70s," *American Fabrics*, no. 96 (Winter 1972–1973): 74–75.

13. Mountaineering Industry Reunion, transcript.

14. Selections from the Gore story in this chapter were previously published and are included here with permission from the Science History Institute. Rachel S. Gross, "Bob Gore's Cozy Revolution," *Distillations*, December 1, 2020, www.sciencehistory.org/distillations/bob-gores-cozy-revolution.

15. Synthetic fibers are a distinct category from man-mades. The first man-made fiber was rayon, sold commercially in the 1920s, which was made from cellulose (wood pulp). It was a natural fiber but man-made. Nylon was the first synthetic man-made fiber, meaning it was both a product of test tubes and a petrochemical product.

16. On Bill Gore, see Alex Ward, "An All-Weather Idea: GORE-TEX," *New York Times*, November 10, 1985. For background on the Gores, see also "Background Information on W.L. Gore & Associates," n.d., ECT Corporate Affairs, Gore. On the tactics of advertising "better living through chemistry"—which helped DuPont revamp its image from merchant of death to purveyor of synthetics for consumer products—see Andrew M. Shanken, "Better Living: Toward a Cultural History of a Business Slogan," *Enterprise and Society* 7, no. 3 (September 2006): 485–519.

17. Gore, *The Early Days*, 10.

18. Gore, *The Early Days*, 11.

19. E. Corbellini, "Comfort in Clothing for Outdoor Activities and Multi-Filament Poly-Propylene Yarn," in *Polypropylene Fibres and Textiles* (London: Plastics and Rubber Institute, 1987), 32/2, SHI.

20. For Bryant, see Nelson Bryant, "Outdoors: Staying Warm in Bitter Cold," *New York Times*, February 5, 1979. For narratives of death, see Earl Gustkey, "The Cold Facts of Freezing to Death," *Los Angeles Times*, January 7, 1978; Robert Istler, "4 Dead Hikers Were Lightly Dressed," *Los Angeles Times*, September 8, 1978; and David Arnold, "Many Saved Each Year in N.H. Mountains: Carelessness Keeps Rescue Teams Busy," *Los Angeles Times*, October 31, 1981.

21. "GORE-TEX," *New York Times*, November 10, 1985. On the special properties of PTFE, see also W. L. Gore & Associates, Corporate brochures, 1988 + 1999, ECT Corporate Affairs, Gore. On DuPont and PTFE, see Hounshell and Smith, *Science and Corporate Strategy*, 485.

22. Though Bob Gore officially joined the firm in 1963, while still in college he had contributed to his parents (and then patented) the idea for making PTFE-insulated ribbon cables, which enabled them to start the company. See W. L. Gore & Associates, Corporate brochures, 1988 + 1999, ECT Corporate Affairs, Gore.

23. Gore, *The Early Days*, 104.

24. On the invention of ePTFE, see Ward, "An All-Weather Idea"; Gore, *The Early Days*, 92–93; and "A Visit with William Gore," *Signpost*, May 1980, Folder #15, F3.1 COF: External Communications, 1975–1991-General, Gore.

25. "Expanded PTFE: It's a Whole New Ball Game," *Plastics World* 29, no. 7 (July 1971): 40–42, SHI; Gore, *The Early Days*, 103; and Robert Sorrels, "The Culture of Innovation: An Ethnography of W.L. Gore & Associates" (Ph.D. diss., 1986), 106, SHI.

26. On Gore's plans, see Company Description, ca. 1970, ECT Corporate Affairs, Gore. On holding water, see "GORE-TEX," *New York Times*. On applications of the laminate, see "GORE-TEX(r) A Breakthrough," by Joseph Tanner, 1977, Folder #1.2, F2.1 COF: Product Training/Information 1970s–1989 (North America), Gore.

27. For "ideal target," see "Beginnings of GORE-TEX(r) Fabrics for Military Applications," meeting with Wayne von Stetten, December 8, 2011, GCA. For "best candidates," see "Evaluations of 6 Proposed Wet Weather Coveralls," July 24, 1974, Military Ergonomics Laboratory, USARIEM, Gore. For market pivot, see Newspaper and Magazine Articles, 1982, Folder #18, F3.1 COF: External Communications, 1975–1991-General, Gore.

28. For instance, DuPont invested $500 million into the development of Kevlar in the 1960s, and then twenty years later was producing forty-five million pounds a year. Pamela G. Hollie, "Space Age Clothing's Debut," *New York Times*, July 28, 1983. On investments, see "A Visit with William Gore," *Signpost*, May 1980 + Letter from Bill Nicolai of Early Winters, Folder #15, F3.1 COF: External Communications, 1975–1991-General, Gore.

29. *Early Winters*, catalog, 1977, Folder #1, Box F1.3 COF: Marketing Materials, Catalogs (North America), GCA; *Banana Equipment*, catalog, Spring 1977, Folder #1.2, Box F1.3 COF: Marketing Materials, Catalogs (North America), Gore; Marmot Mountain Works, Ltd., Catalog, 1977, Folder #1.1, Box F1.3 COF: Marketing Materials, Catalogs (North America), Gore.

30. For "Holy Grail," see Fletcher, *The Complete Walker III*, 405. For "revolutionary," see Marmot Mountain advertisement, *Backpacker*, October 1976, 71.

31. Gore, *The Early Days*, 68.

32. For advertisements, see GORE-TEX fabric binder, Peter Gilson, n.d., Gore. On technical ads, see Maryann Ondovcsik, "High Performance," *American Fabrics and Fashions* 133 (1985): 41–45.

33. Manning, *Backpacking*, 97.

34. On reactions to Gore-Tex, see Steve Netherby, "Wet Suits," *Field and Stream*, March 1982, 59–60. On seam sealant, see Frostline catalog, 1979, and Trent Bush, interview by Chase Anderson, *Highlander Podcast*, opdd.usu.edu/podcast.

35. Steve Shuster, conversation with author, August 2015.

36. For Owens, see Netherby, "Wet Suits," 59. For "botched," see Colin Fletcher, *The Complete Walker III*, 3rd rev. ed. ([New York]: Knopf, 1984), 406. For "leakage," see David Sumner, "Field Report," *Backpacker*, February/March 1979, 63.

37. "GORE-TEX," *New York Times*.

38. On Gillette's goals, see Rita Ricardo-Campbell, *Resisting Hostile Takeovers: The Case of Gillette* (Westport, Conn.: Praeger, 1997). On Johnson Wax, see "Backpacking Industry Annual Report," *Backpacker* 5, vol. 2, no. 1 (Spring 1974): 32.

39. Maurice H. Pomeranz, "Backpacking Becomes Big Business," *Backpacker* 5, vol. 2, no. 1 (Spring 1974): 33.

40. On Gore-Tex profits, see Kief Hillsbery, "The Second Coming of Gore-Tex," *Outside*, [198X?], Newspaper and Magazine Articles, 1980, Folder #16, F3.1 COF: External Communications, 1975–1991-General, Gore. On $100 million, see Hillsbery, "The Second Coming of Gore-Tex."

41. For $4 million, see "GORE-TEX"; for returns, letters from customers, Folder #7.1 Box 4.4, Gore. For "easy to put on," see Karl Neumann, "Hot Tips on the Cold," *Los Angeles Times*, February 7, 1988. For "unparalleled," see Tina Sherman Harnden, "For Boaters, New Gear Makes the Trip Drier," *New York Times*, January 13, 1985.

42. Fletcher, *The Complete Walker III*, 406–407.

43. For "dated," see Johnson, *Frostline*, 44; Frostline catalog, 1981.

44. For "Denali," see unnamed gear company owner, quoted in Johnson, *Frostline*, 44. For "store-bought," see Karl Neumann, "Hot Tips on the Cold," *Los Angeles Times*, February 7, 1988.

45. "GORE-TEX"; Witherell, *L.L. Bean*, 326.

46. For Barnes, see Johnson, *Frostline*, 43. For cyclist, see online forum, "Frostline Kit Vintage DIY Panniers," www.bikeforums.net/classic-vintage/999673-frostline-kit-vintage-diy-panniers-lets-see-them.html, accessed July 10, 2020.

47. On Gore-Tex's success in the 1980s, see Philip H. Dougherty, "Advertising; High-Tech Textile Campaign," *New York Times*, February 22, 1985; and "Wilbert Gore, Inventor of Waterproof Fabric," *New York Times*, July 31, 1986; see also Sorrels, *The Culture of Innovation*.

48. Nelson Bryant, "Outdoors: Keeping Warm Is Easier than Ever," *New York Times*, December 26, 1982.

49. On trickle down, see Ondovcsik, "High Performance," 41–45.

50. For Whittaker and Nicolai, see Netherby, "Wet Suits," 60.

51. *The Graduate*, directed by Mike Nichols, 1967; Harvey Manning to Bob Cram, August 10, 1979, Box 13, Harvey Manning Papers, UWSC.

52. Ward J. Irwin to Harvey Manning, Box 19, Harvey Manning Papers, UWSC; Nelson Bryant, "Outdoors: Learning Winter Camping Skills," *New York Times*, December 29, 1985.

53. Accession 2002.005.0005—Shirt, Folder: Apple Annie, ADK.

54. Sue Whitcomb to Adirondack Museum, September 14, 1998, ADK.

55. Woods and Waters display sign, Apple Annie Update 2000, ADK.

56. On the science of clothing, see "Goretex Fabrics Represent the Contribution of Science to Functional Outerwear," *Esquire*, June 1983, Marketing Materials—1983 (North America) Folder #7, Gore. On gear as stylish, see "Fabric Laminate Rides Fashion Wave," *New York Times*, May 14, 1984.

Chapter 9. Bean Boots and Puffy Jackets

1. David K. Shipler, "The Affluent Lose Their Cool During Abercrombie Sale," *New York Times*, July 23, 1968; "The Theory of the A&F Class," *New York Times*, November 19, 1977; Isadore Barmash, "Abercrombie & Fitch in Bankruptcy Step," *New York Times*, August 7, 1976.

2. Richard Wolkomir, "High-Tech Materials Blaze Urban Trail for Outdoorsy Duds," *Smithsonian*, January 1985, 122.

3. On total leisure time per capita decline, see "Executive Summary: Outdoor Recreation in a Nation of Communities," March 1988, A Report to the Task Force on Outdoor Recreation Resources and Opportunities to the Domestic Policy Council; H. Ken Cordell et al., USDA Forest Service, General Technical Report RM-189. On mall locales, see Price, "Looking for Nature at the Mall." On lifestyle and consumption, see Binkley, *Getting Loose*, and Mike Featherstone, "Lifestyle and Consumer Culture," *Theory, Culture & Society* 4, no. 1 (February 1987): 55–70. On lifestyle and sports, see Belinda Wheaton, "Introducing the Consumption and Representation of Lifestyle Sports," *Sport in Society* 13, nos. 7–8 (2010): 1057–1081; and

Tolga Ozyurtcu, "Living the Dream: Southern California and the Origins of Life-style Sport," *Journal of Sport History* 46, no. 1 (Spring 2019): 20–35.

4. On nostalgia and national identity and appealing to an authentic past, see Grainge, "Advertising the Archive." On heritage as exalted past values that shape modern life, see Herwitz, *Heritage, Culture, and Politics in the Postcolony.*

5. For instance, Limerick, *The Legacy of Conquest.*

6. M. R. Montgomery, "The Marketing Magic of L.L. Bean," *Boston Globe Magazine,* December 27, 1981.

7. Montgomery, "The Marketing Magic of L.L. Bean."

8. Rita Reif, "A Rustic Store That Became Awfully Chic," *New York Times,* November 25, 1972; Ron Alexander, "Fabled Boots Now a Fashion Fad," *New York Times,* February 20, 1979.

9. Greta McDonough, "Thanks to Mr. Bean, I was Preppy Before I Knew the Term," *Owensboro Messenger-Inquirer* (Kentucky), November 3, 2010; Joyce Cohen, "A Higher Grade of Campus Dress," *New York Times,* October 11, 1981. On the rise of conservative sportswear styles in the 1980s, see English, *A Cultural History of Fashion in the 20th Century.*

10. Birnbach, *The Official Preppy Handbook;* Gorman, *L.L. Bean.*

11. On the fashion cycle, see "Unfashionably Chic," Forbes.com, October 19, 2006, www.forbes.com/2006/10/19/leadership-retail-fashion-lead-manage-cx_tw_1019llbean.html#6e01bf7d3597. Gorman quoted in Witherell, *L.L. Bean,* 326. For "average guy," see Thomas Ehrich, "Homey Hustlers," *Wall Street Journal,* December 5, 1973.

12. Montgomery, "The Marketing Magic of L.L. Bean."

13. For "unique core values," see "Unfashionably Chic"; on the A&F core, see Reif, "A Rustic Store"; for "rugged individualism," see "L.L. Bean, Inc.: Corporate Strategy," HBS Case Study, 1; for "guaranteed disaster," see Montgomery, "The Marketing Magic of L.L. Bean"; for End, see "L.L. Bean, Inc.: Corporate Strategy," HBS Case Study, 8.

14. On the rise of mail order, see "L.L. Bean, Inc.: Corporate Strategy," HBS Case Study, 2; and Andrew N. Case, "The Solid Gold Mailbox: Direct Mail and the Transformation of Buying and Selling in Postwar America," *History of Retailing and Consumption* 1, no. 1 (March 2015): 40.

15. On Bean's mail-order approach, see "L.L. Bean, Inc.: Corporate Strategy," HBS Case Study, 5–6; Witherell, *L.L. Bean,* 338; Mowen, *Consumer Behavior;* and Case, "The Solid Gold Mailbox," 41.

16. On the Coty award, see Wolkomir, "High-Tech Materials." On reporter and internal Bean reactions, see Jim Dudas, "L.L. Bean Is Stylish to Boot," *Cleveland Press,* October 13, 1976, quoted in Witherell, *L.L. Bean,* 274.

17. Witherell, *L.L. Bean,* 283, 351, 354.

18. Customer quoted in Montgomery, "The Marketing Magic of L.L. Bean." For *Corporate Cultures,* see Witherell, *L.L. Bean,* 312.

19. Wolkomir, "High-Tech Materials."

20. Maryanne M. Garbowsky, "Speaking Personally; Heading for the North Woods . . . By Mail," *New York Times*, November 8, 1981.

21. Jill Gerston, "Rough 'N' Ready-to-Wear," *Philadelphia Inquirer*, August 20, 1989.

22. "L.L. Bean, Inc.: Corporate Strategy," HBS Case Study, 5.

23. On the merger, see Boyd Burchard, "Eddie Bauer to Merge with General Mills," *Seattle Times*, January 5, 1971, EB. For "Cadillac," see McPhee, *The Survival of the Bark Canoe*, 76. On expedition advertising, see Rachel S. Gross, "Logos on Everest: Commercial Sponsorship of American Expeditions, 1950–2000," *Enterprise & Society* 22, no. 4 (December 2021): 1067–1102. On sending MBAs, see Spector, *Legend of Eddie Bauer*.

24. On Bauer and fashion, see Patricia Peterson, "Fashion," *New York Times*, September 12, 1976. On expansions, see Glenn Bischoff, "The Eddie Bauer Way," *Outside Business* 11, no. 7 (October/November 1986), EB. On growth, see "Evolution of a Down-Wear Retailer," *New York Times*, March 12, 1981.

25. On product offerings, see "Evolution of a Down-Wear Retailer," *New York Times*, March 12, 1981. On the Suburban Sports Parka, see "EB Parka Review," EB.

26. Bischoff, "The Eddie Bauer Way."

27. On the partnership proposal, see Eddie Bauer/Ford Bronco Speech, EB-Ford Communiques, EB. On the appeal of the truck, see Joseph Malinconico, "Ford Truck Has Touch of the Outdoors," *New York Times*, January 29, 1984.

28. On gear bags, see Abbie Anderson to Edsel B. Ford II, March 9, 1983, EB-Ford Communiques, EB. On mailing insert, see Jim Nystrom, "Ford Bronco Promotion," June 19, 1984, EB-Ford Communiques, EB. On estimates, see Donald Woutat, "Detroit Auto Makers Try to Increase Sales to Young Professionals," *Wall Street Journal*, September 27, 1984, EB-Ford Communiques, EB. On sales numbers, see Dwight McCade, "Ford Bronco Promotion," June 6, 1984, EB-Ford Communiques, EB, and "Mullinax Ford Dealership Pilot Program," pamphlet, EB.

29. On the general outdoorsperson, see Abbie Anderson to Beryl Stajich, April 25, 1984, EB-Ford Communiques, EB. On Boomer masculinity, see McCarthy, *Auto Mania*. On doctor and lawyer market, see Joe Skorupa, "In Search of Eddie Bauer," *Popular Mechanics*, February 1994.

30. For 50 percent, see "Gear in Stores: A Review of Changing Presence," EB. For men as customers, and new president, see Carol Pucci, "Eddie Bauer: New President Signals Change at Area Retailer," *Seattle Times*, September 4, 1984, Eddie Bauer executives, EB. For lifestyle as barbecue, see Frank Dever to Mark Willes, "Eddie Bauer Article in a Japanese Magazine," November 5, 1987, Eddie bauer pr old, EB.

31. On store layout, see "Gear in Stores: A Review of Changing Presence," pamphlet, EB. For Rayden's reflections, see "REI, Eddie Bauer Expand; Outdoor Specialists Explore New Territories," *Chain Store Age Executive with Shopping Center Age*, August 1987, 46.

32. On taking down, see Robin Updike, "Apparel Retailer Moving Away from Founder's Concept," *Seattle Times*, August 8, 1988, Eddie bauer pr old, EB. On guns, see Rebecca Case, "Eddie Bauer Remade," *Journal-American* [?], Eddie bauer pr old, EB.

33. On "traditional lifestyle," see Robert Spector, "Eddie Bauer to Present Home Goods Division," *HFD-The Weekly Home Furnishings Newspaper* 64, no. 51 (December 17, 1990): 1. On scents, see "Eddie Bauer Inc. Tries on Men's Fragrance," *PR Newswire*, August 26, 1993, 0826SE001.

34. Eddie Bauer catalog, EB. See also Spector, *Legend of Eddie Bauer*, 92.

35. On "the real thing," see Judy B. Rollins, "Catalog Cowboy," *Salt Lake Tribune*, February 21, 1992. On "wanna-be attire," see Gerston, "Rough 'N' Ready-to-Wear."

36. Gerston, "Rough 'N' Ready-to-Wear"; Lawrence Teacher obituary, *Philadelphia Inquirer*, March 27, 2014.

37. On "upscale" and "outdoorsy," see Joe Skorupa, "In Search of Eddie Bauer," *Popular Mechanics*, February 1994, and April Christofferson, *Edgewater*, 1998, www.google.com/books/edition/Edgewater/zdbzeCfP7jkC?hl=en&gbpv=1&dq=%22eddie+bauer+type%22&pg=PT134&printsec=frontcover. For Quindlen, see Anna Quindlen, "Public & Private; Not So Itsy Bitsy," *New York Times*, August 31, 1991. On the catalogs, see James Adams, "Embarrassment of Riches," *Sunday Times*, March 27, 1994. For projected sales, see SGB retail registry '94, *Sporting Goods Business* 27, no. 3 (March 1994).

38. "Eddie Bauer Comes Home to Flagship Seattle Store," *PR Newswire*, April 16, 1992, 0416A9330.

39. On predictions, see Robert E. Carr, "Some Good News and Bad News for the Nineties," *Sporting Goods Business*, May 1991, 8. On imitators, see Martin Forztenszer, "On and Off the Beaten Path; Outdoor Gear Isn't Just for the Adventurous Anymore," *New York Times*, May 16, 1998; Carr, "Some Good News and Bad News"; and Kathleen Kiley, "From Intimates to the Great Outdoors," *Catalog Age*, November 1994, 9.

40. On the rise of hip-hop fashion, see Rizzo, *Class Acts*. On the postwar Black marketplace, see Greer, *Represented*.

41. On the appeal of hip-hop style, see Rizzo, *Class Acts*.

42. "Our Story," *Timberland*, www.timberland.com/about-us/our-story.html; on RZA, see Jake Woolf, "Wu-Tang's RZA on Timberlands, 'The Boots That Paved the Way,' " November 6, 2014, www.gq.com/story/wu-tang-clans-the-rza-on-timberland-boots?; Michael Marriott, "Out of the Woods," *New York Times*, November 7, 1993.

43. Justin Monroe, "Timberlands," *Vibe*, September 2005, 244; Woolf, "Wu-Tang's RZA on Timberlands"; "A Brief History of Rappers Co-Signing Timberlands," *Finish Line* blog, blog.finishline.com/2014/12/02/a-brief-history-of-rappers-co-signing-timberlands/.

44. Lei Takanashi, "How the North Face Took Over '90s New York," *The Cut*, October 31, 2018, www.thecut.com/2018/10/the-north-face-new-york-style.html; www.

highsnobiety.com/p/the-north-face-nuptse-jacket/; Julia Szabo, "Geared for the Grocery, or Mount Everest," *New York Times*, March 9, 1997; "The North Face: Nuptse," vimeo.com/239848438; "Fly Out" lyrics, genius.com/Yl-rap-fly-out-lyrics.

45. Szabo, "Geared for the Grocery"; Takanashi, "How the North Face Took Over"; Marriott, "Out of the Woods"; Tierney, "The Big City."

46. For brand stories, see Enstad, *Cigarettes, Inc.* For tree-stamped, see Monroe, "Timberlands." For lifestyle aspiration, see Jon Caramanica, "The Gang That Brought High Fashion to Hip-Hop," *New York Times*, June 28, 2016. For Just Blaze, see Hua Hsu, "The Brooklyn Street Crews That Boosted Ralph Lauren and Invented Their Own Style," *New Yorker*, July 8, 2016. For Ones, see Samuel Hine, "Meet Joey Ones, the NYC Survivalist and World's Most Loyal North Face Collector," *Garage*, February 21, 2018, garage.vice.com/en_us/article/a34jqe/joey-ones-north-face-collector.

47. For sales increase, see Adams, "Embarrassment of Riches." For Swartz's reaction, see Marriott, "Out of the Woods."

48. Marriott, "Out of the Woods." On distancing, see Leslie Kaufman, "Trying to Stay True to the Street," *New York Times*, March 14, 1999.

49. For co-opting, see Szabo, "Geared for the Grocery"; for appropriating, see Andrea Felsted and Alan Rappeport, "Abercrombie Sees Off Awkward Brand Situation," *Financial Times*, August 19, 2011. For "devotees," see Marriott, "Out of the Woods." For "fantasist," see Adams, "Embarrassment of Riches." For "corrupting," see Barney Jopson, with Vanessa Friedman, "Hip-Hop Adoption Leaves . . .," *Financial Times*, June 15, 2011.

50. Debra Sykes, "Courting Diversity," *Sporting Goods Business*, November 1993, 48; Tamara Jones, "The Shirt Off His Back," *Washington Post*, September 26, 1997.

51. Jones, "The Shirt Off His Back."

52. Jones, "The Shirt Off His Back."

53. For guards, see Adams, "Embarrassment of Riches." For Tent & Trails, see Takanashi, "How the North Face Took Over." On scrutiny, see Jeffrey B. Swartz, letter to the editor, *New York Times*, November 21, 1993, and Violet E. Gill, letter to the editor, *New York Times*, December 5, 1993.

54. On models, see Adams, "Embarrassment of Riches." On racialized outdoor leisure identities, see Derek Christopher Martin, "Apartheid in the Great Outdoors: American Advertising and the Reproduction of a Racialized Outdoor Leisure Identity," *Journal of Leisure Research* 36, no. 4 (2004): 513–535, and Finney, *Black Faces, White Spaces*, 27.

55. Michiko Kakutani, "Common Threads," *New York Times Magazine*, February 16, 1997.

56. On the 80–20 rule, see Hal Espen, "Fleeced," *New York Times Magazine*, February 15, 1998.

57. SGB retail registry '94, *Sporting Goods Business* 27, no. 3 (March 1994).

58. Bobby Allyn, "The Patagonia Vest Endures in San Francisco Tech Circles, Despite Ridicule," NPR, March 31, 2022, www.npr.org/2022/03/31/1089994672/patagonia-

vest-tech-workers-san-francisco; Karen Dacre, "Gorpcore Trend Peaks Again as Extreme Outdoor Wear Hits Pub and Park," *The Guardian,* November 26, 2021, www.theguardian.com/fashion/2021/nov/26/gorpcore-trend-rises-as-extreme-outdoor-wear-hits-pub-and-park; Jonathan Evans, "The North Face x Gucci Is Back and Ready for You to Take a Long, Strange Trip," *Esquire,* December 5, 2022, www.esquire.com/style/mens-fashion/g41175234/north-face-x-gucci-chapter-3/.

59. Guy Trebay, "Storming the Catwalk in an L.L. Bean Boot," *New York Times,* February 5, 2020.

Epilogue

1. Candace Dantes, "Made Together: Outdoor Afro + REI Co-op," *Uncommon Path* blog, September 13, 2022, www.rei.com/blog/hike/made-together-outdoor-afro; "We Are Nature," Outdoor Afro x REI Co-op product line, www.rei.com/b/outdoor-afro-rei-co-op; Outdoor Afro 2022 Annual Report, outdoorafro.org/wp-content/uploads/2022/12/2022-Annual-Report.pdf.

2. Nneka M. Okona, "Black Oases," *Uncommon Path* blog, www.rei.com/blog/outdoor-afro-black-oases; Finney, *Black Faces, White Spaces.* A marketing think-piece published by *The Atlantic* and paid for by REI directly uses Finney's research to frame an argument for making the outdoors more inclusive. "Five Ways to Make the Outdoors More Inclusive," *Atlantic Re:Think,* www.theatlantic.com/sponsored/rei-2018/five-ways-to-make-the-outdoors-more-inclusive/3019/.

3. "Continuing Our Commitment to Change," www.eddiebauer.com/content/be-the-change; "NativesOutdoors," www.eddiebauer.com/campaign/nativesoutdoors; NativesOutdoors, natives-outdoors.com/.

4. The Venture Out Project, www.ventureoutproject.com/#what-we-do; Blackpackers, blackpackers.org/about/; Fat Girls Hiking, fatgirlshiking.com/; Alpine Curves, kinsaactive.com/; Unlikely Hikers, unlikelyhikers.org/.

Alexander, Kimberly S. *Treasures Afoot: Shoe Stories from the Georgian Era*. Baltimore: Johns Hopkins University Press, 2018.

Anderson, H. Allen. *The Chief: Ernest Thompson Seton and the Changing West*. College Station: Texas A&M University Press, 1986.

Angier, Bradford. *Home in Your Pack: The Modern Handbook of Backpacking*. Harrisburg, Pa.: Stockpile Books, 1965.

Anishanslin, Zara. *Portrait of a Woman in Silk: Hidden Histories of the British Atlantic World*. New Haven: Yale University Press, 2016.

Ante, Spencer E. *Creative Capital: Georges Doriot and the Birth of Venture Capital*. Boston: Harvard Business Press, 2008.

Aron, Cindy S. *Working at Play: A History of Vacation in the United States*. Oxford: Oxford University Press, 1999.

Baime, A. J. *The Arsenal of Democracy: FDR, Detroit, and an Epic Quest to Arm America at War*. Boston: Houghton Mifflin Harcourt, 2014.

Banet-Weiser, Sarah. *Authentic™: The Politics of Ambivalence in a Brand Culture*. New York: New York University Press, 2012.

Barthes, Roland. *Mythologies*. Trans. Richard Howard and Annette Lavers. New York: Hill & Wang, 2012.

Beard, Dan. *The Book of Camp-Lore and Woodcraft*. Garden City: Garden City Publishing, 1920.

Bederman, Gail. *Manliness and Civilization: A Cultural History of Gender and Race in the United States, 1880–1917*. Chicago: University of Chicago Press, 1995.

Belasco, Warren J. *Americans on the Road: From Autocamp to Motel, 1910–1945*. Cambridge: MIT Press, 1979.

——. *Appetite for Change: How the Counterculture Took On the Food Industry*, 2nd updated edition. Ithaca, N.Y.: Cornell University Press, 2006.

Berghoff, Hartmut, and Adam Rome, eds. *Green Capitalism? Business and the Environment in the Twentieth Century.* Philadelphia: University of Pennsylvania Press, 2017.

Binkley, Sam. *Getting Loose: Lifestyle Consumption in the 1970s.* Durham: Duke University Press, 2007.

Birnback, Lisa, ed. *The Official Preppy Handbook.* New York: Workman, 1980.

Blaszczyk, Regina Lee. "Styling Synthetics: DuPont's Marketing of Fabrics and Fashions in Postwar America." *The Business History Review* 80, no. 3 (Autumn 2006): 485–528.

———. *Producing Fashion: Commerce, Culture, and Consumers.* Philadelphia: University of Pennsylvania Press, 2008.

———. "Rethinking Fashion." In *Producing Fashion: Commerce, Culture, and Consumers,* edited by Regina Lee Blaszczyk. Philadelphia: University of Pennsylvania Press, 2008.

———. *American Consumer Society, 1865–2005: From Hearth to HDTV.* Wheeling, Ill.: Harland Davidson, 2009.

Boag, Peter. *Re-Dressing America's Frontier Past.* Berkeley: University of California Press, 2011.

Boorstin, Daniel J. *The Image: A Guide to Pseudo-Events in America.* New York: Atheneum, 1980.

Bourdieu, Pierre. *Distinction: A Social Critique of the Judgment of Taste.* Translated by Richard Nice. London: Routledge & Kegan Paul, 1984.

Boyle, Gert. *One Tough Mother: Taking Charge in Life, Business, and Apple Pies.* With Kerry Tymchuk. New York: Carroll and Graf, 2007.

Breck, Edward. *The Way of the Woods.* New York: G. P. Putnam's Sons, 1908.

Brimmer, F. E. *Autocamping.* Cincinnati: Stewart Kidd, 1923.

Brinkley, Douglas. *The Wilderness Warrior: Theodore Roosevelt and the Crusade for America.* New York: HarperCollins, 2009.

Brower, David, ed. *Going Light with Backpack or Burro.* San Francisco: Sierra Club, 1951.

———. *For Earth's Sake: The Life and Times of David Brower.* Salt Lake City: Peregrine Smith, 1990.

Brown, Elspeth. "Marlboro Men: Outsider Masculinities and Commercial Modeling in Postwar America." In *Producing Fashion: Commerce, Culture, and Consumers,* edited by Regina Lee Blaszczyk. Philadelphia: University of Pennsylvania Press, 2008.

Bryan, George S., ed. *The Camper's Own Book.* New York: Log Cabin, 1912.

Bryson, Bill. *A Walk in the Woods: Rediscovering America on the Appalachian Trail.* New York: Broadway Books, 1998.

Bushman, Richard. *The Refinement of America: Persons, Houses, Cities.* New York: Vintage, 1992.

Cabela, David. *Cabela's: World's Foremost Outfitter: A History.* Forest Dale, Vt.: Paul S. Ericksson, 2001.

Canfield, Michael R. *Theodore Roosevelt in the Field.* Chicago: University of Chicago Press, 2015.

Case, Andrew N. *The Organic Profit: Rodale and the Making of Marketplace Environmentalism.* Seattle: University of Washington Press, 2018.

Chamberlin, Silas. *On the Trail: A History of American Hiking.* New Haven: Yale University Press, 2016.

Chatelain, Marcia. *Franchise: The Golden Arches in Black America.* New York: Liveright, 2020.

Cheney, Theodore A. *Camping by Backpack and Canoe.* New York: Funk & Wagnalls, 1970.

Childers, Michael W. *Colorado Powder Keg: Ski Resorts and the Environmental Movement.* Lawrence: University Press of Kansas, 2012.

Chouinard, Yvon. *Let My People Go Surfing: The Education of a Reluctant Businessman.* New York: Penguin Books, 2005.

Clarke, Alison J. *Tupperware: The Promise of Plastic in 1950s America.* Washington, D.C.: Smithsonian Institution Press, 1999.

Clemente, Deirdre. *Dress Casual: How College Students Redefined American Style.* Chapel Hill: University of North Carolina Press, 2014.

Cohen, Joanna. *Luxurious Citizens: The Politics of Consumption in Nineteenth-Century America.* Philadelphia: University of Pennsylvania Press, 2017.

Cohen, Lizabeth. *A Consumers' Republic: The Politics of Mass Consumption in Postwar America.* New York: Vintage Books, 2003.

Cohen, Valerie Mendenhall, ed. *Women on the Rocks: The Mountaineering Letters of Ruth Dyar Mendenhall.* Bishop, Calif.: Spotted Dog, 2007.

Coleman, Annie Gilbert. *Ski Style: Sport and Culture in the Rockies.* Lawrence: University Press of Kansas, 2004.

——. "The Rise of the House of Leisure: Outdoor Guides, Practical Knowledge, and Industrialization." *Western Historical Quarterly* 42, no. 4 (Winter 2011): 436–457.

Collingham, Lizzie. *The Taste of War: World War Two and the Battle for Food.* London: Allen Lane, 2011.

Cook, Daniel. *The Commodification of Childhood: The Children's Clothing Industry and the Rise of the Child Consumer.* Durham: Duke University Press, 2004.

Cronon, William. "The Trouble with Wilderness; or, Getting Back to the Wrong Nature." In *Uncommon Ground: Rethinking the Human Place in Nature*, edited by William Cronon. New York: Norton, 1996.

Cross, Gary. *An All-Consuming Century: Why Commercialism Won in Modern America.* New York: Columbia University Press, 2000.

Cross, Gary S., and Robert N. Proctor. *Packaged Pleasures: How Technology and Marketing Revolutionized Desire.* Chicago: University of Chicago Press, 2014.

Crowley, John E. "The Sensibility of Comfort." *American Historical Review* 104, no. 3 (June 1999): 749–782.

Cunningham, Gerry, and Meg Hansson. *Light Weight Camping Equipment and How to Make It*. Ward, Colo.: Highlander Publishing, 1959.

——. *Light Weight Camping Equipment and How to Make It*, 4th ed. Denver: Colorado Outdoor Sports Corp., 1968.

Davenport, Eugene. *Vacation on the Trail*. New York: Macmillan, 1923.

Davis, Joshua Clark. "Activist Businesses: The New Left's Surprising Critique of Postwar Consumer Culture." *American Historian*, May 2017.

——. *From Head Shops to Whole Foods: The Rise and Fall of Activist Entrepreneurs*. New York: Columbia University Press, 2017.

De Abaitua, Matthew. *The Art of Camping: The History and Practice of Sleeping Under the Stars*. London: Penguin Books, 2012.

Deloria, Philip J. *Playing Indian*. New Haven: Yale University Press, 1998.

Denning, Andrew. *Skiing into Modernity: A Cultural and Environmental History*. Berkeley: University of California Press, 2014.

Dole, Minot. *Adventures in Skiing*. New York: Franklin Watts, 1965.

Domosh, Mona. *American Commodities in an Age of Empire*. New York: Routledge, 2006.

Elmore, Bartow J. *Citizen Coke: The Making of Coca-Cola Capitalism*. New York: W. W. Norton, 2015.

English, Bonnie. *A Cultural History of Fashion in the 20th Century: From the Catwalk to the Sidewalk*. Oxford: Berg, 2007.

Enstad, Nan. *Ladies of Labor, Girls of Adventure: Working Women, Popular Culture, and Labor Politics at the Turn of the Twentieth Century*. New York: Columbia University Press, 1999.

——. *Cigarettes, Inc.: An Intimate History of Corporate Imperialism*. Chicago: University of Chicago Press, 2018.

Ewen, Stewart. *Captains of Consciousness: Advertising and the Social Roots of the Consumer Culture*. New York: McGraw-Hill, 1976.

Fanger, P. O. *Thermal Comfort: Analysis and Applications in Environmental Engineering*. Copenhagen: Danish Technical Press, 1970.

Farber, David. "Self-Invention in the Realm of Production: Craft, Beauty, and Community in the American Counterculture, 1964–1978." *Pacific Historical Review* 85, no. 3 (August 2016): 408–442.

Farish, Matthew. "Creating Cold War Environments: The Laboratories of American Globalism." In *Environmental Histories of the Cold War*, edited by J. R. McNeill and Corrina R. Unger, 51–84. New York: Cambridge University Press, 2010.

——. "The Lab and the Land: Overcoming the Arctic in Cold War Alaska." *Isis* 104, no. 1 (2013): 1–29.

Fenichell, Stephen. *Plastic: The Making of a Synthetic Century*. New York: HarperCollins, 1996.

Fink, Paul M. *Backpacking Was the Only Way*. Johnson City: Research Advisory Council of East Tennessee State University, 1975.

Finney, Carolyn. *Black Faces, White Spaces: Reimagining the Relationship of African Americans to the Great Outdoors*. Chapel Hill: University of North Carolina Press, 2014.

Fletcher, Colin. *The Complete Walker: The Joys and Techniques of Hiking and Backpacking*. New York: Alfred A. Knopf, 1971.

——. *The Complete Walker III: The Joys and Techniques of Hiking and Backpacking*. New York: Alfred A. Knopf, 1994.

Folk, G. Edgar. "The Harvard Fatigue Laboratory: Contributions to World War II." *Advances in Physiology* 34, no. 3 (September 2010): 119–127.

Ford, Tanisha. *Liberated Threads: Black Women, Style, and the Global Politics of Soul*. Chapel Hill: University of North Carolina Press, 2015.

Fordyce, Claude P. *Trail Craft: An Aid in Getting the Greatest Good Out of Vacation Trips*. Cincinnati: Stewart Kidd, 1922.

Frank, Thomas. *The Conquest of Cool*. Chicago: University of Chicago Press, 1997.

Friedman, Danielle. *Let's Get Physical: How Women Discovered Exercise and Reshaped the World*. New York: G. P. Putnam's Sons, 2022.

Friss, Evan. *The Cycling City: Bicycles and Urban America in the 1890s*. Chicago: University of Chicago Press, 2015.

Fussell, Paul. *Uniforms: Why We Are What We Wear*. Boston: Houghton Mifflin, 2002.

Gelber, Steven M. *Hobbies: Leisure and the Culture of Work in America*. New York: Columbia University Press, 1999.

Gladwell, Malcolm. *Outliers: The Story of Success*. New York: Little, Brown, 2008.

Goldstein, Carolyn M. *Do It Yourself: Home Improvement in 20th-Century America*. New York: Princeton Architectural Press, 1998.

Gordon, Sarah. " 'Any Desired Length': Negotiating Gender Through Sports Clothing, 1870–1925." In *Beauty and Business: Commerce, Gender, and Culture in Modern America*, edited by Philip Scranton. New York: Routledge, 2001.

Gore, Robert W. *The Early Days of W. L. Gore and Associates*. [Newark, Del.]: W. L. Gore & Associates, 2008.

Gorman, Jim. *Guaranteed to Last: L.L. Bean's Century of Outfitting America*. New York: Melcher Media, 2012.

Gorman, Leon. *L.L. Bean: The Making of an American Icon*. Boston: Harvard Business School Press, 2006.

Gould, John Mead. *How to Camp Out*. New York: Scribner, Armstrong, 1877.

Grainge, Paul David. "Advertising the Archive: Nostalgia and the (Post)national Imaginary." *American Studies* 41, no. 2/3 (Summer/Fall 2000): 137–157.

Green, Nancy L. *Ready-to-Wear, Ready-to-Work: A Century of Industry and Immigrants in Paris and New York*. Durham: Duke University Press, 1997.

Greer, Brenna Wynn. *Represented: The Black Imagemakers Who Reimagined African American Citizenship*. Philadelphia: University of Pennsylvania Press, 2019.

Grinnell, George Bird, and Eugene L. Swan, eds. *Harper's Camping and Scouting: An Outdoor Guide for American Boys.* New York: Harper & Brothers, 1911.

Hagedorn, Hermann. *Roosevelt in the Bad Lands.* Boston: Houghton Mifflin, 1921.

Hallock, Charles. *Camp Life in Florida: A Handbook for Sportsmen and Settlers.* Forest and Stream Publishing, 1876.

Halsted, Homer. *How to Live in the Woods.* Boston: Little, Brown, 1948.

Hammett, Catherine T. *Campcraft ABC's for Camp Counselors.* New York: Girl Scouts of the U.S.A., 1941.

———. *Your Own Book of Campcraft.* New York: Pocket Books, 1950.

Handley, Susannah. *Nylon: The Story of a Fashion Revolution.* Baltimore: Johns Hopkins University Press, 1999.

Hart, John. *Walking Softly in the Wilderness: The Sierra Club Guide to Backpacking,* 1st rev. ed. San Francisco: Sierra Club Books, 1984.

Harvey, Mark W. T. *A Symbol of Wilderness: Echo Park and the American Conservation Movement.* Seattle: University of Washington Press, 2000.

Heggie, Vanessa. *Higher and Colder: A History of Extreme Physiology and Exploration.* Chicago: University of Chicago Press, 2019.

Henderson, Howard. *Practical Hints on Camping.* Chicago: Jansen, McClurg, 1882.

Henderson, Kenneth. *Handbook of American Mountaineering.* Cambridge, Mass.: Riverside, 1942.

Herman, Arthur. *Freedom's Forge: How American Business Produced Victory in World War II.* New York: Random House, 2012.

Herwitz, Daniel. *Heritage, Culture, and Politics in the Postcolony.* New York: Columbia University Press, 2012.

Hill, Daniel Delis. *American Menswear: From the Civil War to the Twenty-First Century.* Lubbock: Texas Tech University Press, 2011.

Hittel, John S. *Yosemite: Its Wonders and Its Beauties.* San Francisco: H. H. Bancroft, 1868.

Hoganson, Kristin L. *Consumers' Imperium: The Global Production of American Domesticity, 1865–1920.* Chapel Hill: University of North Carolina Press, 2007.

Holding, Thomas Hiram. *The Camper's Handbook.* London: Simpkin, Marshall, Hamilton, Kent, 1908.

Horowitz, Daniel. *The Anxieties of Affluence: Critiques of American Consumer Culture, 1939–1979.* Amherst: University of Massachusetts Press, 2004.

Horowitz, Roger, and Arwen Mohun, eds. *His and Hers: Gender, Consumption, and Technology.* Charlottesville: University Press of Virginia, 1998.

Hough, Emerson. *Out of Doors.* New York: D. Appleton, 1915.

Hounshell, David A., and John Kenly Smith, Jr. *Science and Corporate Strategy: Du Pont R&D, 1902–1980.* Cambridge: Cambridge University Press, 1988.

House, William P. "Mountain Equipment for the U.S. Army," *American Alpine Journal* 6, no. 19 (1946).

Howard, Vicki. *From Main Street to Mall: The Rise and Fall of the American Department Store*. Philadelphia: University of Pennsylvania Press, 2015.

Iarocci, Louisa, ed. *Visual Merchandising: The Image of Selling*. London: Routledge, 2013.

Isserman, Maurice. *Continental Divide: A History of American Mountaineering*. New York: W. W. Norton, 2016.

Jacobs, Margaret D. *White Mother to a Dark Race: Settler Colonialism, Maternalism, and the Removal of Indigenous Children in the American West and Australia, 1880–1940*. Lincoln: University of Nebraska Press, 2009.

Jacobson, Lisa. "Manly Boys and Enterprising Dreamers: Business Ideology and the Construction of the Boy Consumer, 1910–1930." *Enterprise & Society* 2, no. 2 (June 2001): 225–258.

Jacobson, Timothy C., and George David Smith. *Cotton's Renaissance: A Study in Market Innovation*. Cambridge: Cambridge University Press, 2001.

Jaeger, Ellsworth. *Wildwood Wisdom*. New York: Scribner, 1945.

Jakle, John. *The Tourist: Travel in Twentieth-Century North America*. Lincoln: University of Nebraska Press, 1985.

Jarvis, Christina S. *The Male Body at War: American Masculinity During World War II*. DeKalb: Northern Illinois University Press, 2004.

Jasen, Patricia. *Wild Things: Nature, Culture, and Tourism in Ontario, 1790–1914*. Toronto: University of Toronto Press, 1995.

Johnson, Bruce. *The History of Gear: Holubar Mountaineering, Ltd*. N.p.: Blurb, 2010.

———. *The History of Gear: Gerry: To Live in the Mountains*. N.p.: Blurb, 2011.

———. *The History of Gear: Frostline of Colorado*. N.p.: Blurb, 2013.

———. *The History of Gear: Warmlite: Still Controversial After All These Years*. N.p.: Blurb, 2017.

Kaiser, David, and W. Patrick McCracy, eds. *Groovy Science: Knowledge, Innovation and American Counterculture*. Chicago: University of Chicago Press, 2016.

Kasson, John F. *Amusing the Million: Coney Island at the Turn of the Century*. New York: Hill & Wang, 1978.

Kemsley, William, Jr. *Backpacking Equipment: A Consumer's Guide*. With the editors of *Backpacker* magazine. New York: Collier Books, 1975.

Kennedy, Paul. *Engineers of Victory: The Problem Solvers Who Turned the Tide in the Second World War*. New York: Random House, 2013.

Kephart, Horace. *The Book of Camping and Woodcraft*. New York: Outing Publishing, 1906.

———. *Camp Cookery*. New York: Macmillan, 1918.

Kerouac, Jack. *The Dharma Bums*, repr. ed. London: Penguin, 2000. Originally published 1958.

Kidwell, Claudia B., and Margaret C. Christman. *Suiting Everyone: The Democratization of Clothing in America*. Washington, D.C.: Smithsonian Institution Press, 1974.

Kirk, Andrew G. *Counterculture Green: The* Whole Earth Catalog *and American Environmentalism*. Lawrence: University Press of Kansas, 2007.

———. "The New Alchemy: Technology, Consumerism, and Environmental Advocacy." In *The Columbia History of Post–World War II America*, ed. Mark C. Carnes. New York: Columbia University Press, 2007.

Klingle, Matthew. *Emerald City: An Environmental History of Seattle*. New Haven: Yale University Press, 2007.

Koehn, Nancy F. *Brand New: How Entrepreneurs Earned Consumers' Trust from Wedgwood to Dell*. Boston: Harvard Business School Press, 2001.

Kohlman, Oley. *Uphill with the Ski Troops*. Cheyenne, Wyo.: Pioneer Printing and Stationery, 1985.

Kotler, Philip, and Waldemar Pfoertsch. *Ingredient Branding: Making the Invisible Visible*. Heidelberg, Germany: Springer, 2010.

Kreps, Elmer Harry. *Camp and Trail Methods: Interesting Information for All Lovers of Nature*. Columbus, Ohio: A. R. Harding, 1910.

Kropp, Phoebe. "Wilderness Wives and Dishwashing Husbands: Comfort and the Domestic Arts of Camping in America, 1880–1910." *Journal of Social History* 43, no. 1 (Fall 2009): 5–30.

Lasc, Anca I., Patricia Lara-Betancourt, and Margaret Maile Petty, eds. *Architectures of Display: Department Stores and Modern Retail*. London: Routledge, 2018.

Leach, William. *Land of Desire: Merchants, Power, and the Rise of a New American Culture*. New York: Pantheon Books, 1993.

Lears, T. J. Jackson. *Fables of Abundance: A Cultural History of Advertising in America*. New York: Basic Books, 1994.

———. *No Place of Grace: Antimodernism and the Transformation of American Culture, 1880–1920*. Chicago: University of Chicago Press, 1994. Originally published 1981.

Leechman, Douglas. *The Hiker's Handbook*. New York: W. W. Norton, 1944.

Le Zotte, Jennifer. *From Goodwill to Grunge: A History of Secondhand Styles and Alternative Economies*. Chapel Hill: University of North Carolina Press, 2017.

Limerick, Patricia Nelson. *The Legacy of Conquest: The Unbroken Past of the American West*. New York: W. W. Norton, 1987.

Linderman, Wanda Taylor. *The Outdoor Book*. N.p.: Camp Fire Girls, 1947.

Löfgren, Orvar. *On Holiday: A History of Vacationing*. Berkeley: University of California Press, 1999.

Long, J. C., and John D. Long. *Motor Camping*. New York: Dodd, Mead, 1923.

Look, Dennis. *Joy of Backpacking: People's Guide to the Wilderness*. In collaboration with Arthur S. Harris, Jr. Sacramento, Calif.: Jalmar, 1976.

Lubar, Steven. "Men/Women/Production/Consumption." In *His and Hers: Gender, Consumption, and Technology*, edited by Roger Horowitz and Arwen Mohun, 7–37. Charlottesville: University Press of Virginia, 1998.

Luther Hillman, Betty. *Dressing for the Culture Wars: Style and the Politics of Self-Presentation in the 1960s and 1970s*. Lincoln: University of Nebraska Press, 2015.

MacCannell, Dean. *The Tourist: A New Theory of the Leisure Class*. Berkeley: University of California Press, 1999.

Maher, Neil M. *Nature's New Deal: The Civilian Conservation Corps and the Roots of the American Environmental Movement*. New York: Oxford University Press, 2008.

Manko, Katina. *Ding Dong! Avon Calling! The Women and Men of Avon Products, Incorporated*. New York: Oxford University Press, 2021.

Manning, Harvey. *Backpacking: One Step at a Time*. Seattle: REI Press, 1972.

——. *Backpacking: One Step at a Time*, 4th ed. New York: Vintage Books, 1986.

——. *REI: 50 Years of Climbing Together*. [Seattle?]: Recreational Equipment Inc., 1988.

Marchand, Roland. *Advertising the American Dream: Making Way for Modernity, 1920–1940*. Berkeley: University of California Press, 1985.

Martin, George W. *Modern Camping Guide*. New York: D. Appleton-Century, 1940.

Martin, Richard. "All-American: A Sportswear Tradition." In *All-American: A Sportswear Tradition*. New York: Fashion Institute of Technology, 1985.

Marx de Salcedo, Anastacia. *Combat-Ready Kitchen: How the U.S. Military Shapes the Way You Eat*. New York: Current, 2015.

Mason, Bernard S. *The Junior Book of Camping and Woodcraft*. New York: A. S. Barnes, 1943.

May, Elaine Tyler. *Homeward Bound: American Families in the Cold War*. New York: Basic Books, 1988.

McCarthy, Tom. *Auto Mania: Cars, Consumers, and the Environment*. New Haven: Yale University Press, 2007.

McKenzie, Shelly. *Getting Physical: The Rise of Fitness Culture in America*. Lawrence: University Press of Kansas, 2013.

McNeish, Cameron. *The Backpacker's Manual*. New York: Times Books, 1984.

McPhee, John. *The Survival of the Bark Canoe*. New York: Farrar, Straus and Giroux, 1975.

Mendenhall, Ruth Dyar. *Backpack Techniques*. Glendale, Calif.: La Siesta, 1967.

Meyer, William B. *Americans and Their Weather*. Oxford: Oxford University Press, 2000.

Middlefeldt, Sarah. *Tangled Roots: The Appalachian Trail and American Environmental Politics*. Seattle: University of Washington Press, 2013.

Miller, Warren H. *Camp Craft: Modern Practice and Equipment*. New York: Charles Scribner's Sons, 1922.

——. *Camping Out*. New York: D. Appleton, 1925.

Mitman, Gregg. *Breathing Space: How Allergies Shaped Our Lives and Landscapes*. New Haven: Yale University Press, 2007.

Montgomery, M. R. *In Search of L.L. Bean*. Boston: Little, Brown, 1984.

Moreton, Bethany. *To Serve God and Wal-Mart: The Making of Christian Free Enterprise*. Cambridge: Harvard University Press, 2009.

Mowen, John C. *Consumer Behavior*, 4th ed. Englewood Cliffs, N.J.: Prentice-Hall, 1995.

Muir, John. *The Story of My Boyhood and Youth.* Boston: Houghton Mifflin, 1925.

Murray, William H. H. *Adventures in the Wilderness; or, Camp-Life in the Adirondacks.* Boston: Fields, Osgood, 1869.

Nash, Roderick. "The Cult of the Primitive." *American Quarterly* 18, no. 3 (1966): 517–537.

——. *Wilderness and the American Mind.* New Haven: Yale University Press, 1967.

Nelson, Hugh. *Making Your Own Backpack and Other Wilderness Campgear.* Athens, Ohio: Swallow Press, 1981.

Neuzil, Mark. *The Environment and the Press: From Adventure Writing to Advocacy.* Evanston, Ill.: Northwestern University Press, 2008.

Nordhoff, Charles. *California for Health, Pleasure, and Residence.* Franklin Square: Harper & Brothers, 1874.

O'Connor, Kaori. *Lycra: How a Fiber Shaped America.* New York: Routledge, 2011.

Ohmann, Richard. *Selling Culture: Magazines, Markets, and Class at the Turn of the Century.* New York: Verso, 1996.

Oldenziel, Ruth, and Karin Zachmann, eds. *Cold War Kitchen: Americanization, Technology, and European Users.* Cambridge: MIT Press, 2009.

Orkney, Janna. *Growing Up with G.I. Joe's: From War Surplus Store in a Tent to Multi-Million Dollar Retail Chain—How My Father, Ed Orkney, Built G.I. Joe's.* Agoura Hills, Calif.: Columbia Press, 2016.

Orvell, Miles. *The Real Thing: Imitation and Authenticity in American Culture, 1880–1940.* Chapel Hill: University of North Carolina Press, 1989.

Overy, Richard. *Why the Allies Won.* New York: W. W. Norton, 1995.

Packard, Vance. *The Hidden Persuaders.* New York: D. McKay, 1957.

Paoletti, Jo B. *Sex and Unisex: Fashion, Feminism, and the Sexual Revolution.* Bloomington: Indiana University Press, 2015.

Parsons, Mike, and Mary B. Rose. *Invisible on Everest: Innovation and the Gear Makers.* Philadelphia: Northern Liberties Press, 2003.

Peiss, Kathy. *Cheap Amusements: Working Women and Leisure in Turn-of-the-Century New York.* Philadelphia: Temple University Press, 1986.

——. *Hope in a Jar: The Making of America's Beauty Culture.* New York: Henry Holt, 1999.

Pendergast, Tom. *Creating the Modern Man: American Magazines and Consumer Culture, 1900–1950.* Columbia: University of Missouri Press, 2000.

Perkins, Leigh. *A Sportsman's Life: How I Built Orvis by Mixing Business and Sport.* With Geoffrey Norman. New York: Atlantic Monthly Press, 1999.

Petrzela, Natalia Mehlman. *Fit Nation: The Gains and Pains of America's Exercise Obsession.* Chicago: University of Chicago Press, 2023.

Pettit, Michael. *The Science of Deception: Psychology and Commerce in America.* Chicago: University of Chicago Press, 2012.

Petzoldt, Paul. *The Wilderness Handbook*. New York: W. W. Norton, 1974.

——. *The New Wilderness Handbook*. With Raye Carleson Ringholz. New York: W. W. Norton, 1984.

Philpott, William. *Vacationland: Tourism and Environment in the Colorado High Country*. Seattle: University of Washington Press, 2014.

Pinkerton, Kathrene. *Woodcraft for Women*. New York: Outing Publishing, 1916.

Pitcaithley, Dwight T. "A Dignified Exploitation: The Growth of Tourism in the National Parks." In *Seeing and Being Seen: Tourism in the American West*, edited by David M. Wrobel and Patrick T. Long. Lawrence: University Press of Kansas, 2001.

Pitkin, Thomas M. *Quartermaster Equipment for Special Forces*. Washington, D.C.: Historical Section, Office of the Quartermaster General, 1944.

Porter, Theodore M. *Trust in Numbers: The Pursuit of Objectivity in Science and Public Life*. Princeton: Princeton University Press, 1995.

Prendergast, Tom. *Creating the Modern Man: American Magazines and Consumer Culture, 1900–1950*. Columbia: University of Missouri Press, 2000.

Price, Jennifer. "Looking for Nature at the Mall: A Field Guide to the Nature Company." In *Uncommon Ground: Rethinking the Human Place in Nature*, edited by William Cronon. New York: Norton, 1996.

——. *Flight Maps: Adventures with Nature in Modern America*. New York: Basic Books, 1999.

Przybyszewski, Linda. *The Lost Art of Dress: The Women Who Once Made America Stylish*. New York: Basic Books, 2014.

Rabinovitch-Fox, Einav. *Dressed for Freedom: The Fashionable Politics of American Feminism*. Urbana: University of Illinois Press, 2021.

Raibmon, Paige. *Authentic Indians: Episodes of Encounter from the Late-Nineteenth-Century Northwest Coast*. Durham: Duke University Press, 2005.

Rappaport, Erica. *Shopping for Pleasure: Women in the Making of London's West End*. Princeton: Princeton University Press, 2000.

Reidy, Michael. "Mountaineering, Masculinity, and the Male Body in Victorian Britain." *Osiris* 30 (November 2015): 158–181.

Reiger, John F. *American Sportsmen and the Origins of Conservation*, 3rd ed. Corvallis: Oregon State University Press, 2001.

Rethmel, R. C. *Backpacking*, rev. ed. Minneapolis: Burgess Publishing, 1972.

Richardson, Eudora Ramsay, and Sherman Allan. *Quartermaster Supply in the European Theater of Operations in World War II*. Vol. 3, *Outfitting the Soldier*. Camp Lee, Va.: Quartermaster School, 1948.

Ringholz, Raye C. *On Belay! The Life of Legendary Mountaineer Paul Petzoldt*. Seattle: Mountaineers Books, 1997.

Risch, Erna. *The Quartermaster Corps: Organization, Supply, and Services*. Vol. 1. Washington, D.C.: Center of Military History, U.S. Army, 1995. Originally published 1953.

Risch, Erna, and Thomas M. Pitkin. *Clothing the Soldier of World War II*. Washington, D.C.: U.S. Government Printing Office, 1946.

Rizzo, Mary. *Class Acts: Young Men and the Rise of Lifestyle*. Reno: University of Nevada Press, 2015.

Roach, Mary. *Grunt: The Curious Science of Humans at War*. New York: W. W. Norton, 2016.

Roberts, David. *The Last of His Kind: The Life and Adventures of Bradford Washburn, America's Boldest Mountaineer*. New York: Harper, 2010.

Roberts, Mary Louise. "Gender, Consumption, and Commodity Culture." *American Historical Review* 103, no. 3 (June 1998): 817–844.

———. *D-Day Through French Eyes: Normandy 1944*. Chicago: University of Chicago Press, 2014.

Robertson, Thomas, and Richard Tucker, eds. *Nature at War: American Environments and World War II*. New York: Cambridge University Press, 2020.

Rome, Adam. *The Genius of Earth Day: How a 1970 Teach-In Unexpectedly Made the First Green Generation*. New York: Hill & Wang, 2013.

Roosevelt, Theodore. *Hunting Trips of a Ranchman*. New York: Current Literature Publishing, 1907.

———. *Ranch Life and the Hunting-Trail*. New York: Century, 1911.

Ross, William F., and Charles F. Romanus. *The Quartermaster Corps: Operations in the War Against Germany*. Washington, D.C.: Center of Military History, 2004. Originally published 1965.

Rothman, Hal K. *Devil's Bargains: Tourism in the Twentieth-Century American West*. Lawrence: University Press of Kansas, 1998.

Rugh, Susan Sessions. *Are We There Yet? The Golden Age of American Family Vacations*. Lawrence: University Press of Kansas, 2008.

Rustrum, Calvin. *The New Way of the Wilderness*. New York: Macmillan, 1958.

Saijo, Albert. *The Backpacker*. San Francisco: 101 Productions, 1972.

Scanlon, Jennifer. *Inarticulate Longings: The Ladies' Home Journal, Gender, and the Promises of Consumer Culture*. New York: Routledge, 1995.

Schmitt, Peter J. *Back to Nature: The Arcadian Myth in Urban America*. New York: Oxford University Press, 1969.

Schorman, Rob. *Selling Style: Clothing and Social Change at the Turn of the Century*. Philadelphia: University of Pennsylvania Press, 2003.

Schrepfer, Susan R. *Nature's Altars: Mountains, Gender, and American Environmentalism*. Lawrence: University Press of Kansas, 2005.

Schwartz, Alvin. *Going Camping: A Complete Guide for the Uncertain Beginner in Family Camping*. New York: Macmillan, 1969.

Scott, William R. "California Casual: Lifestyle Marketing and Men's Leisurewear, 1930–1960." In *Producing Fashion: Commerce, Culture, and Consumers*, edited by Regina Lee Blaszczyk. Philadelphia: University of Pennsylvania Press, 2008.

Scott-Nash, Mark. *Playing for Real: Stories from Rocky Mountain Rescue.* Golden, Colo.: Colorado Mountain Club Press, 2007.

Sears, Clare. *Arresting Dress: Cross-Dressing, Law, and Fascination in Nineteenth-Century San Francisco.* Durham: Duke University Press, 2015.

Sears, George Washington [Nessmuk]. *Woodcraft,* 12th ed. New York: Forest and Stream Publishing, 1900. Originally published 1884.

Sears, John F. *Sacred Places: American Tourist Attractions in the Nineteenth Century.* New York: Oxford University Press, 1989.

Seton, Ernest Thompson. *The Book of Woodcraft.* Garden City: Doubleday, Page, 1912.

Sfraga, Michael. *Bradford Washburn: A Life of Exploration.* Corvallis: Oregon State University Press, 2004.

Shaffer, Marguerite. *See America First: Tourism and National Identity, 1880–1940.* Washington, D.C.: Smithsonian Institution Press, 2001.

Shanken, Andrew M. "Better Living: Toward a Cultural History of a Business Slogan." *Enterprise & Society* 7, no. 3 (September 2006): 485–519.

Shapiro, Aaron. *The Lure of the North Woods: Cultivating Tourism in the Upper Midwest.* Minneapolis: University of Minnesota Press, 2013.

Shelton, Peter. *Climb to Conquer: The Untold Story of World War II's 10th Mountain Division.* New York: Scribner, 2011.

Sievert, Jane. *Unexpected: 30 Years of Patagonia Catalog Photography.* Ventura, Calif.: Patagonia Books, 2010.

Simon, Gregory L., and Peter S. Alagona. "Beyond Leave No Trace." *Ethics, Place and Environment* 12, no. 1 (March 2009): 1–34.

——. "Contradictions at the Confluence of Commerce, Consumption, and Conservation; or, an REI Shopper Camps in the Forest, Does Anyone Notice?" *Geoforum* 45 (2013): 325–336.

Spector, Robert. *The Legend of Eddie Bauer.* Seattle: Documentary Media, 2011.

Spring, Ira, and Harvey Manning. *100 Classic Hikes in Washington.* Seattle: Mountaineers Books, 1998.

Stanton, Shelby L. *U.S. Army Uniforms of World War II.* Harrisburg, Pa.: Stackpole Books, 1991.

Stole, Inger L. *Advertising on Trial: Consumer Activism and Corporate Public Relations in the 1930s.* Urbana: University of Illinois Press, 2006.

——. *Advertising at War: Business, Consumers, and Government in the 1940s.* Urbana: University of Illinois Press, 2012.

Strasser, Susan. *Satisfaction Guaranteed: The Making of the American Mass Market.* New York: Pantheon Books, 1989.

Strayed, Cheryl. *Wild: From Lost to Found on the Pacific Crest Trail.* New York: Alfred A. Knopf, 2012.

Sumner, David E. *The Magazine Century: American Magazines Since 1900,* 2nd ed. New York: Peter Lang, 2010.

Sutter, Paul S. *Driven Wild: How the Fight Against Automobiles Launched the Modern Wilderness Movement*. Seattle: University of Washington Press, 2002.

Swiencicki, Mark A. "Consuming Brotherhood: Men's Culture, Style and Recreation as Consumer Culture, 1880–1930." *Journal of Social History* 31, no. 4 (Summer 1998): 773–808.

Taylor, Joseph E., III. *Pilgrims of the Vertical: Yosemite Rock Climbers and Nature at Risk*. Cambridge: Harvard University Press, 2010.

Tedlow, Richard S. *New and Improved: The Story of Mass Marketing in America*. New York: Basic Books, Inc., 1990.

Theobald, Brianna. *Reproduction on the Reservation: Pregnancy, Childbirth, and Colonialism in the Long Twentieth Century*. Chapel Hill: University of North Carolina Press, 2019.

Toll, William. "Acclimatizing Fashion: Jewish Inventiveness on the Other (Pacific) Coast, 1850–1940." In *A Perfect Fit: The Garment Industry and American Jewry, 1860–1960*, edited by Gabriel M. Goldstein and Elizabeth E. Greenberg. Lubbock: Texas Tech University Press, 2012.

Turner, James Morton. "From Woodcraft to 'Leave No Trace': Wilderness, Consumerism, and Environmentalism in Twentieth-Century America." *Environmental History* 7, no. 3 (July 2002): 462–484.

Tuttle, Dorothy E. L. *Official Training Book for Guides at the American National Exhibition in Moscow, 1959*. N.p., 1959.

Tynan, Jane. "Military Dress and Men's Outdoor Leisurewear: Burberry's Trench Coat in First World War Britain." *Journal of Design History* 24, no. 2 (2011): 139–156.

———. *British Army Uniform and the First World War: Men in Khaki*. London: Palgrave Macmillan, 2013.

Ugolini, Laura. "Consumers to Combatants? British Uniforms and Identities, 1914–1918." *Fashion Theory: The Journal of Dress, Body, & Culture* 14, no. 2 (June 2010): 159–182.

Wall, Sharon. *The Nurture of Nature: Childhood, Antimodernism, and Ontario Summer Camps, 1920–1955*. Vancouver: UBC Press, 2009.

Walton, Izaak. *The Compleat Angler; or, The Contemplative Man's Recreation*. London: J. M. Dent & Co.; New York: E. P. Dutton & Co., 1920. Originally published 1653.

Warner, Patricia Campbell. *When the Girls Came Out to Play: The Birth of American Sportswear*. Amherst: University of Massachusetts Press, 2006.

Weaver Robert W., and Anthony F. Merrill. *Camping Can Be Fun*. New York: Harper & Brothers, 1948.

Whitaker, Jan. *Service and Style: How the American Department Store Fashioned the Middle Class*. New York: St. Martin's, 2006.

White, Dan. *Under the Stars: How America Fell in Love with Camping*. New York: Henry Holt, 2016.

White, Stewart Edward. *The Forest*. New York: Outlook, 1903.

———. *The Mountains.* New York: McClure, Philips, 1904.

———. *Camp and Trail.* New York: Doubleday, Page, 1911.

Wilson, Mark R. *Destructive Creation: American Business and the Winning of World War II.* Philadelphia: University of Pennsylvania Press, 2018.

Witherell, James L. *L.L. Bean: The Man and His Company.* Gardiner, Maine: Tilbury House, 2011.

Woloson, Wendy. *Crap: A History of Cheap Stuff in America.* Chicago: University of Chicago Press, 2020.

Wrobel, David M., and Patrick T. Long, eds. *Seeing and Being Seen: Tourism in the American West.* Lawrence: University Press of Kansas, 2001.

Young, Phoebe S. K. *Camping Grounds: Public Nature in American Life from the Civil War to the Occupy Movement.* New York: Oxford University Press, 2021.

Young, Terence. *Heading Out: A History of American Camping.* Ithaca, N.Y.: Cornell University Press, 2017.

Yowell, Skip. *The Hippie Guide to Climbing the Corporate Ladder and Other Mountains.* Nashville: Naked Ink, 2006.

Zakim, Michael. *Ready-Made Democracy: A History of Men's Dress in the American Republic, 1760–1860.* Chicago: University of Chicago Press, 2003.